'Soultracker'

Following Beauty

LEO DOWNEY

LIBRARY OF CONGRESS CONTROL NUMBER:		2014917468
ISBN:	HARDCOVER	978-1-4990-7809-1
	SOFTCOVER	978-1-4990-7810-7
	EBOOK	978-1-4990-7808-4

Rev. date: 11/24/2014

To order additional copies of this book, contact:
Xlibris
1-888-795-4274
www.Xlibris.com
Orders@Xlibris.com
548982

CONTENTS

Introduction 11

'Following Beauty' 13

'Road Dog' 17

'To Be Beautiful' 20

     Winter 2014

'Weirdosyncracies' 23

'Soultracker's' 26

'Staying Together' 29

'Wandering in the Spirit' 33

'The Autobiography of a Soul' 36

First Vision Quest 39

'Can You Hear Them?' 42

'Holiness' 45

'True Intellect' 47

     Winter 2014

'I Got It' 50

'The Artist' 52

     Winter 2014

'Brainwashing' 54

'Bully' 56

'There Was a Man' 59

'Give Me Something Beautiful' 61

'Soulpath's' 66

'Answers' 68

'The Sacred' 72

'The First Commandment is to Be an Artist' 73

'This One Answer' 75

'Where He Took Me' 77

'I'll Follow You' 81

'Californian' 85

'A Boner' 88

'The Middle Road' 91

'The Last Frontier' 94

'The Shivers' 97

'Opposites Attract' 100
'Virgins' 101
'God is the Artist' 103
'A Better Reason' 105
    Winter 2013
'Soulguardian's' 110
'Another Kind of Ecstasy' 114
'Tough' 117
    Summer 2013
'The Beauty of It' 121
'A Creature' 123
'Dad' 125
'Montecito Rats' 127
'Confession' 129
'The Bells' 131
'Our Lady of Love' 133
'My First Bad Review' 135
'Grizzly' 141
    Fall 2013
'She Showed Me What a Woman Was' 144
'I Fall in Love With Her' 146
    Fall 2013
'Two Mothers' 148
    Winter 2014
'Everything's Alive' 151
'Pope in the Box' 153
'For A Woman' 155
'A Coyote Story' 157
'The Monastery' 161
'Who You Want To Be Is Who You Are' 165
    Winter 2014
'The Orchestra' 167
'God Thinks' 169
    Winter 2014
'Medicine Man' 171
'Religious' 176
    Winter 2013
'What I Want' 180
    Winter 2013
'The Monastery ~ Predator and Prey' 184
'A Spider in the Center' 188

'Tunnel Rat'.. 192
'The Last Detail' 196
　　　Winter 2014
'Indian Nation' 199
'An Idea'.. 203
　　　Winter 2014
'Practical' 209
'Get Lost' 215
'One Man' 218
The Path of the Buffalo ~ Part I 225
'The Path of the Buffalo' ~ Part II 227
'Buffalo & Horses'.. 231
　　　Winter 2014
'Down the Alley' 234
'Conception Sky'... 237
'Elk Spirit Woman'.. 239
'Canadian Winter Account'... 245
'Freedom to Choose What We Eat' 248
'InSpiration' 252
'Chester'.. 257
　　　Christmas 2012
'The Voice of Creation'... 258
'Free Will' 264
　　　Winter 2014
'Why'... 267
'Ours to Hold' 269
True to Our Nature.. 270
'We Are Altars'.. 271
'We'd Love What We Wanted'.. 273
'Fight'.. 275
'The Most Important Thing a Man Can Have'............................ 281
'Be Small' 283
'A Bridge'.. 285
'Falling'... 287
'Mud Spelt Backwards...'.. 290
'It's You'.. 292
'One Again' 294
'Impossible'... 295
God and People 297
Does God Know What He Means? 299
'The Only Sacrifice'.. 301

'Precision' 305
'Into The World' 306
'A Confucian Slip' 307
'Kintsukuroi' 311
'Beautiful Reason' 313
'The Bear' 316
'Funny' 317
'How I Pray' 318
'Find Yourself' 323
'Chip Monk' 325
'The Most Beautiful Thing You Can See' 327
'A Different Way to Live' 328
'One at a Time' 329
'Strong' 333
'Big Balls' 337
'Mother's Day' 339
'Addiction' 340
'To See Her Beauty' 342
'Hitting Bottom' 345
'Sacred' 346
'Love' 348
'Communion' 349
'What Makes It Perfect' 351
'Thinks' 353
'Freedom' 356
'Yet' 358
'Real Thing's Are Alive' 361
'Beauty' 364
"My Whole Life, It Has" 365
The Most Astonishing Miracles 367

I dedicate Soultracker to my son.

Introduction

Thank you for taking the precious seconds to read Soultracker, I don't want you to waste a single one of them.

Art is the description of beauty. I am an artist. My story is the voice of a soul I've tracked my whole life for the why of beauty. Whatever you believe and believe you don't believe, if you read this book, slowly, I hope you will laugh and cry and get the shivers like I have, and I pray, it will help you find your why. I've found mine, I track them. There is no one better, no one even close. The souls I track change why from a question to a reason, a meaning and a purpose that no one and no circumstance can take away.

'Following Beauty'

I went through different phrases for the second part of the title to my book, like, 'Soultracker' ~ Wandering in the Sprit and Stubbing Your Toe, and a bunch I can't remember and then the second to last one I came up with was, 'Soultracker' ~ Tracking Creatures to Their Creator. I like the, '~', but it was hard making my mind up on the rest. Really what Soultracking is, is, 'Following Beauty.' So that's what ended up on the cover.

I've followed beauty my whole life. It started before I fell in love with the guitar and the beauty of music. I felt beauty in moods that drifted and whispered to me like angels on the coast of Iceland and Big Sur, in my Dad's car where music of the late 60's first brought me to tears. I felt it with my whole life force in girls!, they were so beautiful to me they became my inspiration. As a child, I felt it's subtle nuance in expanses of green and I felt it as a young man when I began to follow beauty into the wilderness. I loved to be all alone with her like a woman. I loved Earth, like a woman, and she loved me back, asking for everything I am, testing, but never judging me, only loving and inspiring me with her beauty. I think it's why God had to be alive with feelings to be beautiful to me, everything else beautiful was, girls were, animals, insects and plants were. Life came before opinions.

I wouldn't want you or me to believe anything unless it's the most beautiful thing we can find. An artist expresses the beauty he finds. The reason I care about the details of God is because they are beautiful. The idea that since people have some similar ideas about God, they're all the same, and that the details don't matter, is an idea we think is respectful of peoples freedom, and I agree we have to be free to believe whatever we want to the most, but the reason the world says the details don't matter, is because it loves what it wants more than who's giving it. To me it's like saying, well any woman will do, it doesn't matter who she is, believe whatever you want about her, call her what you want, there's a bunch of woman and they're similar so they're the same. I guess that would be true if all I care about is what I can get from her, but it would be false and make no sense to me at all if I loved her, and she loved me.

My experience has been like Earth to the world, I find it the opposite of almost everything I read and here. To me the details are the most important thing about anything I believe, and God, the same way they are about music or you, or a woman I've fallen in love with, or any kind of art. No detail is too small if it's beautiful. The world wants to simplify everything to a cliche, and call similar same, because the world thinks relative thoughts based on assumptions instead of choosing the most beautiful thing to believe. It looks for solutions outside itself. But the soul of beauty isn't relative, it isn't limited by existing, by taking form and being alive, either are we, when I look at Christ, or Mary, or you, that's what I see.

All that makes beauty different is that she loves more. Beauty's answer is never outside herself because she gives. Beauty doesn't need a 'cause,' she is her own. Beauty doesn't compare herself to anybody. I loved that about the wilderness, it was just me and her, we had each other all to ourselves like lovers, but our inspiration was something beautiful we could share with everyone else. Beauty changes the world by not changing herself, not reacting. She doesn't jump around and yell. She doesn't compete, she believes and creates. When she surrenders to love she conquers everything, especially me.

All I'm doing is describing what I see, don't believe me unless it's beautiful, and if it's not, help me, give me and everyone something more beautiful in every way beauty exists! That includes intellectual integrity, a partial truth is like a broken string, like a train of thought with no destination. Partial truth is not truth that sets me free. Don't believe me unless you think it might be beautiful, but the souls I'm tracking are absolutely breathtaking and they're alive, really. I'm not making it up, I'm just pointing to the tracks. You can follow your own or somebody else's, but it is impossible to not follow because every thought is whispered to you, and you take others wherever you go with you. If you don't think the souls I track and love are beautiful, describe someone that is, show me what's at the end of the tracks, show me the living thing that is making them.

The world says, 'What is beauty, it's whatever we say it is, it's porno or a signed toilet'. You know, I think it can be a junk yard and I see it in even the most sad and forlorn people, love is what makes beauty and only what is alive can love. But the angels around me hear tone in an endless harmony that touches even to our intellect, the way a master hears it on a guitar. Most people can't tell the difference and it doesn't matter to them, and you can't force somebody to care, but a master reaches for the tone anyway, because he or she is an artist and by reaching through the fear of failure and judgement and rejection, and doing it anyway, they inspire the rest of us.

Wisdom holds the scales of justice. To weigh beauty and ugliness all she has to do is open her exquisite hands. All she has to do is touch me with them and I feel the difference between beauty and ugliness, light and dark, warm and cold, life and death. Her intellect is thousands of years old. Her line is an unbroken succession handed down by the laying on of her hands. God married her and they became one flesh, one body. To see, she opens the eyes of souls. All those that have gone before are here and just as important as us. I'm in love with her and so are the angels. She measures what I believe by its beauty. She's taught me my intellect is not for thinking but for choosing, the highest beauty I can find every second in every way beauty exists. Her beauty is how I can know whether what I believe is true or false.

To me, Life is sound before it's matter. It's why first there was a Word and the word was God. He sings us, into existence. He is an artist first and a critic last, but he is a Lover always and a lover lives for beauty. The most positive thought is a beautiful reason. I may doubt what I think I want and don't want, what to ask for and decide to do, but I don't doubt a molecule of the life that lives in you. I don't doubt Christ and the Body his soul inhabits, I don't doubt a word he says, because of his beauty. I don't doubt an atom of the New Adam, because his love is beautiful to me beyond measure. His intellect is perfect, even here on Earth. He is in the lions I've looked into, he stands with the buffalo, he sleeps warm and newborn, between a mother and a father. I hear him like I hear wind a mile away on the wings of a condor, in the silence of an owls flight, and the haunting call of one lonely and wise, last night.

An artist is like Earth to the world. They don't whine because beauty is hard to reach for. They don't solve the problem by making everything ugly, and then being satisfied with it. It takes their life, their whole heart, mind and soul and, their body. Beauty takes an artist's body like tone takes a guitar. Beauty took Christ's body. He said we can know the truth and it will set us free, do you think he lied about that too? All I have to do is listen like my life and yours depends on it; to find that it does.

When I was young and just beginning, I played at a wedding. I was nervous and afraid, but I tried as hard as I could, I cared, and it was good. Then a man with a beard stood, and sang the Lords prayer, something I've almost always thought was better left said, but this time it was beautiful. He looked into my eyes and the eyes of everyone their, the bride and the groom, there was nothing put on, it was honest, his voice was deep and sincere, and simply, beautiful.

I told him that I loved it, he said thank you and then he asked me why when I sang I didn't look him or the others in the eye? I said, "I don't know... I don't want to make them feel uncomfortable." He said, "No, Leo, you don't know what they feel like, you don't want to make you feel uncomfortable" and I said, "Yeah.... you're right" and then I said, "But I don't want people to think I'm full of myself" And he said, "No Leo, give it everything, they want you too, it shows them that they can too, they want to, we all do." That's what I love about art, it doesn't matter how 'good' you are, what makes it art is that you give it everything. Everything. It's what makes it beautiful. Life is art.

'Road Dog'

My friend Randy Cobb invited me backstage to a show he opened for Bonnie Raitt. I sat on a road case drinking a beer hoping she might come sit next to me. She walked over and put her hand out for me to help her up, knocked my beer over and said, "Oh, sorry did I get you wet?" I amused her with a typical road dog kind of reply I don't really want to repeat. We rode around L.A. that night checking out bands she knew. I'd been dating Kymberly Herrin, a Playboy Bunny and actress from Santa Barbara, Bonnie said, "I must seem like a rare squash compared to her." Bonnie is smart and funny and I almost fell off my motorcycle. We were staying at the home I rented in the foothills above Santa Barbara at Painted Cave. We had our guitars and I played her 'Have Mercy on Me' a song off my Heaven and Hell CD. She liked it and said she'd help me get a publishing contract and introduce me to her manager. Her record, Nick of Time had gone Gold a few days earlier. Bonnie is friends with Jane Fonda so we rode up the hill to her house and she did a radio interview over the phone for a show she was doing at the Lobero while I sat with Jane and her two kids in the kitchen. Jane asked me about my times alone in the mountains. I tried to tell her. I wanted to tell Bonnie, I wanted to tell everybody, but I couldn't. From the first time I went alone into the wilderness as a teenager, things began to happen that aren't supposed to happen. Miracles change your orientation, they transform your reality, every thought, every word you hear and person you meet, all your desires grow roots into a different kind of earth.

I was afraid to share the heart of my vision for different reasons. It is a living beauty revealing itself, but it involves facing fear, wanting to know a Truth beyond opinions, about God, ourself, the Earth, and the world. I've come to believe something that in certain ways is the opposite of what almost everyone I know and love believes. The subtle precision of how it all fits together, like a perfect body, like nature itself, in endlessly increasing perfection, is like looking into the most beautiful face. Like art, this body and this face is an inspiration that takes my whole being to begin to express. It is something so beautiful it brings me to my knees, but it doesn't seem like anybody wants to be on their knees. We'd have to look up to someone. It seems like the world wants a disembodied energy, without feelings, unlike us, not a living being to actually be loved, because then we'd have to care what someone else felt. But I have feelings, and I felt like a bad dog telling the other dogs we had to be good. I couldn't explain my experience to Bonnie, to Jane, to my band, I felt like a mystery to myself. I see now, somehow, I'm living this mystery and I've lived it my whole life, even the times I fell.

I've been tracking creatures of a living Communion in heaven and on earth, I want to be one of them, they all point away from themselves, to God, like a Mystical Bride. Being mystical doesn't mean it's not as real as what we call real, it means we don't understand it. A 'Mystic' is a person that enters mysteries and becomes part of them. For me knowing truth is knowing a person. The more deeply I love you, the more I come to know you, truth is the same, truth is a virgin, she won't give you herself unless you love her enough to marry her. The mystery is not only spirit, it is blood, because the mystery is here too, it has come to Earth. We can't begin to know this mystery until we enter Her, as God has, in glorifying surrender.

The spiritual world and its creatures are identical in many ways to the natural world. Earth and the creatures that walk here were teaching me to track. The unseen world and its creatures are Soultrackers, they inhabit the deserts of our heart. It can be unfathomably dark there. We can become the light darkness can't comprehend, in our own hearts and in the hearts of those we love. Wandering in the Spirit is seeing by faith. Christ's blood flows there in a river of lives the way water flows to the sea, we evaporate and rise, into a sky moved to tears by the beauty of one holy soul, and rain pours down on Earth's face. No one enters their heart alone, everything alive lives there, inside, really, not symbolically, not what we see but what it means, because what it means is what it is.

From Earth back to the world. Bonnie did a show in New York and the guys from KISS were on the plane with her flying back to L.A. She said one of them wanted her to sit on his lap and let the other guys take a Polaroid. We were in the elevator at the Granada, she was laughing and kind of humming, in that sexy blues droll of hers she said, "Those guys are real road dogs" I'd never heard that before and I said, "What's a *road dog*?" and she said, "You're a road dog!" Lol, it was one of those musician type conversations. So I wrote this song called *'Road Dog'* I gave her half the rights, and everything I'd been working for began to happen. I was thirty years old, I had a rock band, I wanted to live it, to be the real thing. My idea of what an artist is, is inextricably tied to my idea of what a man is. Back then my idea of what a man was, was a man Bonnie and a Playboy Bunny and other beautiful women I liked and loved, wanted! I wanted them too. I had people say, "Are you crazy, go for it!" In my heart I knew it's never been about giving up what I want, it's about giving up who I'm not to become who I am. I began to see how sleeping with a woman I wouldn't give my soul to and life for was not reaching for the highest love, but teaching the whole universe we are less than what we are. I admired and liked Bonnie, I thought she was beautiful, I didn't care what I could 'get' from her, I cared about her. I wasn't ready for what we might have had, but I didn't explain it well and we lost touch.

I've been deeply in love. It has always been a woman's soul I wanted to join. Being in love with God is like being in love with a woman's soul. I write a lot of love songs, if you keep that in mind when you listen to my songs, you'll feel more of what I'm feeling and who it is I'm singing to. Through my manager Tony McIlwain, and Chis Pelonis, at Sony Records, I was offered a three record deal and a promotional contract with Budweiser. I'd worked very hard for this and I was humbled to be recognized by two men I respected. I saw this dusty crossroads I'd seen so many times in my dreams. A few months before, my mom returned from a trip she took with her sisters to Croatia and told me about a beautiful young woman she and her sisters met. I could see how meeting her changed them, as if they'd absorbed her beauty. My mom wanted us to meet. She invited her, she came, and we fell in love. She is a 'perfect creature', every human quality is perfected in her, the most exquisite, sensitive, loving, woman I've ever met. Her humility is irresistible, a glimpse of her eyelash is ecstasy, a virgin and a mother, mine and Gods. The angels call her 'Full of Grace' I call her Mary. She's not a spirit or an idea or a goddess, she is a 'Woman' like you, except that she loves more. In the end, I think God does it all for a woman, his Bride, and she does it all for him. That's what I mean by loving a woman's soul is like loving God. She changed everything. She was showing me what a woman is, and through this, slowly like life, what a man is.

I asked her, how would I feel if I were you? She showed me love the world hasn't seen an eyelash of; yet. The surface is symbolic, all we are able to know is what something means to us, its meaningfulness or its meaninglessness. I will only believe in the most beautiful, meaningful reality I can find each second, because anything less is meaningless. Let that faith and that being be whoever it is, that's who I want because that is who it has to be and that is who she is. Faith, loyalty and obedience like this does not limit our intellect or our experience anymore than love does and it has nothing to do with how worthy or unworthy we think we are. Knowing what we believe is knowing who we love, they are inseparable, because everything real is alive. The more sincerely I enter the mystery, the more I find what is most true, what is highest, until the mystery enters me, and becomes a miracle. What is a miracle's effect? To confront us with ourself. Miracles define reality. They rise up and come down like Gods gavel. The time of the miracle is eternal, and it's here.

'To Be Beautiful'

WINTER 2014

My story is a journey, the progression of a boy to a man. Each step leads to the next in a way I learned I was tracking souls with a heart. It started with animals and the human animal, woman. She has taken me to the Animator of animals. Soultrackers track souls to God and find their own, kind of like those drawings of an ape turning into a man.

Earth was a breathtaking creature. My first memories are Iceland and the Arctic Sea. The brilliant green and the brilliant white, where the sun sleeps on the horizon. The summer sky crystal blue where the Blue Angels flew. The ocean gave birth to volcanoes. The ash made the beach black and the sun dried the fish. My father smiling in his flight suit when my mom gives him a kiss. I saw good in the world and I loved it.

Time changes quickly now like it's all made of plastic, but then the cars were heavy and metal. The Cigars that smelled good in Paris when I was three, are still there for me. The world was in a romantic mood. Everything about it seemed beautiful and good. The incense and Cathedral, the grotto where Mary stood, smiling at me with her outstretched arms, that priest, quiet with the tears when he lifted the cup, everyone silent but the Gregorian chant, kneeling, believing, facing a God who was sacred, and someone buried beneath me, where we sat with his name carved in the stone. It was seamless.

I felt Earth and the world she gave birth to, I was a Californian, it was art, the Big Sur Coast, the shades being drawn on both sides of freedom, bodies finding souls, long hair, leather and tattoo, the cold redwood canyons they roared through. I thought Hells Angels were from heaven and men were cowboys in the Salinas Rodeo. I wanted to play the guitar with everything I had to give, and after a while I did.

Light My Fire, played for the first time on the radio in my dad's Ford Galaxy 500. It was night and I cried for the beauty. I looked out the window and saw me on a motorcycle beside us. My Dad was a Commander in the U.S. Navy, a pilot in World War II, a genius in the top 99.999 percentile of world I.Q. level, 156, they say Einstein was 160. He flew canvas bi-planes to the first jet fighters. He was tough, especially the way he used his mind, he'd crashed with steel nerves that kept him alive. He mellowed and blossomed when he turned fifty and stopped drinking, I did too.

I was a kid with ideas about what a man was. A man was a creature, like a lion, an artist, he was strong, tough, but to fight for someone else, to love and endure, not to hurt anybody. He was tough enough to let the deepest things in him show. I was just the beginning of a man. I thought, if you can call it that, 'I should do whatever I want as long as it doesn't hurt anybody', but it hadn't sunk past my skin that we were more than a body, and mine was so full of passions it was hard to feel anything else.

I fell in love once a couple times when I was a young man. They were the love I was in. I'd drink their air and breathe their skin, it was pure and clean and inebriating. I felt them as exquisite expressions of perfect beings, nothing seemed more beautiful than these works of living art, they were one with the soul of the Earth. They magnified her and became one with me. I held them like a horse that wants to run. This mood would engulf me to create. I captured them the way that notes awake, and go to sleep, with their lips against my fingertips.

I recorded my first CD, 'Carmel', if you listen with your soul to each note, as if it's you that play, the way we held them to give them away, to the harmony, until it's said what it longs to say, and then lays down and rests, maybe you'll hear how I heard the Earth and touched her too. I gave Earth everything I had. I loved her and her animal, the woman, and then one day, someone took Earth away, from my world, a man, by the will of a different kind of creature, and I encountered 'evil' for the first time. Evil the world denies is there, like a God without feelings. I'm not that interested in ideas, I'm interested in beings, they are the beauty I am here to express.

The heart of my story is a living 'vision' in the wilderness. A vision is a miracle that never ends. It changes our reality. A miracle is a gift, given with a price, the cost of knowing. It's not that we have to believe to be given a miracle, it's that we have to believe after we are given a miracle. This is the Cross of Light 'Believers' bear.

I see now how it's all an infinite gradient of beauty. The soul is a kind of body snatcher. We give our body to our soul like we give it to a woman. You are meant to love her enough to marry her, to create with her, to become the love of God for her children. This is where the souls sense of beauty comes in, like tone to a musician. We are created to know and love our Creator, not only because we're pathetic in every way if we don't, but because of the beauty! When the children ask Mary, "Why are you so beautiful?" She says to them, "Because I love." I like her beauty secret.

Having no sense of the difference between 'sin' and love is like a musician not hearing the nuance of tone, it's more than good and bad, it's a gradient of beauty beings embody with their souls for ours. Mercy, Forgiveness, Glory and Faith, are Gods 'Grace' like the grace of a perfect woman, like the notes and the words and the tears of someone who has reached. It's not about getting in trouble for not being good enough, it's not about fixing ourself. But it is about the nature of Earth and the Universe, as the living form of angels, creatures, beings who are the children of a Father and a Mother with hearts like ours. Maybe you can have a free ride with a guarantee, I don't think so, nothing in nature is like that, I want to ride a giant.

Evil is the mystery of imperfection, and no one explains imperfection perfectly. But anyone that's seen it walk up a wall backwards and hang there, smelling the incontinence of atheists, and begging a priest to go away and leave it alone, knows it's a creature with a will that wants theirs. I live in a world of sovereign creatures, they aren't my ideas any more than you are.

We are only responsible for what we know, only the conscious free choice of sin can kill a soul, but even the unconscious sin we freely choose spreads like a virus and curses Earth. It disrupts the balance of her harmony, her creatures and all the rest of us, all the way to the innocent and unborn. Sin teaches us to be ugly. It manifests chaos. The soul is a child gestating in a body for a lifetime, waiting to be crowned and born at the moment of death with the breath of God, to become one with his creation, like a flower, like a 'Woman', not to transcend an illusion, but to make everything sacred. If you look at the way Christ and Mary love each other and enter their love, their words, their life, their bodies, with your heart, the way you listened to the notes, you will see they aren't asking us to give up anything we want. They are asking us to be beautiful.

'Weirdosyncracies'

The things I write and the things I'm passionate about, God, beauty, Earth, art, creatures, the mystery of a man and a woman, I'm sincere, but I know I've got weirdosyncracies.

One of my friends says, "Leo! Art, it'z a wvaste of time!' "Wverk! Wverk! be praktikal!" I love him. He's got some funny weirdosyncracies, but he's got a point. He's saying live in the real world. Music, spirit, faith, they're invisible, but when the invisible world of faith steps into this one, it leaves tracks, and it becomes the real world. Its purpose is to express who is creating it. Near death experiences, encounters with angels, miracles, apparitions, and most of all, visions, transform what we call real. For me, the material world is the symbolic world.

I've lived on both sides, the Earth and the world, the Spirit and the flesh. In the Monastery where I intended to live the rest of my life, I heard a call to be a bridge. Beginning in the wilderness and then in the world, when miracles happened, I saw that with our life, we hold everyone's life in our hands, our ancestors, those here now, and those to come; this is the 'burden' of the Cross, the burden of Light. Through real love, the eternal and holy kind, the world can have everything, if we listen, pray, and follow the way of the ones who are there already. I'm a crummy example, but maybe that's good, it proves crumminess can't stop you. I want to try. It was the same way with music, all the good and beautiful things about the world, the wilderness, condors and buffalo, with all that life has been, sometimes it has been heartbreaking, but you already know, love is worth it, 'Love makes up for a multitude of sins.' The only thing it can't make up for is insincerity.

Art isn't a waste of time, life is art. To love with our whole heart, mind and soul, is to be an artist, it's what it takes to be creative and it's the first Commandment. I find out if what I believe is true, because only what's true, sets me free. Everything my holy ancestors believe and teach me is for a purpose; Freedom. There is nothing better, nothing even comes close to Freedom and no one appreciates freedom more than someone who has experienced slavery. For me it came in the form of addiction, but really it was accepting a bribe in exchange for my soul.

My passions are horses, they want to run and I can't always control them, it might be why I'm a little jaded with horses, they're always on the edge, but they are passionate. Prayer can turn weirdosyncracies into gifts. I have kind of a linear dyslexia, I don't go in a straight line because I've always wanted to approach from the Center. That's what Wandering in the Spirit is, it happens out on Earth, alone. I forget the world and my whole desire is to follow God wherever he takes me. He takes me into his kingdom on Earth. I say 'whatever happens, my breath is yours, let me be your prayer...' I don't know where my next step will land, you're tracking Gods soul with yours, I think it was the normal state of many of the Native people that lived in those mountains. Things happen, the laws of nature suspend, the unseen world enters this one, that's what a Vision is, a miracle, they change our reality, they are a great gift and also a burden of light. Once you know, you can't rationalize, generalize and compromise everything the way the world does.

I've seen a side of my tribes story, mystics, saints, angels, priests, not fake ones, real medicine men, it's a whole other world, if you ever meet one, you'd see, it's not what you think, they love, till they bleed, they change the identity of a man, miracles happen around them, it's not what they say, it's who they are, who they love, but it seems almost totally lost on the world today, it's like a bad cartoon. There is a hidden beauty there just like the hidden beauty of the Earth, and I want to tell my story about it, because it's different, it's something I think we're missing.

Soultrackers follow a Holy Communion of beings instead of themselves, they're all going to the same place, wild animals are there all the time, the Center, Gods mystical body, unlimited, even by the limit he takes on out of love, his Son, the New Adam. His word and ideas are perfect, but he left us infinitely more than his ideas. He left us his Communion on Earth, his Spirit, his breath, his sacred flesh and blood to become ours. These are the ancestors of my tribe, not symbolic ancestors, real ancestors. They are proof his word does what he says and they are among us.

The world is busy and cluttered with thoughts and people are thinking them too fast. They jump from one to another without precision, coming to circular conclusions based on what they believe they don't believe. I believe the only way we can help Earth is to sanctify ourselves. First comes the natural man. It begins with a decision to love the truth more than wanting to be right and more than what we think we might prefer.

Loving the truth allows us to go to the Center in a prayer of the heart. Prayer of the heart is like love, like music, like Earth, like God, I go there as a child, I don't have to be any better than I am, but I lift up everything in myself, my heart and my love, and also my lack of love and the tragic things about me, Christ called sin; to the light. Becoming aware of desires born from a lack of love is part of the illumination of our conscience. Every breath is being born again in a conversion of my soul. This place, in our soul and our heart, with all our faults, and with every ounce of what is sincere in us, is the place we help save each other and the world, doing doesn't do it unless we do it from there, because this place is the State of Grace. Even here in the world, it can feel as beautiful as walking out onto the Earth alone.

It's being's I follow, not ideas, there's something profoundly emancipating about recognizing my nothingness, I don't have to be more than I am to be with them. I believe everything I say, but then I fall and I'm not always faithful to them. Our brothers, the angels and saints are here right now with us, they keep their distance for our glory and freedom. To help us become one of them, they let us see with their vision, by faith, like they do, we create.

It's painful to love enough to care how they feel. But what are we going to do, keep forsaking the innocence of Earth for the world? Betray Christ with our life for a bribe? You know what it does when I fall, and it's not an excuse, in the end, after the pain, it humbles me. Don't accept yourself as an excuse, accept yourself as an act of humility. I follow them the way I follow beauty, the way I've fallen in love with a woman, I can't help it, they are their own proof, they are limitless. They are the opposite of what the world thinks. They are the fire of prayer I throw myself into like a piece of wood.

I want to end with the most beautiful creature I know, and this is the most important thing about her, she is a Woman. Please get this or you miss her entire, total, whole point; She doesn't have to be more than she is and either do you, she doesn't have to be a goddess so she can be better than a woman, she doesn't want to be worshipped, she wants to be loved! Like you. That is what she lives, loves, and cries to reveal to you; yourself. Her greatness is her humility, her beauty is her love, and it's ours when we decide to believe. She's not a bunch of dumb ideas, she's a woman, a daughter and a mother.

In her apparitions happening around the world, the Blessed Virgin, The Woman Clothed with the Sun, The Living Ark of the Covenant, The first Christian, who's soul magnifies the Lord, who said 'Yes,' to the angel that knelt with Gods proposal to be his Bride, who loved God as her baby and as her Creator, who's humble heart is pierced to reveal the thoughts of ours, Mary, the Mother of Heavens Children, our Mother, the New Eve, Gods greatest work of art, the Great Sign in Heaven, the Woman who's offspring keep the commandments of God, calls the world to her Son, and says, "Pray with your heart until prayer becomes your joy." Anybody can do it, even somebody like me, and if that's not a miracle nothing is. Luckily, it's not about being better than somebody else. When prayer becomes our joy, we become what I mean, by a Soultracker.

'Soultracker's'

A 'Soutracker' is not a leader, but they are who I follow. They don't claim to be or want to be. They point away from themselves to the tracks and the souls that are already there, pointing away from themselves too.

Soultracking is an art where the artist is the medium. I learn it like music, but it takes more than my lifetime, it takes my life. It is a total commitment and can't be turned off. You can't turn off your blood. Animal, human, angelic, they are one. To find our soulpath is to find our family and walk with them in two worlds at once. It's living with the awareness that it takes life to give life, and looking back, yeah, I guess it isn't easy, I've needed a lot of help.

When I was a kid it was sacred. There was incense and a lonely flame. People knelt in a solemn and beautiful silence, the way I have in the wilderness. There was something there so far beyond men and the good and bad they do, but gradually like the wilderness, the world infiltrated it and raped away its innocence. Now the tracks are so faint, they're almost gone, but not quite. Soultrackers find them.

When I was a teenager I looked for it again. I walked into a sacred place where evil lurked, licking its lips and rubbing it's face. Of all the places left, this has to be the last place, it's the way evil works. I wouldn't wish it on my worst enemy, but I've learned a lot from evil. A few statues were left with tears in their eyes. Before I turned away and left, I remembered, I'd asked my mom if they were sad. She said, "No Leo, their tears are of the deepest joy, Love..." She was a Soultracker.

You've probably never known a real one but I have. It would take a life to describe their Medicine, but nobody believes or even wants to anymore. We don't need a man anymore for anything, or a woman either. I sat naked and still once in the sand, tired and sad, and then a big black bear found my track with his nose, and in a second, me, with his eyes. I'd let him walk right up to my face, we looked into each other's eyes, he was beautiful like that lonely flame. We were sacred even if the whole rest of the world jumped up and down and shot their guns in the air, and lying, conniving fake priests perfected evil in holy places. When they came after me, they made me stronger and I'm friends with real ones. As long as there are good ones, bad musicians can't make music bad. Truth will win in the end and it's beginning. I've known the real ones, the bear is one, I pray I'm one and I pray you're one too. We're not good, but we want to be, and we're sincere down to our last tear.

I laugh as hard as I love, but a soul is the most precious thing anybody has. Every living thing is an altar. Time is a trillion dollars in my hands I can spend any way I want, but only a soul has life. You already possess more than you could ever think to want. Medicine men and bears have it in their eyes, that's how I tell if they're Soultrackers...and anybody that wants to can be one.

'Staying Together'

I think I was eight years old in Monterey, wandering around the woods between our houses one Saturday when I saw Mrs. Vurnamen on her back porch and told her she had a 'mangy old cat!' I didn't expect her to come running after me, but she did. It was a long way through the trees and fields back to my house and I was surprised and scared at how fast she could run in that dress.

A few days before, I'd told her that my Dad was a meteorologist and he said the sun was further from the earth in the summer than the winter and it made her really mad. She got all shaky and red and said, "Well, 'My' dad is an optometrist and he said it's not!" She meant to say her 'husband'. She was all worked up. I think it was the first time I'd gotten a response like that out of an adult.

I played with her boys, Jim and Tim. Their bedrooms smelled like pee and they were the only fat kids I knew. Well there was this one other fat kid named Greg who sat across from me in fourth grade and would open his mouth really wide whenever I asked him because I was amazed and told him it was the size of a whale. When I was a kid, there were hardly any fat kids, we all ate peanut butter and jelly sandwiches and a lot of us had freckles…and it was okay to say fat.. and I liked fat kids just as much as skinny kids.

I ran up the back stairs of our deck, through the door and into the kitchen where my Dad was having a cup of coffee. He looked up and said, "What's the matter Lad?" I said, "I told Mrs. Vurnamen she had a mangy old cat and she chased me through the woods and she's right behind me!" His eyes twinkled and he grinned. I ran to my bedroom and hid.

I heard him walk out on the back deck and Mrs. Vurnamen's footsteps coming up the stairs. He said, "Hi Mrs. Vurnamen, how are you?" Then there was some muttering. Mrs. Vurnamen's footsteps went back down the stairs. I heard Dad walk into the house and call for my mom, "Betsy…" She said, "Who was that?" There was some more muttering and then they both started laughing so hard and I came out and started laughing too! My mom said, "Really Leo!" but she couldn't stop laughing. My Dad was strict and very serious about us being respectful, but we couldn't help it. Once on a trip through Europe in a big cathedral at mass, I stuck my tongue out at my aunt Jeanie. She got really mad too, I was only three or four, but they were still laughing about that a few years before my Mom died. My sister told me I could be a real pill, and I knew what she meant, but I think I had a lot to do with my mom and dad laughing and staying together when it was hard. Whether you're a kid or a grown up, I think, if you can do that you should.

'Wandering in the Spirit'

I loved what I found beautiful in the world, but since I was a kid, I wanted to 'live like an Indian'. As a teenager, I began to wander alone into the desert mountains of California. As much as I was able I made every breath I took there a prayer. I let each next step take me wherever I was led, pacing myself with my breath. I would end up in deep, silent canyons where everything stood still. I found sand floored caves where California Condors had nested and others strewn with arrow heads and flint knapped pieces of colored stone as if the people that had lived there for thousands of years had just stepped out and might come back. Sometimes I would stand for a very long time before my next step, sometimes I would cover miles crawling through bushes and up mountain sides to places so beautiful, so peaceful and so sacred, I would weep. The tears came from a place of innocence, a place of joy and dignity where everything was as perfect as I could dream, including me. I felt as if I was participating in a hidden heaven on Earth waiting only for all of us to finally stop judging each other and start loving each other. God was speaking to me and loving me through his creation. God was showing me he was real, the purpose of miracles and visions. Eventually I recognized and called this, 'Wandering in the Spirit'.

My relationship with the earth, plants, animals and insects that surrounded me, took on a transcendent quality. I experienced 'miracles' and life became mystical. As much as I could, cherishing my own ancestors, I wanted to experience the life the Native Americans that lived in the same mountains for thousands of years before me had lived. I survived on what I could gather and hunt, mainly rattlesnakes. Hunger was a profound teacher. Once I snatched a rabbit from a red tail hawk.

The trails there are ancient and faint, I got lost and in finding my way, I would find myself. I'm looking back on my journey now from one of those places and times, where getting lost becomes a way of finding myself. There are so many kinds of lost. It's a long trail of grace, but I strayed so far off of it and got so lost that it almost killed me. As I find my way, I hope somehow I can help you find yours. I tell my story and begin my journey from where I am, where I have been and where the Spirit leads me when I follow.

Finding my way has been following a Spirit. Though it's a Spirit that seems to keep asking me to give everything I have and am and want, to him, the more I do, the more he shows me my true self. You may think you're free of 'beliefs' and 'religion' and that you follow your own path, but everything I've learned says no, that is just not true. Everyone follows a spirit and has religion, their religion is whatever they believe about reality and the ones that say they follow their own way or no way or some 'other' way are just as religious about it as someone that follows the way of his own ancestors. It's not how many people believe in something, or how passionate they are about it that makes it ugly, what makes it ugly is its lack of beauty. What matters most to me about the Spirit and the Way is how beautiful it is, ultimately, Beauty, in every way that beauty exists is the measure of Truth. What makes something true in the end is, 'What it means', but meaning has lost its meaning today, we hardly even know what meaning means anymore. We don't know what we believe or why and we don't think we should care, let's just get along. It's sort of like playing bad music badly and trying to solve the disharmony by not listening too closely. The wilderness, music, and 'religion' keep teaching me the same thing, the opposite, to 'Listen.'

> I've known deep joy here
> Love and moods of the aesthetic
> Exquisite verging on the ecstatic
> Is how I would describe moments like these
> That have accompanied me the way Earth does;
> With light that flickers through the trees
> The tears of mist sparkling on leaves
> Webs the spiders have helped me weave
> Lions have looked into me
> Behind it all invisible
> Angels must have dropped to their knees
> To pray they could breathe
> And know what it means to be a man
> And believe

Friends would joke with me asking what the heck are you doing back there wandering alone in the woods? I'd say I'm working hard, it's just that it's invisible work. The most beautiful things I have to give are all invisible, love, faith, music and even these words, it is what is invisible about all of it that is its treasure. It seems impractical, it's not 'of this world' but I can't really help it, when I glimpse the Spirit, I feel something so beautiful resisting it is like being unfaithful to, or resisting a lover. If I could give some of this to others and watch them feeling it and seeing it, I would feel complete like I am doing the last thing I have to do before I leave. I want to try, I never stop praying, whatever I'm doing, asking to be who I was created to be. It's like the whole place is disappearing but I'm more here than I've ever been.

I've awakened from nightmares that were so real somewhere they must have been, but when I woke up what was real was here and they weren't and I have never been so grateful. People that think hell only exists if they believe in it haven't woken up as grateful as me. But I don't want to preach, reason can be divine and meaning can be full but it is never enough, I want to create and to be something beautiful. I want to be like a field of white and purple sage you lay down and fall asleep in, that dreams with you. If I can believe enough for me I can believe for you. If it's all true, do you get a glimpse of what it means?

'The Autobiography of a Soul'

My book is about a vision, mine and yours. Don't read it if you don't want a vision of your own, or you'll end up like I did, a Walking Dead Man. To promise you this is to bare my soul. What I have shared isn't mine, it's ours, theirs. Something is happening on Earth only a tiny percentage of people know anything about, it heals lives, it converts hearts, it transforms souls, and it transubstantiates bodies. It reaches the Alpha and the Omega. It is more important than anything else. It is better than anything I could ever have dreamed, more beautiful than eyes of galaxies. I've held it back, for you, cryptic on purpose. Like getting a sick buffalo calf away from its mother in time to save it, it takes great restraint, to stalk up with Earth on the spirit of the world, and not spook its prejudice. Enter it with one moment of sincerity, and you'll begin to become its beautiful consequence. *Soultracker* is an autobiography that's not about me, it's about us.

To write the way I speak, the way I think, I use comma's, to slow down and discern the gradients of beauty in each thought. Each is important, and leads to the next, my path is my stories context, the way tracks lead to a creature, but I've tried to make each chapter stand on its own too, so you can enter it and wander. Read it slowly okay... enter it like the wilderness, like the first man, and the last woman. When I Wander in the Spirit my pace is my breath, slow, deep, still, peace. Miracles happen and become visions. I hope you'll read my words like tracks, and find the creature that left them, with your soul. I hope I find yours. It's the most beautiful thing we have to give.

The most important part of writing and performing music for people is loving them. It's incognito, but it's what it's all about. When I track an animal, the most important thing I do is love it. I've been very hungry many times, it's part of my story and what brought me to Canada. Like a curse, living on earth means killing. It can seem almost impossible to live up to the life I take. To me, not living up to it is what sin is. It's what the Sundance is about, and it's what my holy ancestors have believed for two thousand years. Only life gives life, life kills and eats life everywhere on Earth, animals, insects, plants, even God becomes food, to those that believe him. We become the beauty we consume, the Creator becomes the creature. The artist becomes the art.

I stopped discerning beauty, instead of believing in Gods body I believed in my own, and became food for a different kind of predator, one that believes in his 'body' instead of Gods. I followed their whispers like tracks without discerning their meaning. I forgot what the intellect is for, to choose, only the highest, most beautiful thing I can find every second. All around me they say, "Think or don't think this way and you'll get what you think you want." We can't know what we want till we know what we are, and it's absolutely amazing. It's not a positive thought, a memory, a symbol, or an idea, it's not mind over matter, it's soul over mind, it's alive, that's the whole point. Life is what a soul finds when it tracks, and it's art to express with words, how much better life is than an idea.

I've tried to tell the truth, the good and bad, the funny, the sad, the sinful, the serious, the beautiful, the passionate, the guilty, the innocent, the agonizing and ecstatic. I don't like drama but I've left some in, like sin in myself, for some to say I'm too pious and others not pious enough. We are a composite of animal~spirit. Christ makes both sacred by asking me to reach like an artist, with the precision of caring, with all my intellect, body and soul. He didn't want to do the most beautiful thing he ever did. Christ and Mary didn't live to get what they thought they wanted, escape suffering or recognize form as illusion, they lived to love and make Earth sacred. My art is tracking creatures to their souls.

If you sense something good in my soul, track it. For the man, I hope you'll have some affection and forgive my sins. Please don't try and take them from me though, because I'm moved to tears for the beauty of forgiveness. If you find even the slightest error in what I believe, inspire me with the beauty of what you believe. Be a saint and prove it's true. Take whatever's good in me, like a breath.

I'm not a leader, I'm a follower, but to follow the souls I do takes my whole heart and intellect, my body and my soul. They don't point at themselves. I don't want to either. What's worth saying is not thought, but revealed. The only way to guide is to follow, animals, angels, and a communion that's already there, that's what I mean by Soultracking. It's a man or woman that follows a living vision. Not an idea vision, and not a thing you are in control of, the vision of living creatures to their source. It's kind of hard, like art... it asks for everything. I look back and I see, wow, to follow the creatures and the souls I've followed, and follow right now, required something different, that I believe truth exists, perfect, sovereign and alive. To know it by its beauty is to be...an artist.

We all have it and are made for it, not by trying to be bigger, by being smaller. Every sacred mystery is the opposite of what the world thinks. We're already so unbelievably amazing, we carry God inside us the way Mary's Son did, by wanting to like he did, and it's this oozing, deep ochre Earthy red blood dripping passionate living presence... of a mountain lion, a buffalo, a woman, an angel, mine and yours. I've wanted to live for it since I was a kid that wanted to live like an Indian. I want to die for it too.

Thinking positive is better than thinking negative, but it's not about thinking, it's not more ideas and ways to think, no matter how positive they are, they're dust to a bug. It's alive. It's praying, with my heart, till I become a prayer, because that's what they are. It's putting your nose in their tracks until you walk their path and smell them like faint incense, breathe their breath, you feel their presence, you really do. It makes the hair stand up on your neck and gives you the shivers like a mountain lion, like a beautiful fear. It's here, already right now, it's singing a song. Sometimes I can hear it with them. Our Creator is becoming his Creation.

He's alive and he's in love with a woman, her beauty, his art, her flesh, his body. They 'Love' each other! You have to be willing to risk your life to track them, even your soul, because they make every breath, thought and second infinitely valuable. That is what holiness is. It is the caring of love taking every track to its source. It takes guts, you've got more than me, it's all been grace, it's falling in love.

I don't follow souls that guess. I track souls that are already there, but they are in the least of my brothers. I found out by becoming him, heartbroken, in jail, addicted, chained, not to my brother, to a demonized angel, really. Our issues aren't what we think they are and our answer is better than we can imagine.

The souls therapy is spiritual, the souls doctor, a Medicine Man, a true Priest like Christ, the souls medicine, angelic. My healing had to take place in my soul, for my will to be free, and the souls I track healed me. Gods will is free will. The greatest gift we give each other is ourselves and the way is to be free. Not free from others, free for them. That's what Soultracking is.

The why of Soultracking is the how. Discerning the tracks is the art of living for beauty. It waits for me and comes for me when I follow it, the way wolves have, there's something in them that wants to be seen. The intellect is not for thinking but for choosing, only the most beautiful tracks, and then leaving ours on the path. We walk for them all when we're free. You can be it alone or in a family, sick, strong, with everything and nothing. It's a different kind of prayer, that began with Wandering in the Spirit alone on Earth, and I don't know how I could have done it without her, but I'm praying it's in me and I can share it with people that live in the world.

To write my book took my whole life. I entered The Heart of All Things, the Sacred Heart, your heart and mine, its desert, snow, rivers, lions, its savannah and its Woman. It's alive. The souls I track are free, and we will be. They live for the highest beauty. They make music, they make love, they make sense, they make me, One with them. They're as real as you, that's why I love them.

First Vision Quest

I was sixteen the first time I went alone into the desert mountains of California. I had my Dads big navy survival knife and this feeling something was going to jump out of the woods and try and kill me and eat me any minute. There was something wonderful about going alone into the woods and feeling like that.

The reason I was alone in the woods happened a few months before, I'd been invited to a promotional thing with a real pumped up motivational guy that wanted us to come to a seminar called EST. He was jumping around telling us how great 'It' was, but not telling us what 'It' was, which is kind of funny because the whole slogan of 'It' was, "I got It". He seemed so sincere and positive and everything, I figured 'It' must be good so I signed up and paid a deposit to get 'It' too. But then I heard about a dear friend that got 'It' and seemed kind of cold afterwords. So I got second thoughts about 'It' and for some reason I decided to go into the woods for three days alone and ask Jesus to tell me whether he thought I should get 'It' or not.

I'd never heard of what the Native Americans call a vision quest and I didn't think that much about Jesus. I didn't read the bible, I didn't have one of my own. My parents had a great big old leather one. They read it and knew a lot more about the whole thing than they had told me. We were Catholics, Jesus and God to me were these sacred beings I felt when we went to what we called the Mass. Everybody was quiet and prayed, the priest seemed to spend most of the time praying too, but at the start he would read out of the bible and talk about it for a while. I wanted to go outside and play and I don't remember what he said. The part that stuck with me was how holy it seemed and how I felt different. In a kind of innocent and naive way, I always felt Jesus around me. By the time I was twelve or so, that holy and mystical feeling of it changed, they sang songs everybody seemed to like but me, it didn't sound sacred like it used to. It used to be real quiet, but now it seemed kind of noisy. I didn't want to go anymore and my parents didn't make me.

On my first day in the mountains I found a pool at the foot of a two hundred and fifty foot waterfall cascading down a face of smooth sandstone. A feral goat showed up and climbed away. I soaked up the essence, the lichen painted rocks and insect tracks in the sunlit sand made joy spill from me. In the evening I looked for some twigs to make a small fire. The creek bed was scoured clean by the winter floods that thunder through. I looked next to some boulders and far down under them I saw a little flash of white that caught my eye. I reached in as far as I could and pulled out a little bible. I thought, hey that's interesting, I came back here asking Jesus for an answer and I find a little bible... I started reading it but the print was small and the sun was setting. I flipped to the back and read a prayer in larger print asking Jesus to take over the throne of my life, in my innocent way I felt he already was but I prayed it and asked for that and then I looked across the canyon and asked Him for a sign He had heard me. I was hoping some bushes on the far ridge might do something, but nothing happened and then I said, 'It's okay, I know you have heard me' and I really did. Then for some reason I turned around and looked up two hundred and fifty feet to the top of the waterfall and standing in the water, looking down at me over the edge was that mountain goat. I turned away and looked back and he wasn't there anymore. I asked, 'Please show me a sign again that you've heard me' I looked back up and there he was again standing in the water the same way looking down at me...

I went to sleep that night under the stars feeling happy, a little scared and brave and the beginnings of what the wilderness became to me. I had a very powerful dream. In it I walked into an abandoned ranch house and into a room full of occult stuff on the walls. A voice in the dream said, 'The occult things in this room were the downfall of the man that lived here'. I woke up under a full moon. I knew from my sisters help that dreams were a symbolic language and that a house usually represented yourself. I had been experimenting with some occult stuff, Rune Stones and Astrology and some stuff like that and I had witnessed remarkable synchronicity and answers through them, but in the dream this voice said they were the downfall of the man that lived there. I asked Jesus, 'Please tell me what this means' and in the full moonlight I opened the little bible randomly and put my finger down. It was a quote of Jesus and I still am not sure exactly where it was or the exact words, but I remember clearly that what it meant to me was, 'To have all you need, put All your faith in me'.

I thought... I've put my faith in you, but I've also put my faith in these other things, these things in the dream and I've seen they can work, but you're saying put 'All' my faith in you, like, put all my eggs in one basket, that's asking a lot but, it feels right somehow, hmmm, Okay, I'll do it! and then I thought, Hey, that's the answer to my question!! If I put all my faith in you, I don't need EST! I had always thought of God as within myself just as much as I thought of God as outside myself, to me He was everything good. But all these things... I was young, I had no guidance, I was finding my own way alone in the wilderness, I was deeply loved but I hadn't been taught much about the Spirit and God.

I spent the remaining three days in the innocent joy of my very first experiences of 'Wandering in the Spirit'. Then I came home and called the guy from EST and told him I wasn't coming. He badgered, cajoled, intimidated, lied, told me I was afraid and not a man of my word and used every trick in the book to get me to come and finally I gave in and said okay. I didn't know I was going against my 'vision'. I didn't know the holy Communion of my ancestors and what they pass down to us. I didn't know how the Native Americans honored and prepared for the vision quest under the 'authority' not just the guesses, opinions and suggestions, of their Medicine Men and the tribe, and how they called a man that went against the vision he received a, 'Walking dead man'. I became a zombie before it was popular. I've always been on the cusp of things.

'Can You Hear Them?'

I wandered in two wildernesses, both filled with creatures, one is a wilderness of the soul, with creatures that are angels, as real as you and me. It's taken a long time to realize, that I can feel their presence, just like a buffalo or a rattlesnake; they are here beside me all the time, with a blessing or a curse.

When we listen to the ones that bless us, we become their blessing. They show me, my life is not so much about thoughts, it's about Beings. They are a treasure, they are everything we could ever wish to want, it's not about the thoughts we think, it's about the thoughts we listen to. That is what the buffalo have whispered to me, one in particular, a great big bull that became a kind of angel to me. I used to think of angels as delicate and ethereal, they aren't. They are the persons, the souls, of the stars and planets and bears and waves, all the power we could dream a breath of is ours in the angels.

He tried to give me his strength one night in these 'dreams' I'd have with him. He killed another bull that was going to kill me. He jumped up on him and peeled the hide down off his hump and over his head slowly, and then stood back. The bull fell to his knees and shuddered in the steam that rose off his white skull. It was such an awesome strength he showed me, and wanted to give me, I wish I could show you, but I wasn't ready to take it.

God gives us his power, his presence in us, in proportion to our having the guts to take it. He doesn't compromise himself to be in us. It takes guts to carry God around. It's not macho guts, it's the kind of guts animals have. Thinking life is about thoughts is like thinking music is about notes. Music is about feeling and choosing with my whole being, you can feel angels like a song.

I'm a very Earthy person, and I'm talking about real Beings, persons. We are all wandering in their wilderness, but hardly anyone knows it, I didn't. Many of our thoughts and feelings aren't our own. Learning through an experience that almost destroyed me, that what we hear and feel are the presence and whispers of Creatures, has taught me how to hear the beautiful ones. They are so beautiful and so powerful, all I want to do is listen to them and tell you what I hear them say.

Angels are what it means to pray. It's not something we do, it's Beings we put ourselves in the presence of. What I am learning to do, is to take my will from the ones that curse, and give my will to the ones that bless. They aren't ideas! They aren't your or my truth! They are their own, like a bear. When I let them be their own, they come. When you limit them to ideas, you judge them instead of love them. I call them, and they come, but not so much with my words or my thoughts, I do it with my being, my heart, my soul. You make yourself a prayer like they are, and they come.

To make ourself a prayer, we have to let go of everything, everything, but even for a second is enough. The creatures on Earth have been trying to teach me this my whole life. It took years for the buffalo to accept me like one of them. They stay wild, they don't lose their wild instincts, they stay true to their wild nature, but they know me. They can remember the face of a person they come to know like me for three years without seeing me. They'll charge strangers, they still charge me sometimes, they know how you feel.

Animals have taught me about angels that bless and angels that curse. Real priests have too, priests that faced them down, the same way I've done with a buffalo or a mountain lion. It's amazing what facing something does to it and to me. When you face something, you put yourself in its presence. It takes guts, a mountain lion makes the hair on the back of your neck stand up, even before you know he's there. But you know what, I've been very afraid about a lot of things in my life, many of my friends are braver and stronger than me, but I don't know if they know it, they inspire me, whether they believe what I believe or not, I've prayed to be sincere.

Sincerity is the prayer that calls angels. Every sacred mystery I enter is the opposite of what it appears to be, every single one, every single time. And it never stops, it always keeps being the opposite of how it appears, like something turning itself inside out. Wisdom used to rest in people, books hardly existed till a few hundred years ago, and very few people could read. Because persons were the deposit of our faith and our treasure, they were like the tree of life, they handed truth and faith down to us, in an unbroken line of succession, and knowledge came with wisdom and with authority, that is the soul of a 'tribe'.

I said I wanted to 'live like an Indian' I'd sit in their caves and it was like they'd just left. They had such pure wisdom, they knew that each thing was a 'person' and that they sat in the Creators hands every second. My ancestors knew this too, it's all right there, but because it's only in books for most of us now, it does not come with the wisdom of elders that actually live it and prove it. They are here, but hidden and rare. So the blind follow the blind, wasting life re-inventing the wheel, and thinking of this like freedom to choose their own path. It's so dumb! I don't want to do what a fake or an amateur tells me to do, but what if he's real?

What if we have true Saints to speak to us? What if it's true and they prove it? They do and they are. But will anyone listen?

I really wonder, everybody is so busy trying to convince themselves and others, that they already know, with these cliches we think are philosophies, or theologies. There is a pride so false it hides from everyone. I've really looked, hard, we're dumb! We don't have a clue! But angels do. If you squeak like a hurt rabbit in the woods, predators will come, I've done it many times. It might take a few minutes or all day, but they will come if you keep it up. If you reach for what you know is wrong, what is beneath your dignity, over and over, angels will come that want you. It's not your body they want, it's your soul, they stalk you through your will.

If I took you into my herd, would you listen to me? or would you tell me what to do? If you took me into your office or your work, I'd ask you questions and I'd listen to you. My dad was remarkable, I asked him questions, and I listened! to his answers, all my life. Nobody listens, we are seriously lost, we have lost our faith, we don't even know what our faith is, or what faith is.

The last person on Earth I'd listen to is me; because I can listen to angels, and the Communion of my holy ancestors who have become like them and are with them. When I do, their blessings turn into me, they make us their prayer. They are living and longing and dying if they could, to give us all, their blessing, and turn us into their prayer.

Love is a blessing, hate is a curse. If you're addicted, tormented, hopeless, desperate, sick, perverted, stuck, jealous, angry, resentful, obsessed, proud, greedy, mean, conniving, guilt tripping, malicious, envious, or numb like a zombie, you're listening to angels that are cursing you and others through you, and if others are behaving that way toward you, they are listening to them.

They are real creatures, not idea angels, not positive thoughts and affirmations angels, they're real whether you think you're thinking bad thoughts or good thoughts. And this is the Sacred Mystery unfolding itself right in front of you and me; they are the proof that the angels that bless are also real.

If the whole world knelt down, even one at a time, and confessed, and called them, they would bless the soul of the Earth with our presence on her. They would bless our souls, everything can still turn around, it's never too late for the mercy and love, God became a man, for all of them to see. He made them for us, and gave each of us, our own, to become like. Everything we could ever dream of is ours. Can you hear them?

'Holiness'

To me, holiness is what beauty is in a human being. Holiness is the beauty of love. I've said this before, but when I was a kid and I saw these paintings and statues of saints, often with tears in their eyes, I asked, "Mom, are saints sad?" and she said 'No Leo, their tears are of the deepest joy, love." I never forgot that. I'll say again, when kids that have seen the Virgin Mary ask her why she is so beautiful, she says, "Because I love.' I like that beauty secret. If you want to be beautiful, love.

For me, God had to be all beauty could be, to be God. From the time I was small, I remember listening to the Earth. I'd crawl around in the bushes and feel the sunlight on my skin, Earth smelled good, I'd breathe her in, and want to go in, deeper, further, like an adventure into a kingdom. Everything I heard Earth say was beautiful, even her fear was beautiful, like the storms and waves that roared, north and south of Monterey Bay. We lived all over and I got to see people and places so different, yet the same, there was always this beauty.

I didn't become aware until I was older, I was seeing through the veil of angels. In a way, angels remind me more of animals than of humans. It's not that hard to feel their presence if you discover their nature, and yours. Christ said we will become like angels in the 'next life.' In this life we experience and express everything through our instrument, our body. Love glorifies our body. Our bodies can become like Christ's and Mary's and the angels and saints. Our image, matter-time, our flesh, can become what it symbolizes. This is the mystery and beauty of Christ's body and blood for those that decide to believe in it, but no one has to. For those that don't there is infinite mercy, and also the inescapable likeness to God of Freedom. Mercy is when you forgive someone that doesn't deserve it, for the love of someone that does. Love whatever you want the most, because you will become it. It's not about punishment, it's about the nature and responsibility of freedom and creation. The only way my tracks lead to living beauty, is if I follow living beauty, the souls that make heaven what it is. Without them, I'm a guess, following my own tracks in circles.

Everything on Earth must eat life in form to sustain life in theirs. Christ glorifies form by what he has done out of love. He becomes the image we are created in. He has left more than his symbols, memory, words and ideas, he has left us mystical food, Himself, the food of Heaven, the DNA of heavenly bodies. The world does not realize what they miss, when they believe in other things he says, but not this. To become a mystic, believe in his Mystical Body. He takes the limit of form and turns it into pure beauty. I want to consume beauty knowingly and live for it. When I rose in the prayer of the Angelus, for a moment, I became the music I'd always wanted to create. God becomes his creation. If you decide to enter Christ in your flesh, you become the Soultracker of a Mystical Communion. They are real. Prayer is raising their veil, with tears of joy, and kissing them.

'True Intellect'

Winter 2014

I Exist
I am not a guess
I am an answer
My wonder is my proof

I'm free to believe whatever I want the most, in fact I'm obligated. I've discovered something beautiful I want to share, like pointing to a sunset. What I read and hear today are ways to think and not think in order to get what we think we want. Modern books I read stress that, it's simple and easy if we believe in a few ideas, it's all the same, and the details are meaningless. All I want to be with you is sincere and honest, I find truth, reality, love, life, beauty, peace, passion, art and creativity all proceeding from a mystery that is the opposite of these ideas.

When I judge the beauty of an idea, I do the work of an artist, I'm not judging the person who agrees with the idea, I want to love that person, not judge them. What I have always wanted was to reach for the highest beauty, I find a kind of ecstasy there I want to share. If I tell you how I experience the opposite of almost everything the world tells me to believe and not believe, it's not because I want to make somebody wrong, or feel bad. I've thought and believed some of the same things, but I see something coming from my nature and my experience that gives me an unusual outlook on what it means to exist, like a gift, like a 'spiritual dyslexia', or how the color blindness of a horse whisperer enables him to see shadow and form in extra-dimensional detail. Ever since I was a kid, I felt myself learning from the Earth instead of the world. I experience Earth like a woman I'm in love with.

When I enter her, she reveals herself to me. I wanted to discover her and share myself with her. Her creatures were spirits. Everything was alive and the beauty was far more than material, it was a living breathing beauty creating and being created by a living breathing beauty. I felt she and her Creator were creating it all for me, like the first man, their child, out of the depth of their love for each other, the way a woman and man come together in the life giving act of love. My journey is to bring that into the world.

Impressions, emotions, moods, feelings and ideas I've found most beautiful are never thought, they are only revealed, the same way I came to look at every next mountain range as a living kingdom I was about to enter. A few square inches of Earth and what I saw happening there, as a witness, would bring me to tears of humbling wonder. No detail of anything alive is meaningless, every eyelash counts. I never felt the slightest desire to simplify it. It's core I found infinite, like a heart and soul. I didn't want to simplify my woman and ignore her details, as if it didn't mater Who she was. As if as long as I could get what I thought I wanted from her, they were all the same.

I know I can get what I think I want, I've manifested both my base and my higher desires many times, and every time what I wanted was something else, something who's nature is a continuous surprise, because it's alive. It is a gift. I wanted to give what Creation was giving me. Along with the other creatures, I had to kill and consume life to have life, but they weren't 'wanting' anything, but life. Life is the Beauty. They all seemed to recognize life as their nature, life as their treasure, and ours. We Exist! posing a question, only the beauty of love answers for me, everything else is a guess, calculated on relative assumptions.

I have an intuition I should point something out about how I write, and think. I don't want to waste words or seconds, and I use a lot of comma's. I do that to help delineate each specific thought. If you read what I write that way, stopping for a moment after each comma, to consider what I mean, and then at the end considering how each thought leads to the next, you'll be soultracking. Each thought is a like a track an animal is leaving. By reading their true meaning, slowly, quietly, peacefully, without skipping to conclusions, or assumptions based on prejudices, if you'll just 'listen,' you'll find the living animal, that's what thinking is for. I'll repeat the last sentence of the previous paragraph as an example and ask you to read it that way.

~ We Exist! posing a question, only the beauty of love answers for me, everything else is a guess, calculated on relative assumptions.

I feel kind of bad when I say an idea is dumb. I don't like to say another creature is behaving stupidly, but I sure have had some dumb ideas and acted stupidly. I still do, and I'm learning every second. I think today we are way too easily offended, the language police say we must use the right word of the day, the wrong way, because of a sad and false pride, a pride that allows us to think we can know anything we don't believe. You're here! don't give me your theories, give me your beauty, please. We guess to conclusions we are incapable of knowing. They can only be believed, and believing is a choice we make of what we put our faith in. This is the treasure Earth's creatures seem to know as their nature. They know their identity.

I like to end on a high note, but I hate to pretend. I want the truth more than feeling good, like technique on a guitar. The only way to be dumb is to insist on it. Our ideas can be incredibly dumb, but we aren't ideas. If your God is an idea he's a dumb one, because what you believe in you become. We don't have to be smart, but we really don't have to be dumb.

The true intellect doesn't think anything, it listens and prays, for whispers and visions. It looks away from the world for the worlds sake and from itself for its own sake. It becomes an answer, like Earth. She never simplifies herself or lowers her dignity, she reaches for her beauty, she is no one else in every detail, in a flower, an insect, the imprint of the corners of her claws, the intent in the dust and the dirt she leaves behind, not her ideas, her life, her soul, her God, for a Soultracker to find.

'I Got It'

No one had ever hurt me, I figured the worst it would be was a waste of time.

The EST seminar was a two-weekend event. The first weekend wasn't that bad besides being cramped in a room with 350 people, I don't remember much of it, but the second weekend was a little trip to hell for me. Let me qualify here that as far as I heard from people in the group, the other app. 349 people liked it, although in retrospect I question that. I heard a couple people yell out objections and one person tried to leave. The leader badgered her with peer pressure and got her to give up and stay. I just sat there listening and trying to get my moneys worth like an idiot.

It was done with subtle torture, an integral part of brainwashing. All the chairs were tied next to each other at the legs, they made us take off our watches. They made us sign documents stating that we wouldn't tell anyone else about our experiences there and that we would give up all right to sue them or hold them responsible for anything that happened there. A lawyer stood and said, 'I'm a lawyer and I wouldn't let anyone sign this.' He got peer pressured and cajoled into signing it too. There were three hundred and fifty of us and we went along with this crap cause some guy told us to. I have visions now of confronting the guy and yelling to the crowd, 'Your free, you can go, heavens out the door!' They were sued eventually and they dealt with it by changing the name from EST To the Forum, Sage, and now Landmark, it's just another religion that's main hook is to say it isn't a religion. Materialism, Relativism, Marxism, Maoism, Leninism, Nazism, they're all modern religions who's slogans are the same at the core; i.e. 'Religion is evil and the reason for all our wars, we are here to free you from religion'. For some reason it's not politically correct to point out that those religions killed hundreds of millions more people than all the historic religions combined and they do it in faithfulness to their own teaching. At least when Christian's did it, they were hypocrites.

The guy yelled at us through a shrill p.a. system, telling us, "You're all machines." For four hours he preached, saying that the only thing that made us different from each other was our 'position in space' or our 'point of view'. I'm listening and thinking, we're not machines and this reasoning is dumb, and a few people argue with him that we aren't machines and he argues right back and insists that we are, over and over on and on. Then finally as he turns to the chalkboard to start the next process he quietly says, "You're not really machines" just once like that. I remember thinking to myself did he just say we aren't machines after all that? But it didn't register consciously. I know people that went to EST and they seem to like it or to not care much, but when I left that weekend, I felt like a zombie. I couldn't feel anything. I had regularly cried tears of joy just driving down the road before EST. I wasn't able to cry any kind of tears for years after EST. Whatever the, 'It' was we were supposed to 'Get', I got it and it took me years to get rid of it. The innocent feeling of Jesus and the angels being around vanished, slowly it was replaced with dread.

'The Artist'

Winter 2014

To be an artist is to care. Beauty to me is alive, it's as if she's a woman, showing me what a man is. She is so subtle, like the touch of an eyelash, like the way we put one note to sleep and kiss the next one awake. I want to tell you where Beauty has taken me, how she's taught me, to love her better, how to appreciate her whisper and most of all, how she's taught me to track her.

She led me through the desert. Sometimes I'd find myself in a garden that seemed as though it was tended. Thousands of bees and insects of every kind buzzed, crawled and flew through air the sage breathed out. I was there, all alone, I'd lay down and sleep, I'd crawl beneath the branches and flowers all day and fall asleep again, and again, I was one of them. I'd smell the ground against my cheek, and I felt every holy being, plant, animal, element and spirit was loving me in a way so beautiful and so profound, all I could do was weep.

The painful part of passion, of caring about her, is that she keeps showing me myself. Loving her isn't fixing yourself or making yourself better, it's being loyal to her, what I want is something only she gives me, like a bride. It's letting go when I discover that what is beneath her, is beneath me. Sometimes it's an agony to be true to. I love her so much when I hurt her I feel this pain that goes through my soul. But she forgives me, and that's what I mean, to be next to her is utterly humbling.

She's not a trick question, she's the one God does it for. I want to tell you the truth, the good and the bad, so maybe we can help each other reach, through the most beautiful things in us, the saddest things, and the ugliest, to touch her eyelash. She is teaching us what it is to be sincere, beauty always is.

I've said, the most important thing about her is that she is a woman. When I look into her eyes, I see what she sees, her heart reveals mine. She is beautiful because she loves. Beauty is a little girl with a Father that loves her so much, he trusts her with Earth, the creatures, and the whole universe. He trusts her with himself. Her love transforms me, all of us. If you're afraid, if you think it's impossible, ask her to pray with you, for sincerity. That's what I mean by being a Soultracker.

'Brainwashing'

When I got home from EST, I went to sleep and had a dream. In it there was a big book with a living demons face on it. I opened the book and each page was a mini reenactment of the processes I'd been put through in EST. The difference was that in the dream I was able to see the hidden thing, the subconsciously planted thing that I wasn't able to see when I was actually there going through it. The dream is where I became consciously aware of things that happened like the guy finally saying, "You're not really machines" after hours of insisting that we were.

They made us visualize that we were tiny and crawling up inside a daisy in a big field of daisies. We were all following his detailed description and then we were supposed to crawl out at the top of our daisy and look around at all the other daisies. We were standing with our eyes closed when we did this. Then he said okay now wave to all the other daisies and now open your eyes. Everyone was standing there like a bunch of sheep waving to each other. In the dream I saw how incredibly, 'Lame' this was for lack of a better word. How I had given my dignity and sovereignty over to a man teaching me another mans religion. I had this enlightenment where I realized that no matter how 'good' his religion was, I didn't want it. It was more important to recognize my own innate dignity as a creation of God and as a man than to get some formula that would supposedly give me whatever the, 'It' was they told me I'd get. I didn't care what I could get, if I had to give up my dignity to get it. I remember thinking to myself after the dream that Jesus didn't do that to me. He was somehow different. He was a man I could give my whole self to without losing my own dignity as a man. He had somehow proved this to me even then in my very early, innocent and initial exploration into who Jesus was to me. I remember thinking how incredibly pathetic and lame it would be, how beneath my true dignity as a creation of God it would be, to base my life on some philosophy, some idea, any other man like me came up with. The only being I could bow down to without losing my own infinite dignity was God, and somehow Christ, seemed to embody him. Somehow bowing down to Christ raised me up to God.

The beginnings of the mystery of the incarnation were stirring in me. You may be thinking, 'That's just cause you believe that Leo.' Keep reading, maybe we'll find out if anything is actually 'True' or not.

It's difficult to explain how beneath my dignity, my sovereignty, this whole brainwashed, cult process was. In the dream I experienced this and how I felt about it consciously. The impact is hard to put into words, but there was this incredible loss of dignity. It was like why the hell am I doing what this jerk is telling me to do and acting like a freaking daisy and waving to everybody. God!

The effect carried on and again I realized how no matter how good Werner Earhardt's ideas were, and in retrospect they're pathetically obtuse, I didn't want to base my life and happiness and 'It' on it, them or him. What had he done for me, had he done even an atom of what Jesus had done both historically, archetypically and also personally in the wilderness and in my life with miracle after miracle? Jesus always felt like the only man I could actually 'worship' without losing any of my own dignity. No one else had shown me an atom of the meaning Christ has with his life and with his death. It isn't that I can't learn and be helped and guided in deeply profound ways by others, but I can only worship God. When I worship God I am worshiping my own Creator by loving his creation, his art, the image I have been created in and am being created in. Through Christ's flesh, what he died and rose to leave me, he becomes more intimately and really One with me than any other man or God I know of. When I worship God, I am loving my actual real 'Father' who like every father wants me to have all he has and even more.

When you allow another man, or woman, to be your master that way, the way I allowed myself to be mastered in EST, you give up your dignity as a human being, sovereign in yourself even with the freedom to reject God. God does not usurp that sovereignty. You are able to humbly serve others, you are able to learn and be helped and even healed by others. You are able to be vulnerable and when you're sick, weak. You are able to 'Need' the help of others and ask for it, when it is done in love. I will only submit to a man that I am convinced is submitted to God, in that respect we have a familial and tribal hierarchy on Earth that is part of an angelic hierarchy in heaven. But bowing down to a man and submitting to his 'ideas', giving your sovereignty over to him, teaches you, him, and everyone else, that we are less than what we are. When a woman surrenders to a man in love it is a reflection of what we both are giving God together as one, and the love, the creation of Life that proceeds from the love and surrender of a man and a woman becoming one flesh is just that, a fact and a reality, the fruit of love in us is known by life.

'Bully'

I wander chronologically in this book because I think your knowing me is essential to your understanding what I am trying to share. I was ten years old when we moved to Singapore and I was sent to public school there. It was culture shock to be thrust into an old fashioned Chinese system, very strict with lots of memorization. I remember at the cafeteria all they had was rice and 'Fish Ball Soup' and that was what I thought it was! The kids didn't like me, my hair was long and they said I looked like a girl. Three kids cornered me in the assembly square and one pulled a small knife on me. Nobody else was around, I somehow took the knife away from the kid and they left, I didn't know who the kids were, we all wore uniforms. I thought I would never find any real friends during our stay there. I remember deciding one day, "I'll be my own best friend". It worked and that choice had a profound effect on my life.

When I turned twelve I entered the Singapore International School and I met "Jafa," one of a group of kids from a remnant Scottish military barracks. He was built like a bullfrog and had kind of greasy leathery skin. He was the leader of a loose gang of Scottish kids and he'd yell out at me while he was eating some greasy sausages at the tuck shop, "Oy, Yank, ya want a bit a my botha boots"! I was walking by and looking back at him wondering what he was talking about. I asked my British friend Sean and he said, "He wants to fight yuu, get into a bothahhh with yuu and kick the shit out of yuu." It all started because I had played my guitar in a school assembly, the kids liked it and Jafa got all chesty about it. I was scared of him and full of anxiety. This kind of stuff went on for a couple of weeks with me trying to avoid Jafa and his bother boots. Meanwhile, another friend Robert (an American) who was a lot bigger than me got in a fight with Jafa on the bus and Jafa broke his arm. Robert came to school in a cast. All the kids kept telling me how bad Jafa was and I was scared. They told me he could do a bench press with a kid sitting on either side of the barbell and that he'd jumped off the roof and ambushed some kid at a dance and beat him up bad. I don't know if this was exaggeration or not but he had earned and maintained his authority by beating other kids up. On a Friday, one of Jafa's mate's walked up to me and said

Jafa wanted to fight me the following Monday at lunchtime behind the music hall and that if I didn't show up they would drag me down there.

Finally on Friday evening when my Dad got home I told him about Jafa. Dad said, "I used to box in the Navy, let's go down to the Chinese Emporium and get you some boxing gloves." "I'll teach you a combination and you can practice it over the weekend." He showed me a left jab and right cross combination and coached me to deliver the most power behind my punch. "You don't punch with your arms, you punch with your legs and your whole body, once you start punching, keep punching, that's what a combination is." I have always been grateful to my Dad for teaching me to fight instead of reporting it to the school. I had described Jafa to my father and he must have known there was a good chance I would get beat up, but I think he knew it was more important that I face my fear and stand up to the bully. Almost forty years later I faced another bully. He tried to kill me. I might tell you about that another time.

At lunchtime on Monday I started walking down to the music hall. I'd only been in a few fights before in Monterey and they weren't full on fights. There was a kid at Monte Vista in fourth grade who had a steel plate in his head. He was tough too and talked kind of funny. He would sometimes let another kid drag him across the grass by his hair to show that he was tough. He kept egging me on and one day on the playground he pushed me and I punched him right in the mouth and gave him a fat bloody lip. He respected me and left me alone after that. So heading down to fight Jafa, I was sure I was going to get beaten up but I figured that was better than living another day in dread and having the combination gave me a certain kind of confidence and something to focus on. At the front of the music hall, a couple American kids stopped me and said, "We're not letting you go down there, that guy is gonna beat the crap out of you". I said, "I gotta do it, I just want to get it over with."

All the kids were there waiting to see Jafa give me the botha. I can still hear this cacophony of young voices. The crowd parted and there was Jafa the bullfrog all pumped up with himself and chesty. In this school they had a rule that whoever threw the first punch was the one that got in trouble. I said, "You have to throw the first punch" and he said, "No way Yank" so I said, "Good, then we don't have to fight" and started to turn away then he threw a cheap shot that just skimmed off my chin. I let go with all I had, the left jab and right cross with my body and legs the way my Dad showed me and Jafa fell down into the monsoon drain with me after him. We flailed a bit and I fell back against the sloped side of the drainage ditch as he came over on top of me. I got my foot up between us and pushed him back and off me hard. We scrambled around and somehow I got him pinned down so his neck was locked in my armpit and my foot was braced against the opposite side of the monsoon drain. I punched him in the face repeatedly and asked him to quit, but he just said "Na Yank" so I kept punching him and asking him to quit, saying I didn't want to hurt him anymore and I even told him he could say he won. This went on for a while until a teacher showed up and dragged us out of the ditch. To everyone's surprise, especially my own, I beat up Jafa that day. He got taken to the infirmary and I got taken to the Headmaster Mr. Marshall. He was a great big bearded scary Scott with a long switch in the corner of his office he was allowed to use on some of the kids. He had actually scared the piss out of me once. The school had a uniform and I was wearing black pants instead of brown like we were supposed to. He had warned me and I saw him waiting outside the school in the morning as my bus arrived. I ran to the bathrooms to hide. As I was creeping out the door and about to peek around the corner, he appeared with his hulking mass and growling voice right in front of me and I actually peed a little squirt. Anyway, back to the fight, Jafa missed three days of school. He returned with a broken fat lip and two black eyes. Friends told me the coach came up to him in the locker rooms and said loudly so that everybody could hear, "Oy Jafa, it looks like the Yank gave ya a bit of a lickin". He would nod at me after that when I saw him. It sure felt good to not be afraid.

Twelve is the age of passage for boys to manhood in many tribes going back to the beginning and that rite is forgotten today, it's too bad. I host groups of Native, Metis and all the rest of kinds of kids on my ranch and I try to give them a taste of the good things, mainly I feel so much love for them it brings tears to my eyes. It's hard being a kid today but they are really strong and smart and they want to be good.

I like peace and stillness, arguing never seems to accomplish anything, I let people have whatever opinions they want. You can tell when a person wants to be right more than find the truth, they don't really listen. I've encountered this 'Being', 'the Bully,' he uses, accuses, lies, intimidates, bribes and connives. He hates everything including himself. I've learned some great things from bullies. The thing is they are being bullied themselves by voices that are not theirs and not Gods. In my late forties they almost killed me, but I've learned to recognize their nature and feel their presence the way a mountain lion makes the hair stand up on the back of your neck. They don't like to attack anyone that faces them.

'There Was a Man'

A little while after EST, there was a man, with a kind of authority over me. I felt like he held my music in his hands. Music was my life, if you've given your whole heart, mind and soul for something too, you know what it's like. I'd known the sacred like an angels presence, not like ideas and thoughts, my intellect wasn't really involved, no sin, no guilt, no fig leaf. Before the first betrayal, I was happy, and innocent like a friendly loyal dog.

This man held my world in his hands and I didn't know. I didn't see. I just wanted to play my guitar, I wanted to make beauty drip from the air and touch people, it was all I had left. But the man wanted something else from me. He got it from other kids too, I was seventeen and young, he held what I wanted over my head and manipulated me and it didn't dawn on me, I could just say, "No!" until it was too late. It was far enough, to never be able to come back.

Help came to me in a dream. The man had a demons face and the sun set on his forehead. It dawned on me and I knew, I could walk in with my guitar and say if you want me to play, I will, but I won't do that anymore. I did and it stopped. It's never over but everything, even pure evil, is turned to good for those that love God, Love, the Truth. I think this dream is about to dawn on the world. Earth will wake up and say, you can't do that to me anymore, I'm true to my nature and so are my creatures. I grow innocence in Eden. The birds, the meadows, the unwanted I've adopted, the angels, the planets and the galaxies, the buffalo and the people they grow, are meant for beauty. We will only let those in who can prove to themselves and to us they are sorry. The rest of you can have what you've created, what you've fought, lied, killed, conspired and lived for, and go to hell, because you become what you love the most.

That man didn't hold a gun to my head, and even that shouldn't have made me. I let myself be manipulated and persuaded to do something I didn't want to do for a bribe. I was deceived, without guidance or a code. I said before, I thought, if you can call it that, a person should do whatever they want as long as it doesn't hurt anybody. Now I know, the 'person', is whoever inhabits the soul, and who we let inhabit us, wants to inhabit everyone else. He was inhabited by something that was using him too. I never wished him ill. I forgive him and feel sorry for him, but every sin has a victim and if I speak out about it, it's for the victims, they end up being all of us.

I love people that are attracted to the same sex as much as myself and everyone else. Every statistic proves how challenging it is for them and I want to treat them with the same compassion I'd like to be treated with. Their sins aren't worse than mine, and what about the women that loved me and I left, and the life inside them that never took a breath. No ones sins are worse than our own, but it takes a saint to see that, that's why I listen to saints, they prove what they say is true, the rest of us guess.

'Give Me Something Beautiful'

Somehow, I'd like to reach and lay down like a bridge, to join worlds, yours and mine and everybody's. A bridge is grounded in both sides. Some will say I'm too pious and some will say I'm too worldly. I want to be holy, but I have to be honest, so I'm trying to just be myself and tell you my story.

Some people seem to be able to bring heaven to Earth, it's almost like they've got feathers, but I feel like I grew slow out of a shady place in the desert, like a red Manzanita. It was so hot and dry in parts of the desert mountains, everything depended on finding water. I remember where all the animals and me were coming to the same stinky muddy water hole for miles in every direction. Running out of water is scary and really, horrible, it's much worse than hunger, it induces panic.

There were cliffs and ledges that got a lot of shade and that smooth red bark would feel cool against my skin. I got into a mossy crevice to cool down, it was about three hundred feet up at the top of a box canyon cliff. I could look out over the scrub oaks and sycamores below. Then along came a great big old funny black bear, they can get up to eight hundred pounds in California. He was putting his nose in the air and moving his front paws around the way they do, just looking around, stopping, eating some ceanothus berries. He came to the foot of the cliff beneath me. I could see right down on top of him. I've seen twenty-two different black bears back there, many repeatedly. They always ran away when they saw me. I hung my head out far enough so I could see what he was doing, and he started climbing up the cliff! I'd never seen one do that before. He was climbing straight up this fissured sandstone rock face and using the crevices like there was nothing to it. I got out of the crevice and up on top of the cliffs edge. I didn't want to startle him but I wanted to see him when he came over the top. It was so easy for him to climb I was amazed, and after a few minutes there he was about twenty feet away. I allowed him to see me once he was over the edge, he just stared at me, he wasn't afraid of me like all the other ones, he was looking me over, like maybe he was thinking about putting the chomps on me, but then he ate some berries off the bush next to him.

Anyway, I'm telling you this because it was so neat to see, and because that bear is sovereign, he's not an idea bear. Earth, a tree, scorpions, that red tail hawk I snatched a rabbit from, they are sovereign too, and so am I. This idea, that I create everything with my thoughts, it's thought up by people that think thoughts hold the answers. Good thoughts are better than bad thoughts, but thoughts don't hold answers, love is the answer, thoughts and ideas don't love, Beings do. Beings hold the answer, beings are the answer.

The Native American's knew this, that is why they are called Animists, and closer to my Communion than most realize. They let the soul of the Earth, the life, the Spirit of the creatures teach them. Instead of their own ideas, they'd teach what real Beings gave them. That's what angels do, they move over and onto us like thunderheads, like moods in the redwoods and under the oaks, and they are sovereign. You are sovereign, I am sovereign, I am not your idea, and either is God.

In the Monastery I had a dream where Jesus came to me in a reddish brown robe, he said, "Are you willing to suffer for me?" and instead of saying yes, I said, "What do I have to do?" typical. He said, "Where an open robe" and he opened his robe and pointed where his heart is. I thought he meant to live in the world the way I was trying to live in the Monastery, with his heart.

I see two ways to join, one is to compromise and the other is to rise. Whatever it is I believe, I want it to be the most beautiful thing I can find, but it's being True is the ecstasy of its beauty. That's what faith is, that's what miracles do. They say, not only is this the most beautiful, highest, most glorious reason I could find, it's also, True! Wooohoooooooooooooo!

In the world we face the compromise, do we please each other or do we rise for each other? When I felt the call to leave everything, it was all faith, it was strange you know? On the outside and in every part of me but the heart of my soul, I felt kind of useless, who was I if I left all I'd worked for? but there was this …honor… in it. There was this beauty like I was following an angel and more and more, I believe I was. I was Soultracking.

Angels are Beings with immaterial bodies, I used to think of them in a visual way, but later in encountering the dark ones that tried to destroy me and get me to destroy everything I loved, in a dark night of the soul where God took away grace, it strengthened me, I learned a lot, a ton, like how you learn to walk with rattlesnakes striking in the grass. Angels are more like moods and whispers, they aren't ideas, they are as real as the creatures here, just like a buffalo, what an immense presence buffalo have, especially when they decide to charge you, angels are similar, but without a body, pure intellect and function, not form.

Somehow they are able to appear to us when there is a need and even reach into the physical, I don't know much about that, but I'm learning something about the moods of their presence. Sometimes they're like chocolate in our blood. Do

I tell the truth or what I think people want to hear? Do I say the details don't matter, 'Nothing's really true, lets be nice and let every opinion be equally true, all this believing that something can actually be real or true is the cause of all our problems' Do I say because things are similar they're the same? That it's not nice to let anything be more accurate than something else because then somebody might be wrong sometimes! Everybody gets an A even if it's an F.

That is what the world says, and what does it give us, look around, it's nothing like nature, it's nothing like the animals, it's as far from what Earth gives us as we can get... almost. It is an increasingly ill, self-deceiving, fearful, purposeful mediocrity, a tribe of intellectual zombies that worship ideas, and our dead and dying bodies instead of Life. It's not very beautiful, because it's not True.

It's okay to repeat this, because I don't think too many people believe it yet. We believe whatever we want, whether we know it or not, we have to, everyone has a religion, all it means is whatever we believe and believe we don't believe about the most important things, about reality. There are thirty thousand different religions that all call themselves Christian, but what they believe and believe they don't believe is critically different enough to divide and keep dividing. Some have lots of members and are organized and some have a few and are disorganized, that's got nothing to do with it. Most are sincerely trying to love and do what they think is right, just like most people that don't call themselves Christians.

Whether you're an atheist or a man boy lover or a 'non-denominational' televangelist or anything else, you've got a religion and you're religious, you're totally devoted to whatever you believe you want the most, it's your god and everything you believe about it is your religion. What you believe matters, even the details. What's important to me about it is this; is it the most beautiful thing I can find, and... is it true. If the beauty of who I see and believe doesn't inspire you, I hope I can inspire you to believe what you believe, whatever it is, believe it enough to prove whether it's beautiful and whether it's true or not, to yourself first and then to the rest of us.

Don't compromise it and change it for me, you won't offend me by believing it, it's too late, I've been in the presence of evil, I see now where it's rained on me like acid, I've snuck through temples to Satan, we're not going fix this situation by persuasion. Be as humble and beautiful or as proud and lame as you want, go for it, let the chips fall where they may. Almost no one seems to be willing to learn anything and why the hell should you listen to me? It would be refreshing if you'd offer me something beautiful, not nice sounding words, something that made sense, divine sense. I'd love it for you if you were moved by the beauty I'm moved by, because it is the most beautiful thing I can begin to even glimpse. I actually, truly, believe in the Beings that prove their love to me more beautifully than any ideas or other beings I've ever come close to, but maybe you can work greater miracles than they have, maybe you'll show me something more beautiful, try, please!

Trying to 'get you' to believe in it would be like trying to persuade you to be an artist, you've got to want to be an artist with your whole heart, mind and soul to even have a chance to be an artist. You've got to be willing to give your life for beauty to be beautiful. I don't have to help the souls I track be beautiful, but I love to describe their beauty, their art is mine.

The more accurately an idea reflects the truth the more beautiful it will be, that beauty has every facet of light, it is divinely reasonable, to believe in something stupid is dumb. I've found every sacred mystery I've entered into to be exactly the opposite of how the 'world' sees it, how it first appears, not just different, but the opposite. I've also found it to be perfectly, divinely, exquisitely logical, with both common and uncommon sense, it always holds water without a leak as a perfect concept, it's perfection is miraculous and leads to a perfect Being. If it didn't I'd keep looking till it did, or come to the conclusion that, oh, I guess God isn't real and nothing's actually true, real or perfect, sumpum.

We look at ideas, situations, people and beliefs and make judgments on them that don't make real 'sense'. How do you describe that? How do you help someone to see something they won't look at? It's like music, to begin to actually hear it, you have to work with your intellect and fingers and ears and your 'bits and pieces' and clunk along awkward believing your soul can come through till it does. I have to want to. I can only approach beauty from the Center. My intellect is as beautiful and as important a gift as my heart, my emotions and my body, it's not less or separate.

Animals have gifts and they make use of them, all of them, even a mountain lion that pounces on a deer. The reason people think the intellect is bad and we should just flow with the vibrations, or strum some chords and 'agree on the basics,' that what is similar is the same, that the truth isn't true and nothing is real, that the details are meaningless, is because they've never seen the beauty of the truth the intellect can show them. The only kind of thinking they are doing with it is relative.

Nature doesn't do that, animals live somewhere else, I like it where they live, even the beauty of the fear they give. I have to care about beauty and love truth more than myself, let go of everything and commit myself to it to find out if it's true, before I can begin to really hear it, to see its beauty, and express it. I can do this with all my weaknesses, fears and faults, when I humble myself enough to actually Pray.

Honesty, sincerity, and truth are the beauty and music of angels, real angels, not idea angels. Call them in the name of their God and they'll come. They have as much faith in me as I have in them. I'm calling them. Learn what beauty is. The worst lies I've believed were whispered to me by predators, they hunted my soul through my will. When all our gifts, including our intellect are aligned in the desire for truth, more than being 'right' or what we think we might prefer, and enough to let people think and say all kinds of things about us we wish they wouldn't, our gifts raise us and them, the same way it happens with music, they take us into a different dimension, and we find what it is we are seeking that is beautiful is not a what but a Who. They give me something beautiful I pray I give you.

'Soulpath's'

First I followed their foot prints
The ripples of life around them
They took me into their kingdom of stone
Sky and water
Of Earth
I felt my life there
One alone
With nothing and no one to compare
Or compete with
Nothing was a compromise
I stalked mountain lions in oak savannah
To look in their eyes
I Wandered in the Spirit
Where each step is a moment
And the sun set where it took me
Into miracles that changed reality
My body carried my soul
All I wanted was life
To take what I found back to the world
It has always been art to me
I loved Earth like a woman
But I loved the world like I loved many
I wanted to breathe and drink what was good in it
But 'sin' is like pollution
Impurity is the difference between Earth and the world
I wanted Eve before she fell
I don't know if anyone loved her as much as me
I pray we all feel that way
There's a fire coming of love

Not to be afraid of
To make us pure as living prayers
Like creatures true to their natures
Like angels true to theirs
Everything I tracked was going to my soul

'Answers'

On the outside I was still 'functioning' highly, I was performing and becoming a professional musician, but I was incredibly stressed and confused. First I went through EST, then I had the same kind of thing happen to me that 2.8% of priests did to 86% teenage males, and then my sister who was 6 months away from her Ph.d In Bio-Chemistry and a beautiful, vibrant young woman was struck down with M.S. so severely that in a few months she was in a wheel chair with severe brain damage needing twenty-four hour care. It was so devastating for my entire family, especially my mom. All of us went off into our shells and tried to deal with it. This heavy dark cloud engulfed my family. We didn't come together and pray or talk together about how we were feeling until much later.

When I was fifteen, I had 'Committed Myself to the Truth' I didn't know what the truth was, but I knew it meant I would have to chose what I thought was true over what I might prefer. I hope you will really think about that, because that decision made everything else possible. Once you commit yourself to the truth, everything you do is built on something real. I believed in the golden rule and in the positive thinking kind of stuff, that if you did good things good things would happen. But then I remember thinking, 'Wait a minute, my sister did good things and look what happened to her'. My mother who was an artistic, intelligent, sensitive person had also always been a fearful person. I began to be overcome with anxiety and fear. I thought, 'How can I have a moments peace or joy if something awful can happen any second to me or someone I love.....? and there's no meaning to it...?' The stress got so bad I developed a pain in my solar plexus that actually brought me to my knees a couple of times in public. I also developed a bunch of floaters, little broken blood vessels that float around in the vitreous fluid of the eyeball. I went to the doctor. He did a bunch of tests and then asked me if I was under stress. I said yes, he said he thought that was the cause of it and prescribed tranquilizers for me. I went home without getting the medicine. I'm always very reluctant to take medicine, so much of it has terrible side effects and few people seem to know that misdiagnosis and prescription drugs are the second biggest killer in North America, only after the other man made killer, heart disease. Anyway, I got home and went to sleep. I woke up kind of relaxed but then could feel the stress like butterflies in my solar plexus. My usual automatic reaction was to resist and squelch them down, but for some reason I decided to see what would happen if I just let them go. They got stronger and stronger like a roller coaster ride without the fun. I just let them go without any resistance and in a minute or two they subsided and went away and I never had the pain again.

I didn't know what life was and humans were and what if any meaning there was to it. It is hard to explain how the EST experience bore this. It was a vague fear not of anything in particular but overwhelmingly strong and growing. I remember waking up with dread, like something terrible was going to happen any second and it would have no meaning, no explanation. I remember I prayed for things that I thought would make me happy; to be a great composer, singer etc. but unknowingly until later, I wasn't praying directly for what I wanted, needed, like hope, help, forgiveness, faith, love....I was praying for circumstances I thought I wanted, but what I wanted without realizing it yet, was something beyond circumstances. My prayers seemed to just bounce off God. This went on for several years. The mystery of grace and the mystery of iniquity are critical to 'understand' the life of the soul, kind of like the way an artist has to know his medium. I was only just beginning to know mine, only just beginning to recognize the difference between 'thinking' to 'figure things out', and feeling the presence of angels.

There was something that happened, a bit of inspiration I remember, that helped me along the way. I visited the Palace of Legion of Honor in San Francisco. I went through each room looking at the art and not feeling much except stress, as usual, until I came upon a painting, I can't remember the painter, but it was of a scene from the mountain jungles of Vietnam at sunset. It moved me, deeply, what was it...it was so full of feeling and so breathtaking. It was the only man made creation I can remember through that entire time that really moved me to tears at the beauty. This was a profound event for me because it made me think, maybe there is some meaning and real value to art and if it can move me when I so need to be moved, then it can move someone else also. I thought even if life is meaningless, maybe art can give something of actual value if it's authentic. I was working at my music professionally and functioning as best as I could through all of this period.

Another spark of light entered the darkness of this time. My father gave me a book called the Dancing Wu Li Masters, authored by Gary Zukav and based on interviews he did with a number of the world's leading nuclear physicists. He asked them to explain in layman's terms what they were discovering though quantum mechanics, the study of sub-atomic particles. They used models to describe what they were observing in their experiments. I remember they said that if you enlarged an atom so that its diameter was equal to a 14 story high building, that the nucleus would be the size of a grain of sand and the electrons and protons orbiting it would be the size of dust particles. They said the relative distance between the nucleus and the orbiting protons and electrons was greater than that of the earth to the sun. I saw how even though my prayers were bouncing off God and I was so confused about the nature of truth and reality and why I was hear and what it all meant, that one thing was clear; time, space and matter were not what they appeared to be. 99.9% of everything we thought was real and factual and the hard evidence everybody relied on, was empty space, and it was moving. The same material thing that most of the world was using as its measuring stick for God and everything else, changed its nature, speed and location depending on how you measured it. This was encouraging, it confirmed what my heart and experience were telling me. There was an aspect to the passage I was going through that in hindsight made even the anxiety and confusion of it meaningful. In a way, the meaninglessness became meaningful in this one respect, I had let go of everything I believed and everything I held to be true, even my faith, not by a choice, but by way of wanting the truth more than anything. Letting go of everything you believe in order to find out what's left, what's actually true, is frightening. It's the edge of letting go of your mind and wondering if you're insane. When I see mentally disturbed people, I feel a tender compassion for them. Later I discovered the cause of much mental anguish and illness is spiritual, and the actual attack of spiritual beings, demonized angels, but that comes further on. There was a beautiful diamond that arose out of the trial of losing everything I thought I knew, even my faith, in the end when there was nothing left to hold on to, I'll describe how what was left, was God. God expressed to me as Love and Love as the only pure Truth. The only truth that was not relative. I was learning truth by its own nature, not by my assumptions and attachments or my fears and desires.

This may be the hard way to learn and sometimes I think maybe it's because I'm not as, 'good' as a lot of other people I know, but there is something about living by Wandering in the Spirit into the next step, getting exactly where you want to go without knowing where it is or what it is, with no destination, that is a thrilling way to travel, and a destination in itself because wherever we are going the moment is our destination. This is the sword of the moment, the truth of the moment, each moment is eternal and each moment is not the same, the moment that is heaven is the State of Grace. Wandering in the Spirit is not wandering blindly, it is following the vision only God and the souls that love him reveal to you. It is a reaching for only the most beautiful thing you can find, not something less, and then finding it is a living being. It is what I call Soultracking. It is placing my feet in the tracks as the soul before me leaves them and it takes everything, every bit of myself that is real, that is alive, or I lose the tracks and wander further and further away, off the path of the highest beauty and onto all the other paths I can follow if I want to, but I don't want to. Reaching for the highest beauty hurts the way it hurts to reach for perfection in art.

But this is the thing, an artist doesn't whine about it. They don't say it's not fair that they have to try as hard as they can. They don't say let's make art easier by not caring anymore, let's say everything is as beautiful as everything else so we don't hurt anybody's feelings, beauty's not fair for making us reach, don't judge my work, the validity of my expression, that's unkind, that's bad for my self-esteem. That's the world's attitude toward God and holiness, nothing but a bunch of stupid excuses not to try.

Soultracking is revealed in the miracle, the miracle is the vision. The state of grace is the state of creation, the state an artist must reach, the center, the heart of all things, God's heart and yours. It is kind of like an athlete being in shape, or a martial artist in the center of his discipline, a musicians musicianship, every moment is not the same, just as every idea is not the same, every song is not the same. A touch can be love and a touch can be rape. Wanting to be a good athlete or musician is essential, but it's not enough, being one takes committing myself to the truth. It takes loving the truth, more than what I think I prefer, because the truth is alive, Christ says," I am the truth, the way and the life" because truth and love is not a thing we do, or an idea, it is the living Spirit, the Soul, we become.

It isn't of this world, there is a mountain of pressure against it. I don't think Indians planned out every 5 minutes so they could achieve a goal. I think they lived between steps, and their lives were so full most of us would weep in the recognition that we'd barely ever taken a step, we'd wasted and missed almost every step we'd ever taken rushing toward some goal we'd reach only to rush onto the next, always doing something so we could do something else and never doing something else.

'The Sacred'

I decided to go to the Catholic Church up the street from my house and hoped I might find some spiritual re-connection there. I have vivid memories of the sacred and of my spirit as a child with my parents at the mass. The Latin, the solemnity, the Gregorian chant, the incense and bells, and most of all the reverence, I remember people doing something there they didn't seem to do anywhere else, quietly and deeply, they prayed.

I decided I'd apply to be an usher thinking if I had a job there it would help make sure I went. A priest came to the back of the Church and spoke to me. "You must be Leo, you would like to be an usher"? Yes. A few pleasantries and then he asks me if I've ever been to 'Joe's', a bar and restaurant in town. I said no. He said, "Oh everybody goes to Joe's, it's great, we should go sometime." I'm getting a real weird feeling from this guy and I say, "No thanks I don't have time for anything but my work". Then he says, "Well you know priest's take an oath of celibacy, but there's ways around it" and walks back to the front of the church. I walked out the door and didn't come back for ten years. I remember seeing him driving around in a pink convertible Thunderbird. I didn't think of reporting the guy to someone, I think I responded the way many people do and just got the hell away from him and the Church. I met more false priests like that when I was thirty-three and entered a monastery, but I have to hold off on that till later.

'The First Commandment is to Be an Artist'

I read spiritual, metaphysical and philosophical material from diverse religions and backgrounds and I found wisdom and good ideas, but nothing that really helped. I'd known miracles and joy that verged on the ecstatic, and that was so much more than thoughts and ideas. Finally one day I drove my VW van to the edge of a cliff above Santa Barbara and stopped, looking out over it and wondering if I could go on any longer like this, I was in anguish and beside myself minute to minute. Today people might say, 'You just have to choose to think positive thoughts.' Thinking positively is a lot better than thinking negatively, but honestly, it's not even close to what I am trying to express. As an 'artist', it is this reaching with your whole heart, mind and soul, for the beauty you feel and believe is there, invisible, waiting for you to have the courage to reach as far as it takes, even if it means losing everything, where you reach beyond yourself to find what is within yourself. The why of what I feel, of what I want, is more important than the what, it is the what. My why isn't to feel 'good', it's to feel whatever it takes. Only beings can inspire this, not thoughts.

Passion comes out of the care that is love and it comes out of Vision. The Native American was guided by his elders and the whole tribe under the Medicine Man, who's authority was confirmed by wisdom and signs; to seek his Vision. A Vision is a Miracle. He would do whatever it took to get it because he knew his Vision was his purpose, and then he would live it. Living his vision was his joy and strength, he didn't live for 'getting what he thought he wanted' even with good intentions. It's hard to discern the difference, of course it's good to want something good, but again it's like the difference between craft and art. The more we care the more joy we will feel and, the more pain we will feel. It's learning to think in a kind of harmony. No good thought is one thought, it is always at least three thoughts combined, thoughts are like chords, a chord is notes combined to produce harmony and no matter what the thought, what's important about it is who's thinking it.

Our life carries everything, in a glorious way, through grace, and faith, the whole world rests on each of our shoulders like the mystery of the Cross. I've always felt this in a vague and sometimes vivid way and I'll never stop learning what it is. Why is it important for me to share with you what I think is True, and to point out what I think is a lie? It's a challenge because we've grown up in a world who's new religion is infallible Relativism, nothing is true or a lie, it's like saying all music is the same, none is allowed to be more beautiful than another or someone might have to change and reach beyond whatever it is they think they want in that moment. Okay, maybe you will get to heaven or be 'saved' even if you don't try very hard, or keep choosing something you know is bad for you and others, and born out of a lack of love, but even if you do, is that how you want to live? Anybody can play music, and as long as they are trying I guess that's better than not trying, but does that mean every way is the same? No, the point is to give our whole heart, mind and soul to the beauty, the passion, the meaning and the love. For Christ's sake, you may actually have to feel sorry about something. Relativism says all beliefs and ideas about reality are the same, they're all just 'music' just play some music and get along, don't say anything if the music is a cacophony. It's like singing lies in order to make them sound better, like adds for pharmaceuticals where they sing all the lethal side-effects and ride their bikes around smiling,

For God to be a God worth believing in, I want to be in love with him and have that love be my reason, like the love between lovers. Otherwise what's the point? To get something from him? Is God a tool, or an idea that helps you get what you think you want? Can I be in love with you and not care about how you feel and why, what you think, who you are, and then do whatever I think I want insisting you are not allowed to have any feelings about it? That's the nature of the religion of Relativism, that's the communion of the politically correct, where God must only be ideas and can't have feelings, he must be unlike you. The 'charism' of relativism is to all be the same, but call it diversity. Holiness is the highest individuality there is, because it is the art of becoming One. Holiness is the passion of the truly free individual, in fact it is a love for others so deep that it requires a certain kind of sovereignty. It is a lover holding his hands a hairs breadth from her skin with his 'love sacrifice', looking into her eyes, without carnality, until they rise somewhere together they've never been before and never come back from, that is 'Faith'. The First Commandant is to be an Artist, because what an artist does is love with his whole heart, mind and soul. He 'sacrifices' everything including his flesh and blood. That's what Christ did, he showed and shows me what an artist is, a Creator.

'This One Answer'

If your seconds are precious, if you have been passionate, if you care, you may know the dread and anguish I felt, the confused, stuck, lost, hopeless, desperate, meaningless, purposeless, graceless, seeking of something, an answer I couldn't find. I wasn't purposely not believing in God, I was praying, I thought I did believe in God, but one of the worst things about losing your faith is that you don't know you're losing it. Faith is the fruit of a sincere heart that opens to God's heart, his love is his Grace. Grace is his touch and Faith is our sigh. I can want to be a great musician but that doesn't make me one, faith is the same way, it is the art of love. If you betray your lover out of weakness and you are sincerely sorry and she has the heart of love that forgives you, she helps you and heals you, but your love has to heal her wounds too. The idea of a God that's above it all is just that, an idea. For me, the love of God is like the love of a Lover.

Instead of praying for situations or accomplishments I thought would help me, I finally called out from the core of myself, I said, "Lord, if I can't ever be happy again, I can't go on, please just tell me how to be happy" and then I reached in the glove compartment and pulled out the little bible I had found so many years earlier, I opened it up and put my finger down. It was a quote of Jesus, "To be full of my joy, love each other as I have loved you".

"To be full of my joy, love each other as I have loved you" I wonder to myself, will people get what an infinitely incredibly profound answer this is? Every detail is important, but this answer is the reason I breathe.

I think, of anything I have to say, this one answer is the most important. This one answer is the reason for all the others. I hope you get this one, it's why we're here. Please think about this one, and try doing it, you can do it way better than I can, the thought of you wanting to is a profound comfort. He's telling the truth, he's making a promise. As always, God's Word, Christ, knows what he means when he says what he says and he believes it, and he cares. He is saying if you do this, this will happen, and it does. It's like committing yourself to the truth. Does it mean anything to you?

I was in the deepest darkest cave with no light at all, no way out, no hope and suddenly I saw a little pin prick of light a million miles away, but it didn't matter because it was a way out, even if it was a million miles, it was 'Hope' where there was none. I knew something had happened. I had not asked God to make me happy, I had asked him to tell me how to be happy. He answered as clearly as I could have hoped. I thought wait a minute, I thought I had been loving people and it's important to me that they think I love them, but it's nothing like the way You loved us. You loved us when we were spitting on your mother and torturing and killing you. You loved us before circumstances. You lived to love us, and you're saying that if I love others the way you love me, I will be full of your joy and I just asked you how to be happy. Okay, I'll try it. As I drove down the hill, I saw an old couple walking, I surrounded them in love, I loved them like babies, love that was unconditional, this kind of love I felt Jesus gave, I tried to send them love and blessing like shinning a light, a prayer on them. It was like air to a drowning man, me.

I had to go to the grocery store, a place I had been feeling especially stressed. The previous week, an old man had bumped into me with his cart and I had blown up, yelling at him not to push me! He just looked at me kind of stunned. I went out to the parking lot and wept, not knowing what was wrong with me. Now in the line I silently sent love from the deepest place I could fathom to each person. As I did this, great waves of realization came. Here was the Meaning of and for my life! I was here to love others the way God loves me. This was a purpose that brought such great hope and value, dignity. This was something worth living and dying for. I also realized no one and no thing or circumstance can ever take this away from me. I could be homeless on the street, sick and dying, imprisoned, tortured, confused, forsaken and still do this. I am free to invest my whole life, my whole purpose, and I can do this no matter what the circumstances are, like Jesus on the cross. The amount of fear in me is the measure of how much I am loving and trusting God. No matter what, we can still choose this love as our purpose. It is the only purpose I know that is beyond all circumstance, its meaning and practice exists beyond and before and sovereign over everything. I accepted this as my life's ultimate purpose and a deep healing began that day. I tracked God to his path again. In committing myself to the truth I was learning what truth is, truth is love, and now, I was just beginning to learn what love was.

'Where He Took Me'

It takes a life
To open the eyes
Of a soul
Wrapped in a body
Like a gift

It was warm, my parents loved me
The first time I unwrapped one
My cars weren't toys
They were vehicles
They took me to the world
And the cities
Of my imagination
I was men there
All different kinds
I loved my toys
For who I was with them
When I was eleven I saw it coming
I was growing up
I was kind of sad
To leave my cars where they took me

The coast where I was born
Is haunted with lovers
Breakers rise there
To die in the mist
Ghosts come to sigh
To kiss

Cold in the Canyons
With no bodies to undress
Like gifts under a tree
I unwrapped mine
And I unwrapped hers
Young creatures of Earth
I loved her
I gave her everything
She gave me back
Beauty, that tingled to the tips
of her fingers and trembled on her lips
She loved me
My heart was broken
To leave her where she took me

I loved the world
All the Earthy things of it in me
I drifted like smoke
Things were heavy and metal
Salinas, Big Sur, Carmel, Monterey
I loved Harley's and Hells Angels
I thought that's what I was made of
I liked the moss and rock roofs
That leaned out over the coast
And I wanted one over me
And her
I thought life lasted a long time
Kind of like heaven
I didn't think I'd die
I felt hard to kill
Too strong to give up
Everything I wanted was here
And it was so hard
To leave it where it took me

But my soul can see
Even with my eyes closed
And whenever I left the world
And Wandered in the Spirit
Out onto the Earth

I felt my muscle and my skin
And my heart
Were made of something else
Like a body grows in a womb
A soul grows in a body
When we die, we're born again
It will be hard
To leave me where I took me

God glorifies Earth
With his blood
It runs through our veins
We don't like the sight of it
When I'd eat rattlesnakes
I'd see through their eyes
I pray for the buffalo
But I see myself
And pray to do what they do
They accept everything
Life eats life
I eat prayers
So I have to be one
I consume beauty
With a prayer to be beautiful
Or I eat their life unknowingly
In vain
Bringing condemnation upon myself
And I've done it
It has been very hard
To leave them where they take me

I pray to be Gods Sundance
The Body and Blood of a Man
If you were the last one left that believed him
You'd be him
I'd walk Earth like he did
The blood I left would be his
He told me it is
Who can take that away from me?
They couldn't take it away from him

They couldn't make him stop believing
They couldn't make him stop loving
Even though they hate him
But it must have been sad for him
To leave me where he took me

'I'll Follow You'

In the wilderness I felt as if it was the first day, every next range and valley was like a kingdom to me. I loved to be alone, with who I believed was my Creator, creating everything exactly like he wanted to right in front of me. I found out what and who I believe I am the way I think the people that lived there before me did, through miracles, visions I want to share here with you. They'll happen for anyone that humbles themselves, but like our ancestors, I was able to live away from the 'world' of man, and be alone with what for me is the living meaning of the Earth, the Soul of the Earth, 'Wandering in the Spirit'. Who and what I believe I am is a being created to know and love his Creator by becoming One with who I love. I mean really One, the way the Trinity is One. I do not lose my identity in God, I become sovereign like he is, and find it.

I've described my experience out there by saying I felt like Adam before Eve, before the animals and plants had names, and I could name them. That's what man has done since his soul entered a body, he has given meanings names, with words. This is what I and my ancestors believe God has done also, with his 'Word', the Word of God is not only the living oracle and holy revelation of the Bible, it is Gods expression of himself in Man, Gods word does and is what it says because God is the Artist. He becomes what he expresses, his art, his creation, this is why Christ can say, "I am the truth the way and the life" "I am that I am" Christ is the symbol that is what it symbolizes and everything he does and says is a living Spirit, that's why when he makes a new covenant in his flesh and blood and says, "This is my body" it is.

With his breath, the breath of God, he appoints 'Medicine Men,' Priest's he 'breathed on', and 'sent' as the Father sent him, with his 'authority' to forgive and retain sins, authority that actually does something, who hears you hears me, keys, to loose and bind, like weapons a nation gives soldiers, but these are weapons that deliver and bring life instead of take it. Gods Word isn't more ideas, it is a living being, his Son, he becomes his art. The only reason I hesitate to use his name is because most modern people don't know what it means, and I don't like using it in vain.

In the wilderness, I didn't experience things by their 'names.' It wasn't so much a bear or a mountain lion I encountered, it was a 'living meaning.' We don't realize how we think the word is the meaning, in a kind of obfuscating idolatry of words, but the word is a symbol of the meaning of the 'thing,' and the thing itself, a lion or a bear, is a symbol of itself, of its soul, its 'living meaning.' We are a living symbol of a living meaning and that living meaning is God. That's what it means to be created in the 'image' of God. His soul is ours. He came to show us who we are. Everything creates in its own image. We are so incredibly holy that our sin is a pitiless sacrilege, like a curse we collaborate with. Even though I know and believe this, I still do it, as St. Paul says, 'we do the very thing we don't want to do' That is the nature of a curse and the deceptive affect of a predator.

The Purpose of a symbol is to express the meaning of its creator… I believe that soon, globally, whether we believe truth is true or not, we are going to discover our Purpose. To discover our purpose is an Illumination of Conscience. That can be an agonizing discovery, especially if you still think you 'want' something more than the Truth. I thought I was committed to the truth and it sure was agonizing for me. It might be kind of like what some of my faithful and loving friends call being 'born again' but to be born again, you have to die first and dying is agonizing. For me being born again is a birth that never ends, and by the way, it always takes a Woman, a Mother, even for God. The significance of this is so immense that her veil is the sun. God came to man through a woman, and it seems like almost the whole world is missing their love affair, it's ours!

Love is pure, it is a light that purgates and burns away impurities. We are the windows of our soul. What I and my holy blood brothers, not the liars and predators that seek control in every group under every name, believe, we can and must do is ask Love to make us clean, with our whole heart, mind and soul, so the light can shine through without consuming us. Impurities turn light into heat. Impurity is another word for sin, a grasping for less than what we are, a denial we're afraid to admit and face. We can answer our instinctual fear of punishment by trying to convince ourselves we're not going to hell, or, by trying to convince ourselves hell doesn't exist, we can even try to vote hell away, but our 'living meaning' isn't fear, it's to find the truth we seek and let it be what it is, sovereign like a bear, like God, like Love, and be set free by it, to live, die and believe for the Beauty of Love, like Christ did.

When we are small our world becomes vast, to be first be last, to be great be humble, to be born, die, to gain your life, lose it. It all seems like impractical non-sense for a person that lives for his five senses. Some people sincerely want to have faith and they never experience a miracle, some don't wan't to believe because they think they'll have to change and others lose their faith to gain it back stronger than they ever dreamed.

Prayer is the only way we become convinced of the other world and live for it instead of this one. Prayer takes my whole heart, mind and soul because prayer is art. Prayer deepens the way art does, it starts out kind of course and awkward with a lot of thinking, but slowly, with passion, it turns into love and trust, into a living beauty. Prayer is putting the Kingdom of Heaven first, and your lover 'rewards' you even here on Earth, with miracles and power, beauty and love and with trials that turn us into something real. Until I decide to love Truth more than being 'right', committing myself to it like God, sovereign, I can't experience what 'Oneness' is, because what the sovereign truth does, is what it is, the Spirit and the Life. Everything true is personified like you.

But, maybe you're certain I'm wrong about all of this, maybe we each have our own truth and nothing sovereign exists. Maybe we're all here to vote and guess. Maybe we can all do whatever we think we want with no truth to answer to because we're God and we make up the truth. If that is the case, then what I think we all have a right to ask is this: Show me the beauty of your God and your truth and prove it so beautiful I can't resist it, make it an expression of your living meaning. Make it reveal my purpose to me the way the body of the First Born of the Dead has, the way the Daughter of God has, pierce your heart to show me the thoughts of mine, don't give me your myths and ways to think, give me your flesh and blood and make it exude the fragrance of roses from corpses incorrupt. Bleed from the wounds of Christ, bi-locate, levitate in ecstasies, show me the miracle of the sun after you predict it, sanctify matter with your body, make demons beg and release me. Heal me, love me and forgive me when I'm nailing you to a cross and spitting on your mother and mine. Be the creation that gives her Creator birth, give me birth, and then look into my eyes; but don't be an idea, don't be a symbol, be the Real Presence, show me the love and the beauty she lives for, and I'll follow you, to heaven.

'Californian'

I was born at the beginning of something. It was 1960 in Monterey, California. Married movie stars wanted my sisters. My brother Richard and I were crazy about motorcycles, he taught me to read with motorcycle magazines. I was walking down our hallway when a big earthquake hit. I can still see the walls rolling and waving. I put my hands out and swayed with them. When it stopped I said these words to myself, "If the ground under my feet can shake the only thing I can put any security in is myself." That moment has shaped my life in ways I'm grateful for and in ways that may have made it more difficult than it had to be. The older I get the less faith I have in the, 'world.' I view the things of man as quickly passing. The world I see is the symbolic world, and the real one is in me. Getting married, having a son and raising a herd of buffalo was the exception. It was the deepest happiness I have ever known on Earth, but it forced me to try and find security in a foreign place, not Canada, the world.

Wandering alone in the desert mountains of California I experienced the living and unseen world where there is no inside or outside; Earth. I felt as much a part of it as every creature there, it became the world I put my security in. It was all God talking to me, my culture was a part of it, but my culture wasn't me. Today, it seems like the more visible anything is, the less valuable and real it is to me. Invisible things, what's behind all beauty; songs, ideas, writing, prayer, honoring the ancestors of my faith and its meaning, love we share, the living Earth, "Wandering in the Spirit." These things matter very much to me and seem real, like what I'm here for.

A song is not as important as what it does. It's like a woman's physical beauty. I behold her beauty, I adore her beauty, I'm inspired and life pumps through my veins by her beauty, but I don't love her for her beauty. Her beauty is the outward expression of her soul when she's passionately, deeply and humbly surrendered in love with God. That love makes everyone beautiful and is enough to sustain the love of saints. Theirs is a passion that brings eternity to time, it asks the creature to be a creator, to be willing to break his heart; to give up the very thing he loves enough to die for. The world does not know this is what a true Priest does.

When I was growing up things didn't move with a click, they were metal and heavy, they rusted and took muscle. Steinbeck was alive and lived down the road on the way to the Salinas Rodeo and for some reason I thought Edgar Allan Poe lived in an old stone house on a cliff jutting out above breakers that groan and bellow south of Carmel. Those houses seemed like homes a person could really live in and they still do. I played on Cannery Row. My friend Richie Wagner's dad had a furniture shop in an old cannery warehouse there. There was a three story high room, filled up half with sardine can labels that we'd jump into from a door on the third floor. My brother and sisters were teenagers. Jimi Hendrix, Janis Joplin, Jefferson Airplane, Quicksilver Messenger Service, the Mamas and the Papas, Otis Redding, Eric Burdon, Simon and Garfunkel, the Byrds and Buffalo Springfield were coming to play at the Monterey Pop Festival, and I'll tell you about the Hells Angels in a while.

My Dad was a Commander in the United States Navy, a pilot through World War ll, fighting and killing the worst guys I'd ever heard of. When I saw pictures of what they did, I wanted to kill them too, or make them so sorry they'd change my mind, it's a weird feeling. My country is losing its soul, in a way, it doesn't have a leg to stand on anymore. He had all these medals on his chest, a white hat with a black brim and an eagle holding arrows.

My dad is a genius in the top 99.999% of world i.q. level, 156, they think Einstein was 160, I don't know if you've ever been around a real genius, they're different. He drove a black Ford Galaxy 500 convertible with red leather interior fast. He listened to 'A Boy Named Sue' and laughed. He loved me and our great big dog, Clooey. He loved my mom and my brother and my sisters, but he thought their boyfriends didn't have any 'guts' because they were afraid to go to Vietnam. I didn't wan't to kill those guys…I couldn't even tell who they were, my brother and me watched these numbered ping pong balls on T.V. When students at UCSB burned the Bank of America, he took us to the barber and told him to give us crew cuts. We looked at each other and cried a little as he drove us home. He smoked Chesterfields, he came home in the evening and had a few Martinis, everybody did in those days. Alcohol was the only thing that ever overcame him, and it overcame me, but we quit and went on to live the happiest times of our life and we both mellowed out.

I love California, I love my Dad, I loved having a rock band, being an artist, singing my heart out, the eyes of the women I fell in love with. I still think you have to be willing to punch a bullies lights out, I've got no problem with it, I think you're doing them a big favor. When we were kids bullies liked you if you beat them up. I like the truth, not 'my truth' and 'your truth', truth nobody owns. My outlook on all I've done and how I felt grows with my awareness. I think I was loving the best I could with what I knew.

There's something real wishy washy that seems to be happening to my culture, to men, and women too. I'd love it if someone would respectfully and thoughtfully, explain something that really made sense if they think I don't, but a lot of the time I can't figure out what they're thinking, they don't seem to know themselves, they don't seem to care that much, I mean, they might care about some 'Cause' but not about themselves, like enough to be willing to feel sorry about anything. I don't know what to do about it, except to make sure with my whole heart mind and soul and every next breath, that I believe what I say I do, and prove it, I follow somebody that demands my life, he's taken me back when I've abandoned him, but to be like him demands I give every precious second of my being...I don't live for an idea, I live for a person, God in a man, he's in me and each one of us, and all my holy ancestors, it's hard to do that, but if I don't try, everything feels like a waste of time.

Getting older is beautiful, I love it, I think I'm getting a little bit smarter, I'm less Californian and more me, but all this stuff of Earth, the smokey, bad breathed people I've loved sitting next to me in a bar, beautiful women that waited for me to come home, and loved me, friends that make a future of memories, people that told me the truth, but accepted me, even if I was telling them the opposite of what everybody else did, and loved me for it...it all turns to good for those that love Love, for those whose God is Love, real love, the kind that sometimes says, this is wrong, it's killing your soul, it's 'sin', repent. I'm telling you how it was when I was there and how it is for me now. If I say or do something wrong, stupid, uncharitable, full of myself, explain it to me, with love, help me see truth more clearly. Don't just be quiet, even if you want me to be.

'A Boner'

I was twenty-six. My Carmel CD had just gotten national distribution with Narada Records and was on full rotation on the WAVE FM out of Los Angeles. I'd worked hard and my dream to be a professional musician was coming true. I remember a lot of stress in my early twenties around 'succeeding' and now finally, I felt like I was.

I was driving back up the coast to stock stores that sold my CD. Eselan was selling it in their bookstore. They invited me to do a concert there. I'd always wondered about Eselan and I was looking forward to playing and staying there on my way up the Big Sur Coast, I've spent my whole life trying to express what the Big Sur Coast does to me, I think my Carmel CD is as close as I have come, but I'm still trying.

I pulled up in my old Fiat Spider convertible with my guitars and amps in the back. A young woman with large breasts greeted me at the guard booth and checked my name on her list. She gave me directions to my room and told me I also could use the hot tubs and have a massage if I'd like. She said to walk down to the hot tubs and someone would come and find me for my massage. I dropped my stuff in the room, washed up and went to look for the hot tubs. A long path led down toward the ocean. I could see lots of people on a large deck. As I got closer I began to see that some of them… no all of them… were nude! LOL! Something about the scene struck me as so funny, like I was in a Peter Sellers movie.

I hadn't thought this far ahead and hadn't expected it, but I went into the changing rooms and got nude too. Interiorly I was narrating the whole thing to my friend Joe, who I knew would also think it was really funny, not because people were nude, but because I was nude and Joe knew me so well, he'd know I'd be kind of embarrassed and goofy. There were nude people of every adult age, shape and size, and I was thinking some of them really should keep their clothes on, all the time! I'm just choking, just choking. I amuse myself, I know the animals around my music cabin must think I'm crazy when they hear me laughing like a donkey all alone in here.

The hot tubs were packed full of people but they scooted closer and made room for me to squeeze in, not really squeeze, but there was a bunch of us in there. There was a frizzy red haired lady to my left and an older guy to my right with a big crystal thing hung around his neck he called a grid. They were talking about the UFO's they'd seen the night before. I was dating a playboy bunny at the time and I'd left her at home, which was probably a good thing, although who knows how this story would go if I had of brought her with me? I'm fifty three years old, and I didn't grow up till three years ago. I've never been real comfortable with the nudey beach and nudist colony thing. My bunny took me for a horse ride to the Summerland nudey beach once. We got nude and then she played volleyball. I had to lie on my stomach the whole time! I think maybe I'm some kind of Neanderthal throw back or something, with caveman physiology. I don't understand how all the guys are jumping around with their girlfriends and lying in the warm sun, and rubbing coconut oil on each other, and nobody but me has a Boner! LOL! All kinds of things give me a boner. My mini-bike and all my motorcycles gave me boners, I still get a boner on my tractor, I get a boner for no reason at all! But nobody else does! What up wit dat? Maybe that's why I was focused on the jocularity of the situation, it felt kind of surreal.

I write about all this spiritual stuff and you know I believe it, look at me, I've let it lead my whole life in a funny way that's as serious as it gets. But I'm a really 'Earthy' person. Maybe I'm not sophisticated enough. I remember there were a couple rogue monks that stayed at Esalen some of the time. I found out about that later when I entered the Monastery about thirty minutes down the coast near Lucia...

But anyways, everybody else was just letting it all hang out and flop around like it was no big deal. I told myself, 'Okay, give these guys a taste of their own medicine and if you get a boner be proud'! Maybe I didn't grow up three years ago, maybe at sixty I'll grow up. So I'm sitting in the tub listening to the perfectly normal conversation about reptilians and the sex-therapy workshop a guy is encouraging the management to book. Everybody seems quite serious, when a woman walks up and asks if I'd like a massage. It's the young woman with large breasts that was at the guard booth. She leads me to a table and has me lay down on my stomach. I like the kind of massage where they push in as deep as you can take it. I've gone through the full Rolfing work and it changed my whole life. When I went from my private Catholic high school to Santa Barbara public high school the kids told me I was going to get beat up by all the tough kids. So I worked out all the time and walked around flexing my muscles. I wore overalls with no shirt underneath. I never got in a fight at Santa Barbra High School, I made a bunch of friends and it was great. There were a couple guys that thought about it, but nobody ever did anything. The man that Rolfed me asked me,'Why are you walking around like the hulk?' I said, 'Am I? yeah I guess I am, I think it's cause I'm scared' He said, 'Yes, you don't have to be, let go' and I did, my whole life and my body changed.

She asked me to roll over. The Esalan massage was a real soft thing where they rub you back and forth with long strokes. The sun warmed my skin and she stood at me head leaning over and rubbing down toward my you know what. Each time her hands reached to about my belly button, her large boobs would booble around on my face. I just kept my eyes closed and spoke to myself reassuringly. Soon all hell was breaking loose in my loins region, it was kind of jumpy and erratic like when they blow up those parade floats. There were some quiet comments and a few giggles between her and the masseuse next to us. It seemed like a high-five kind of thing. I kept my eyes closed and said to her, "It seems you've moved me in that special way." Burt Lancaster used that one on Deborah Kerr when they were filming 'From Here to Eternity'. She chuckled some more when I said, 'I guess I should have brought a flag.'

I couldn't wait to get back to Santa Barbara and tell my friend Joe. We shared a house on Mountain Drive. I called before I left San Francisco and recommended he have some Kamikazes waiting. He thought it was even more hilarious than I thought he would. He made me promise to take him with me if I ever played there again. I apologize for my impiety, but I'm trying to tell the truth of who and how I was.

The thing that is so funny about this isn't me getting a boner and all that. It's Joe, I can see him now traipsing around Eselan. Joe has a gift and could walk into an uptight, glum party and have everyone laughing and crying and hugging each other in a matter of a few minutes.

But I never did go back, instead I quit the music business in my early thirties and tried to live as much as I could alone, Wandering in the Spirit, eating rattlesnakes in the desert mountains of California where I grew up. I became celibate and entered a Monastery. Me becoming celibate could be worthy of the Guinness Book of anti-world records. Becoming celibate was one of the 'hardest' things I've ever done. I decided I wasn't going to be with a woman unless I loved her enough to marry her. Five years later God gave her to me... and now here I am, trying to be celibate again and talking about boners.

'The Middle Road'

You can call me a road dog or you can call me a guard dog or you can call me a bad dog, but I think I'm a friendly dog, arf, arf, wag, wag. For a long time I was so friendly, I'd just roll over and hope people would scratch my belly, but then a guy kicked me. At first I couldn't understand why anyone would do that to a friendly dog. I growled and I wanted to bite him, but my owner threw me in her doghouse. I felt blamed for being a dog in the way of a boot. I've still got some scars from that, but I have friends that love me anyway.

He poisoned one of my buffalo, then he tried to kill me, really. I thought he was going to kill my family, so did the police, I walked the fences and watched over my herd and family with a shotgun in the night. It really sucked. I remember creeping around in the dark and saying to myself, "This is sucking all the joy out of our life." He wasn't from around here, a total aberration, that I took personally, but what's more personal than your wife, kids, animals and home? The drama's not important, and it's over now anyway, but as always, there's a reason I'm telling you this; it really wasn't the guy that was the problem, the same way alcohol wasn't the problem I ended up getting addicted to. It was an attack from a kind of creature that is pure spirit and uses us against each other. They get a hold of our will each time we give them a piece. They were attacking both of us and using us for their purpose, chaos, destruction and death. Look around at what is happening, there's a reason. They whisper thoughts we think are our own, they seek our will to enslave our soul. Most of us give it unwittingly, but a growing number make deals and join their league for a bribe. The more the world insists evil and love are the same, the more the polarity will grow. But God will intervene, it's happening already, first through a communion of souls and then directly. In the end, a heart that is Immaculate will triumph. She will crush hatreds head with her heel because she loves God. She calls the world to her Son. Her heart has been pierced to reveal the thoughts of yours.

Sin is the giving of the free will and body God gave us, to a will that isn't free and has no body, so it wants ours. We are composite creatures, animal and spirit. Angels are spirit without the animal, but for me every animal has an angel, in a way, every created thing has an angel and what we are experiencing here is the physical manifestation of it. Its form is its symbol, the image it is created in. Angels exist to express the beauty of who creates them, so do we. They are part of everything, and there are myriad kinds just like the animals, insects and plants. I thought I believed that, but the difference between believing and knowing is the difference between tracks and the creature that leaves them. Thoughts are tracks too, to me what is important about thought is not so much whether I think it's negative or positive, it's who is thinking it. The source matters more than the thought the way you matter more than what you think, because everything real is alive. It almost killed me learning to recognize these tracks, but it changed everything, and with awareness comes grace. They're calling us and pleading for us to pray, to make our life a prayer, until prayer becomes our joy. Prayer is the only way to become aware. Prayer is love, of freedom, of truth, of each other, of the most beautiful highest being we can find every second. Prayer is the process of becoming aware of the source of the most beautiful thought.

I lost the most beautiful thing I had, my faith and my family. I was both blamed and blamed myself for all of it, because nobody knew the nature of its source. This is happening all around us, we personalize hurts and betrayals instead of their cause. We personalize ideas instead of God. It happens especially between men and women. You can put a man in the doghouse, but he'll never be sorry enough to make you happy. He'll end up with his tail between his legs and nobody wants a dog like that. Every man gives away his dignity temporarily, but he gives it to a woman permanently when he lets her take it, and the sad thing is, she doesn't want it. Our sovereignty or separateness is an intrinsic part of what attracts us to each other. I kept thinking, if she'd let me out, and lick my wounds instead of rubbing salt into them, she'd feel my strength, and I could be strong and protect her again.

Soultracking is real. I didn't think it up, the souls I track keep revealing it to me, it's their beauty. It's not some dumb cliche and it isn't a secret or five easy steps to get what you think you want. In my experience it's gotten me more than I ever thought to want or dreamed and has always cost me everything. I keep giving up everything and getting a hundred times more. It's so hard it kills me and so good it's worth dying for. Sometimes it's agonizing and I've crumpled under the immensity of it. The whole universe rests on its weight and each of us carry it like Christ. I follow a path of living souls, beauty for a glimpse of an eyelash, that makes everything else pale. It's hard, like art. I have to love the truth more than being right. I have to fall over and over and not lose hope that truth is love and love forgives forever. I have to believe truth exists and that if I seek it I'll find it and it will set me free; and then become proof it does. I've always been everything or nothing, drinking or loving, sex or solitude, lameness or holiness. I don't write to recommend it, it hurts to be hot or cold, but I think it lends itself to life as art, the reaching for beauty, far enough to fall.

Have you ever watched a man kick up his own dust? There's something kind of beautiful about it, kind of touching, even poignant. When I first began to write Soultracker, my life felt like a confession, for existing in the first place, like I'd been thrown into a fight and I was supposed to apologize for fighting. The politically correct new agey thing that was said to me was that there is no fight, there is no evil, there is no truth, everything is just negative or positive thoughts, myths and opinions, discerning beauty isn't allowed, be sophisticated and nice, walk the middle road... I think they're guessing instead of choosing.

> I think the middle road dead ends at heaven
> And it's backed up to hell
> It's wide, easy, and not worth the ride
> The only guts it takes, are left along its side
> The world will tell you there's two ways to go
> And that you can go both
> But the only way that's true; is in.

'The Last Frontier'

I followed something alive into Canada, I could feel it exhale. There is an earthy, friendly charm here, a wild simplicity. For me, it felt like the last frontier. Big black fins slice the oceans, glaciers feed the salmon run. From the alpine, grizzlies follow them for a harvest and the wolves track the elk down. I want to write like they howl.

Finding this land and the buffalo was like tracking an animal, but I think it was my angel. I track creatures for more than something I want, food for my body, or a glimpse for my soul, I want to give them myself. Soultracking isn't something I can turn on or do like work. It's the way a song comes or I've fallen in love. It becomes seamless with life, but it's a relationship with a free, sovereign creature and Creator. Like the relationship between a man and a woman, it's alive. It used to take me weeks hungry and alone in the woods before I'd begin to enter what I call Wandering in the Spirit, it's close to Soultracking, but different. Wandering in the Spirit is a vivid breathing prayer, where I remain still as I move, it takes a body. Soultracking is walking a living path to the same destination with vivid breathing creatures, that are already there, it takes a soul. The purpose and point of both, is infinitely more than to find them, it's to become them. It's what God does, he becomes what he loves.

To be committed to the truth is to allow them to remain free, to experience them from the inside, to become them by them becoming me. People say, 'God is within.' Really? I think to myself, prove it. A saint is someone who proves what she believes is true. We say, 'God is nature, We are God, God is everywhere,' but my experience of what we really mean is that God can't be anywhere, God can't be free like us, to be a man, so he could have a mother. We think we are un-limiting God by limiting him to an energy or idea, and taking away his body, or that we can control him by making him a myth we invent like me inventing you. As always, with everything sacred and holy, I find it the opposite of what the world thinks. When I allow God to be as much like me as I am, his image in my body and my soul, I allow everyone and everything and every breath to be free. I stop holding, and I start beholding.

I don't seek my thoughts and ideas about a buffalo or a bear or a mountain lion or you. I don't want to guess or vote and I want more than ideas about Christ and faith, I want Christ's faith, I want the truth he says we'll find, I want Gods body to be mine, I want it to achieve what his did, I want to believe what he believes, and what he says, his body does. I want to experience what he experiences and be Gods son. I want all that, but I don't love the way he does. I choose what I think I want more than love, what sin is, a lack of beauty and a pathetic lack of caring. To experience the passion of Christ's heart is devotion the way art is devotion. The more of myself I give it the better it is, but I'm not devoted, well, sometimes I pray with all my heart to be and then I am. Even though it hurts to be miserable at it, it's irresistibly beautiful and able to be wanted without limiting anything.

The world tells me to tell myself how great and good I am, how deserving I am of what I think I want, how I shouldn't feel bad or guilty or ashamed of anything I do, and then I look at a little kid who finds his food in the garbage, who no one loves, abandoned, except for a Sister of Mercy who's hugging and kissing him, and he has this big smile on his face, and I think, I don't love the way I want to, sometimes I've failed miserably at loving my own family and friends and God. That little kid has more love in his heart than I do, he is the least of my brothers, God is within him, and I see it, he proves it! Not because he's a big success that achieves all his passing, pumped up goals, I see the glory of God in him through my tears, because he's gentle, sincere and humble. His is a kind of success the world doesn't want, because we can't sell it, buy it, or take it away.

If you want to feel greatness, feel the pain of your un-lovingness for a few minutes and weep over it. You and I have no idea how ungrateful and un-loving we are. I don't say it to discourage you. You looking at yourself and weeping will impress me a million times more than achieving some goal. To me you will be more beautiful for having been broken, it's an un-bloody way to show me your guts and help me have some too.

Something all creation has waited for, moaning and sighing, is about to happen. We are going to see the consequences of our love, and also of our un-lovingness. I think we are going to glimpse into the greatest thing that's ever happened, and it's going to take our greatness. I hope the world will look at that kid and see what I see and weep, not because he's poor, because he's great. To me, that weeping will be our greatness. If I accomplish anything good in my life, it's by the love of God in me and I'm glad, because this love is limitless. It comes to a man like a woman.

God does the same thing with me, I do with him, he allows me to be myself, free. He tracks my soul. I want it to make him weep for joy the way his does to me. I want him to see me smile like that kid. I want to read tracks from the inside. We are artist's. He proves no one can force him and no one can force me. The only thing I have of my own to give, is our love. I track the most beautiful thing I can find and it's alive.

'The Shivers'

I think one of the purest relationships we have on Earth is with animals. I see them as an example of innocence, as if created in the image of angels, they never 'sin' against anyone or against their own nature, people like that are easy to like and love. When I think about the legendary life and personality, the animating soul of a dominant buffalo bull, I get the shivers.

Yesterday a buffalo cow came at me full speed from a couple hundred yards away and triple charged me. She shook her head and grunted, put her tail up and her head down and stopped about ten feet away, then did the same thing with her head and pounced forward till the third time she stopped a foot away, I had to stomp my boot under her nose and yell some kind of unintelligible cuss word, she backed off real mad with her tail arched up, kicking out to the sides. They do a combination with the tips of their horns that reminds me of my old Karate Sensei, he'd move in close and do this buzz saw thing with hooks and uppercuts and clobber everybody.

They all have a rank and maintain it by enforcing it on each other. They treat me kind of like a cross between another buffalo and a predator. The dominant bull will chase Grizzlies away and stay at the rear of the herd if they run, to fight off wolves. Every herd of buffalo has a guard cow, sixteen years ago this one cow especially would come after me. She also happens to be our ugliest cow, she's kinda homely, I named her Prunella. We've been through a lot together, she kicked a mountain lion off her back a couple years ago. She's getting old now. It's hard enough for me to put them down when they get old or injured so nobody gets named anymore except for the King and his name will always be Chester.

My late bull Chester's son, Chester, has tons of soul and is growing into a beautiful bull. I've seen signs in him since he was born and lately he's showing me who he is and I love it. It would be one of the most beautiful things I can imagine to see him become a giant and walk with him to the end of one our paths like I did with his father. I'm working as hard as I can every second, and praying that he and I can do that here in this setting that is so perfect to share with others that visit us from all over the world. I watch people walk away with a gift, a story and Spirit the buffalo give them and that I try to share with them too.

It's taken a long time for them to accept me, in the beginning I couldn't tell what they were thinking, now they're whispering to me all the time, even in my dreams.

I had a feeling about ten minutes before that cow charged me yesterday, but it's not something I can point out, it's subtle signs on some other level. You learn how to speak with them with your body and your inner-self. They will charge strangers and like yesterday, they still charge me sometimes. Fifty people have been killed and seriously injured by buffalo in Yellowstone Park in the last ten years. Though there are huge fines, signs everywhere and it's dumb, people still get too close to them. Buffalo become accustomed to people in the park but 'too close' can be up to a few hundred yards.

Chester charged my friend Pat Milliken from a hundred yards away. They can run faster than a horse and their horns are like meat hooks, they know exactly where the tips are and they gore predators and each other by hitting and twisting their head at the same time. Cows weigh about a thousand pounds and full grown bulls average about two thousand, Chester was twenty-five hundred and six feet at the hump. He beat up and gored other big bulls we had. A beautiful bull we had disappeared. I found him in the snow and brought him hay with a snowmobile. It was minus 28 one day and his guts were hanging out of the hole frozen, I could smell the gang-green, I had to put him down. I took him to the wolf center a few minutes from here.

In the wild a dominant bull fights hundreds and even thousands of bulls. He has to fight his whole life and win. He knows that about himself and is not afraid of anything, all the other ones know that about him too. Big bulls like that don't mind being alone because they're not afraid of anything.

This cow yesterday never charged me before. I try to avoid getting out in the middle of the pastures, I've been charged helping friends with their buffalo that way. Prunella used to really come after me and I'd run! I'd jump in my truck or over the fence. I called one of my old timer friends that's had buffalo his whole life, he's seen everything and been run over and under, but he's still kicking and it's funny, I guess there's different kinds of people, I don't know if that's smart ones and dumb one or what, but the more I go through this life with them, the more I grow to love them. I said to him, 'I think I've gotta sell that cow, she's so awnry, she keeps coming after me', he said, 'Naaughhhh, that's yer guard cow, every herd has one like that, you've gotta stand your ground and make her stop.' I said, 'really! what if she doesn't stop?' and he kinda growled at me, 'Ahhhhh, they almost always stop.' Hmmmm ... So that's what I had to do. It took dozens of times and a few years for her to stop doing it to me. If you run and don't get away, they'll run you down and twist one of those horns into you like a dull knife.

Buffalo are different from other herbivores like deer and elk who are always looking around for threats and run to survive. They are pretty relaxed and unafraid and they fight anything that attacks them. They'll hook wolves, puma, and slow buffaleros and toss them up in the air. Chester liked to hook fifteen hundred pound round bales of hay when they'd slip off the tractor fork. He could send them in the air spinning. I was pulling off some string frozen to one once, I stepped to the side and yanked just as Chester ran up from the other side out of my vision and sent it flying. I try to be careful and think ahead, but there is always the unexpected with them. A big four year old bull we had broke the sliding steel door off the back of the three thousand pound squeeze, and then sprung the side gate open in front of me. I jumped out of the way. Chester saw his side exposed and slammed into him tipping him and the squeeze with the federal vet on top. They let out a big bellow when they're hit. Chester broke a couple of his ribs and put a hole in his hide that's still there in the thick winter robe.

I'm impressed by animals, by surfers that ride giants, by boxers and bronco bull riders. I'm impressed by people with brain damage in wheelchairs, like my sister. I'm impressed by drug and alcohol addicts that try because I know how hard it is to be overcome, desperate, hopeless. I'm impressed by the least of my brothers, in jail, that were kind to me. I'm not too impressed by me, I need too much help from my friends. I think I'm sincere. I'm impressed by anybody that's sincere.

In the seventies, a person that was gay could feel so unfairly judged and rejected, so condemned that they'd kill themselves. When I was a teenager a gay man got me to do something I felt so bad about I almost did that. I never wished him ill, I prayed for him and felt sorry for him. I'm glad a person that happens too doesn't feel that kind of judgement and condemnation anymore. I live for a God that asks me to only want the highest love I can find, he tells me I can't take a woman's love unless I love her so much I'll marry her and put that before anything, any circumstance, till one of our paths ends. It seems impossible, faith is the only thing I know that gives me that kind of love, but I saw the beauty of what happens when my parents did it. I think they might have done it for me. I've found that I get what I settle for. When your soul entered your body to walk here, it took a thousand times more courage than facing a buffalo. When I think about it, I get the shivers.

'Opposites Attract'

They say opposites attract. They must have known my parents. Dad expressed a clarity of ideas. Mom expressed a clarity of feelings. Dad was color blind, Mom saw more colors than I could imagine, but they were both Colorful. Some feel meaning is complicated, that the intellect is obsolete. Others think it's for choosing what to think and why to believe.

> The only way to show them your beauty
> Is for them to feel my eyes on you
> You know those scales the Lady holds
> That's how my parents held me
> And I'm grateful they were opposites, so am I
> Everything true, is opposite of how it appears
> It's the longing that makes you sigh
> I don't make love with my intellect
> Music is a mystery to me
> Like God & Love it's invisible
> But I feel it when I believe in it
> And when I give my whole heart, mind and soul
> So do you
> Sometimes words are like an awkward lover
> Longing to give everything he is
> His mind, his heart, his soul, his flesh and his blood
> To the Love, he kisses in whispered Words…
> Like notes he puts to sleep with his fingers
> Sometimes they are music

'Virgins'

I had one once, she was my first love and I was hers. She was a ninety-eight pound Mexican Catholic hottie with curves at the end of her straight away guys would drive off the road for, I'll tell you how I did.

She was warm and sweet, the color of Earth when white sage blooms and she smelled like it too. I bought her a rabbit-fur coat and she wore it next to her skin just like the rabbit. Mmmmm, it takes me back to the innocence, to true love before you know what it is.

I loved her and I wanted her so much. I would kiss her and glow like an octopus, I'd grow new hands to feel her with and she'd grow new ones to stop me. One night we were making out in my jacked up Chevy El Camino. I felt like Mount Saint Helens, but she was a good girl and besides how exquisite she was, that's why I loved her. My friend Chris Schapp, he's a big old ol'timer around here, was just telling me about a mountain lion he saw leap twenty feet up into the air onto a snow bank. That was the kind of strength I had pumping through my veins. It's super human and poor old humans can't control it. I was so frustrated I peeled out and then spun around the next corner coming to rest with a telephone pole sunk in my fender. It wasn't too bad, it looked kind of like I had just parked there except for the French kiss it gave my fender. We walked home in the night.

I had this conversation about her with myself, "If you really love her, it shouldn't have anything to do with what she gives you, you should love her before anything else." It was so hard to face this because I wanted to make love to her like Jaws wants to break when a big south swell comes. The only way I could control that force was with love and I did and she loved me for it… and gave herself to me. It brings tears to my eyes right now how beautiful and innocent we were, how much we loved each other, how much fun we had together, the music she inspired in me, but I wasn't ready. It wasn't that I didn't want to be, it happened with Elan too. I was so in love with her and she wanted to be mine. Both of them surrendered with such sacred beauty and I surrendered to them too, but I was not capable of riding their wave and knew I couldn't catch it.

Then I had a wife, I loved her more than I've ever loved anyone, she gave me everything, she gave me a son. I wasn't ready still, I wanted to be, but I got so lost I got sick. It's a power that's super human, it takes balls to have it and balls to get it back. The women weren't ready either.

But this idea of how it's supposed to be, a beauty beyond belief, a virgin that's one with you forever once you find each other, a lover waiting for you to save her, to show her what a man is, like Jesus showed me. A lover who would rather die for you than see you suffer. A daughter who knows her father is God and he's come here to hide in you. It's super human, a love only God could create, it's beyond hate and beyond time so you'll never be ready, it's a new Adam and Eve.

'God is the Artist'

If I could command something on Earth, I would command that we love the Truth with our whole heart, mind and soul, because that would make us all Artists.

In fourth grade, I remember thinking to myself, all I need is a pen and a piece of paper and I can do anything. Compared to music, writing has no rules, this is an open medium, so let me describe my first love to you again, but a little differently, like playing a song with a slightly different feel.

I was fifteen years old when I fell in love with a Mexican virgin. She was exquisite. She smelled so good. Her face was like breathing a Gardenia, her skin was chocolate olive oil. She had a dark brown mane with auburn curls that ended like question marks around her hips. She was an endless curve. I bought her a rabbit fur coat at Sears for her birthday and she wore it for me like the rabbit.

For what seemed like an eternity before that though, she'd only let me kiss and hold her. I've mentioned before how she had more arms than an octopus and she needed all of them to keep me just far enough away to stay virgin for me. I didn't think much about her virginity, I though about how much I loved her. I wanted her as much as I've ever wanted anything. I was like a hundred foot wave ready to wall out on top of her, but with her help, I held myself back. Like the hand of God, she suspended the laws of nature, when she whispered, 'No'. Finally one day I thought to myself, 'If I really love her, it's not for what I want from her, and I do love her, so I've got to accept her wish'. When I saw her, I told her and I meant it. I had a kind of peace. She gave herself to me that night and after that her arms were mine, and they had suction cups.

This is why I told you that, because she inspired art in me, and I've experienced how my sexual drive can be channeled into my creative drive. It poured out as music on my Spanish guitar, but art isn't the music, art isn't the medium. Art is what you see and feel when waves crash and you smell the seaweed. It's the way I'd fall asleep in her dream. The way she was fire, blankets and fog and the Big Sur winter. It's smoke from hippies chimneys in the Garapada Redwoods. It's the earth's soul and the worlds beauty. It's what I gave to her and she gave to me. Art is what you give your whole heart, mind and soul to and what it gives back. It's love, it's only good when it's true and even when I was a kid; I knew.

Art is three things at once. God, or Everything, your self, or Gods body, and the Holy Spirit, the Inspiration, the love that proceeds as beauty. The art of prayer is Love. It takes practice and you have to accept that it's a lifelong pursuit and I'm proof you don't have to fix yourself or be good to do it, but there's an aspect that's work.

One day I thought of prayer like pushups, they don't always feel that good and it's not instant results, but I know if I just do them I'll get stronger, and I did. Like music there are endless forms of prayer, there are structures and melodies we share and silence between the notes, listening and expressing, joy and sorrow. It's a love with someone in you, who is sovereign.

If I tried to convince you how grateful I am for music, how I believe in music even though I only feel it and can't see it, the nuance and precision and the constant 'Discernment' of gradients of beauty, the clarity it demands, the caring to get it 'right,' and there is a 'right,' there is a 'perfect,' without restraint, so subtle; prayer is the love of a Communion of Saints. They're lovers, angels and men and women, and they take it somewhere beyond everything. They make their bodies instruments of the beauty of love. I track them.

'A Better Reason'

WINTER 2013

Sometimes my mom reminded me of a deer in the headlights. She said she was nervous even as a little girl. She was sensitive and artistic, she was humble and spiritual and she loved me. She really loved me, every little curl on my head. The girls I fell in love saw how she was like a deer too and there was something sweet between them. The day she married my dad she said she turned to look back at her mirror where she'd been brushing her hair and saw the image of the Virgin looking back at her, smiling. I remember the look on her face when she told me, it had the joy of a young girl.

When every time you walk out the door your mother is telling you all the things to watch out for you start to think there must be something out there to watch out for. Fear has been proven to be our most inheritable trait. Worry has hounded me and at times overwhelmed me, I'd go into the same spiral my mom went into expecting the worst, but if you really love someone, everything about them turns into a gift and that is what happened. Fear makes a person hard to love and it spreads, it's been really hard sometimes, but I pray in sacred gratitude that my mother gave me life. What I want to describe is something perfect, it forgives perfectly when you are humbly honest, it forgives and asks you to forgive, it is a Child.

When fear is there, it's like a bully, I have to face it or it paralyzes me, and facing fear has taught me things nothing else can. It became a kind of motivation, it was like I had to face whatever it was I was most afraid of. Singing and performing petrified me for the first five years or so of playing professionally, but beauty and passion were irresistible and with time and commitment they turned pure fear to pure joy. Wandering alone in the wilderness at first, especially at night, I was afraid, but I've shared before how everything around me was exactly how God made it in that moment and how in a way it was a 'Beautiful fear' and how I chose to have Faith instead of being afraid. It wasn't faith that nothing 'bad' would happen, it was me offering myself, making myself a living prayer, and discovering what I call and believe is, 'Wandering in the Spirit' and eventually I felt like another one of the critters more happy and at home sleeping in the open out there than I ever felt in the 'world,' and miracles happened.

My father never seemed afraid, he relied on reason. Reason was his art, he was beautiful at it, he used it to find the truth, not to be right. All my life I have asked him questions and listened carefully to his answers. I'm proud of my father and grateful for him. He flew canvas biplanes to the first jet fighters, he fought the Nazi's in World WarII. I mentioned before, he isn't just smart, imagine having Einstein next to you, loving you and trying to answer anything you wanted to ask him, he isn't Einstein, but I could say, maybe because I love him so much, he is a 'saint of reason.' He's 94 years old now and his mind is resting, but it wasn't the answers or the knowledge he taught me that really mattered, it was 'how to think,' it was reason, how to evaluate ideas. He wanted to teach me the reason for reason, the meaning of meaning and what made it meaningful. He wasn't 'artistic' or what I would call particularly 'spiritual.' He believed in God and the faith of our ancestors with conviction, because he found its reason to be totally Divine. I don't remember him talking about miracles he experienced, other than when his neck was healed at a healing mass with Father Ralph Di Orio, totally and permanently healed in an instant after ten years of intense and debilitating pain, x-rayed and needing surgery and barely being able to turn or bend it. It was my dad, we all witnessed it.

If you believe in something with enough faith you can often make it happen, but this is the problem with that; for me it's not a good enough Reason to have faith. So what if I can get what I think I want. I've gotten it before and then I didn't want it, in fact I've thanked God I didn't get some things I thought I wanted. What happened in the wilderness was that every time, the thing I wanted, was a total Surprise! A divine surprise, a miracle, which is what a vision is, a glimpse into an infinite mystery, something that never ends when you get it so you still want it. That's what Wandering in the Spirit is. It's not the faith to get what you want, it's the faith to be who you are. You can get what you think you want with enough faith, but where is the honor in that? What's passionate about that? What a man really longs to be in some way for a woman, for his friends and for God, is a savior, a hero and he can be that for a woman that is humble and gentle, just by truly loving her. The reasons to have faith were all good but somehow, they just weren't good enough. I needed a better Reason and slowly it has never stopped coming.

It's like a work of art, a song or a lover, it's alive and you pursue it, it's God and I want to touch him for the beauty. Often I'm speaking to people of different faiths or that think they have no faith. Sometimes I have resistance to pointing to the Bible as a source of the Truth, because people make judgements about the whole subject based on bad apples and assumptions. But in my life from the first one I found on my first vision quest before I knew what a vision quest was, the first time, when I asked Jesus to give me an answer to something I needed an answer to, it's been a living oracle of infinite wisdom, a sacred door to vision, and although there are other books that are inspired, I have never found one like the bible. It's so much more than, 'Do this and don't do that', it's more than holy thoughts and wisdom, it's a history of the future, a testimony of prophecies fulfilled, the path of my ancestors who's tracks tell a scared mystery, a mystical impressionists masterpiece of reality and a manual for the operation of a soul. For anyone that will humbly enter into it and be quiet long enough to listen instead of blah, blah, blah all the answers they think they already know, it will speak God's mind on multiple levels simultaneously. It's not enough by itself and it was never intended to be and it says that in the bible, but that's another subject, just because something isn't enough by itself doesn't mean it isn't also perfect. What it means is much more than what it says.

I hadn't eaten in a few days, it was 120 degrees, I was sitting in the dirt. I'd gone in as a prayer seeking an answer to what road I was going to walk my life on. Flies were biting my head, I was tired and weak. If I turned around I could have walked out in three or four days, if I continued I wouldn't get back to the coast for weeks more of this. I remember thinking, "Does this really matter? Does God or anybody really care that I'm sacrificing myself and praying? 'Sacrifice' conjures up ideas in the modern and western mind that have nothing to do with what it is. It was particularly difficult on this journey because I had promised to return with a decision of whether to quit the band and the music business or to go on. I tried to adjust my professional life and the scene but it didn't work, I felt like it had to be either all or nothing. It is hard to describe how hard that was for me. I got out the little bible I had found on my first vision quest. I asked God, "Do you care about what I'm doing, does any of this this matter to you!?" I opened it up and put my finger down and it said:

> Now faith is the substance of things hoped for
> The evidence of things not seen
> Without faith it is impossible to please Him. For he that comes to
> God must believe that He is; And that He is a rewarder of those that
> seek Him.

He rewarded me 100 x more than what I gave up and even though it's been really hard at times, he still is.

Christians and religious people and positive thinkers and new agers and even non-believers will say, "You've got to have faith." I think, "Why, exactly, precisely, why?" and "What exactly in?" and "What exactly for?"…Not going to hell? That seems like a lame reason, and it's not because I don't believe there is a state of Hell, I've been there, to my own personal hell, it exists like a rattlesnake or a mountain lion. Hell is a meaning that needed a name. It is a place of utter and complete hopelessness, of no faith and no light to lead the way out. It's inhabitants and offspring prey on and live off the life and hope of lovers. If anyone wants to convince me that the meaning that is called hell, and its minions, can only exist if you believe in it they are welcome to try because one or both of us will learn something. I love it when someone lovingly and sincerely asks me a good question or presents me with an idea that makes sense, it's like a canvas. I've met ideas that are beautiful, ideas I'm repulsed by and some I think are dumb, but never one I was afraid of.

There is the faith you have to have to achieve something in the world. There is the faith you have to have to overcome addiction; addiction is really just faith, but in the wrong thing. There's the faith that you hope keeps you out of hell. There's the faith that helps you get what you hope for, what you think you want, and then there's another kind of faith, the kind Jesus had.

His faith gave faith to others. His faith was ordered by love and it got him crucified. His faith got him something he didn't want and he prayed to be spared from... Sometimes people will say believing in God is for weak people that can't rely on themselves and need a crutch, Jesus got nailed to our crutch and he knew that he had to let us do it to him to show us among others things, there was nothing we could do to God to make him stop loving us, and to prove that he is the first born of the dead. He must have had a different kind of Faith. He must have had a different kind of Reason. I don't know what kind it is, but I pray for him to give it to me. I don't want just any faith, I don't want faith in a lie and I don't want faith in something stupid, I want His Faith. I want to believe everything he believed.

I was worrying again the other day about these practical issues, how am I going to pay all these bills and fulfill my responsibilities and repay and help the friends that helped me when I got sick? How am I going to heal a broken family when we all have so much to learn? How am I going to save this herd of buffalo I love so much and that have so much to give, and it weighs on me, it accuses me along with other voices that say, "You're not good enough, you're bad, there's something wrong with you, you're not smart enough, you deserve to be disrespected and condescended to, others should look down on you too..." and sometimes I begin to succumb to them and think maybe they are right? I turn to this invisible God who I touch through faith and I ask him to help me...help me with all these things I don't know how to do so I can do what your voice calls me to and live for something limitless...but there's a part of me that thinks; well you should be worried, you should try harder, and you should feel bad for needing help and for your failures, are you praying so you can feel better? and I think, yeah, in a way I am, and that's not a good enough reason to believe in anything. Then I read that passage again recently when a wonderful friend sent it to me:

'Now faith is the substance of things hoped for
The evidence of things not seen
Without faith it is impossible to please Him.
For he that comes to God must believe that He is;
And that He is a Rewarder of those that seek Him.'

The way God expresses himself in words, they come alive and mean something new and change everything. I'd been praying for Jesus to give me His faith because I keep thinking why pray for anything else, if I have your faith what else would I need?

I can have faith to feel better or to get what I think I want or to not go to hell, or even to prove faith is real or even to 'find' Heaven, those are good reasons, but they're not good enough, I asked for a better reason and he gave me one; 'To please God; to Be Beautiful, for My Creator.'

Finally here is a reason like love, because it stands on its own not reliant on conditions or anything outside itself for its meaning. I think it's the kind of faith Jesus had, his words say, 'we are one, the kingdom of heaven is within, we live and move and have our existence in God.' Every word I'm saying is like a baby going 'goo goo,' it's a molecule of the divine mystery, but if it's pure, it's also whole. It's the nature of every sacred mystery again, the reflection, the opposite of how it appears, you think you're giving up getting what you want and doing it for somebody else, but you find you are being true to your true self, a new Adam, a son of God. I'm not speaking symbolically and not only spiritually, I mean really a son of God, with his Sons real blood flowing in your veins, really, physically, on Earth. If God's blood is in your veins, you have his life in you, not only his ideas.

It's not about feeling good or getting what you think you want. It's so much more. Sincerity is its nature, but it's like a caterpillar. As soon as I start worrying, "How the hell am I going to fly, I don't know how, I don't have any idea what I'm doing, this is impossible, look how I've failed, what about my body and these immense passions, some people will think I'm full of myself, some won't approve of me" then I stop having faith. I think a caterpillar pleases God and so does a butterfly, that's their Reason, all the creatures, I think that's why they are the way they are, innocent with an innate dignity, true to their nature and messengers to anyone that listens...

I've found this reason and it works like being in love works, like the sacred union of a man and a woman works. If I want to be pleasing to my Creator, I have to have faith for him not for me, because faith is what my Creator finds beautiful. I want to be beautiful and please God so faith becomes something I have for Love not for self, and every time I worry, I'm not having faith, so I'm being displeasing to God, that's what sin is, it's not being beautiful. The kind of Faith Jesus had is beautiful, I'm looking for it and I believe I've found a Reason worth having it.

'Soulguardian's'

It was a time when everything I had worked so hard for in music and my life professionally and as an artist was happening and instead of joy and a sense of accomplishment, I felt like I was about to sell my life to other people, my soul to the world. I didn't trust their judgement or my own and the world seemed like such an unreliable thing to rely on.

I stood at this dusty crossroad I had dreamed of many times before and my heart and soul called me down the one no one seemed to understand, even me, but I felt, "Called' down it by this whispering voice of something so deeply 'honorable', something eternal, but all for this vision of something invisible. It was the same voice and presence I felt alone in the wilderness. I was living my passion and my dreams but I had not aligned them and myself with my Vision, something I first began to receive when I began to Wander in the Spirit alone in the wilderness, a purpose beyond myself and beyond time and space. Many Native American tribes knew a man had to do whatever it took to receive his vision and then live it. God calls and is in every soul, he is Life.

The state I've longed for as long as I can remember and longer is to be in love, with a woman yes, that love of a man and a woman has inspired a beauty beyond me and the world, and a passion to express it, but really to be in love with everyone and everything, that is what being in love does, at first, you see your soul and your lovers soul everywhere in everyone, but then you gradually begin to lose that Vision, and replace it with a wanting, and even soul-mates lose their way, themselves and each other, still I am convinced love can heal anything and does if you both decide to live for it instead of yourselves.

I'm not sure about others, but I need a Vision to live for and for me that Vision has to be for the Love that is God before it is for a woman or even for our children. It's not something I choose, it's something I need. For it to be a vision they can rely on, and to rely on me, its existence can't be dependent on or relative to something else. This is the faith that is love. The thing is that I actually believe in the mystical faith of my ancestors and if it is real, the way the ones that were and are true to it have proved and are proving, it doesn't make sense to make it secondary to anything. For love to remain alive the way I want it to, for life to be art, with passion in every heart beat and every breath, I have to live for my lovers soul and for mine. I see now I have to protect her soul above all and this is where she will love me the way a woman longs to love a man and a man longs to love and be loved. I call that a Soulguardian.

The person I want to see is not only an image in time and space, but that baby with the eyes of wonder I saw in a dream I'll tell you about later. The wonder is a state of grace, creation, it's the state where desire overflows into the passion to give. It's taken me a long time to find that the strength and confidence I have always wanted and wanted to be able to give to my woman, to my children and to everyone, was my Faith.

Faith would be stupid if it didn't work. Words and ideas to faith are good, like craft is to art, but craft isn't art. To teach art you must be an artist and to teach faith you must have it. Faith is the evidence of things unseen, that's miracles. I believe in what I believe ultimately for its beauty. Its beauty is its perfection, beauty is everything good, everything true, existing in a transcendent harmony, a relationship but without separation, like the Trinity and like God in man, but the miracles are the proof and I needed that. I think that is our true purpose, to have so much faith that we prove it's true, because there is this…ecstasy, this realization of reality where we realize that truth actually exists and it's true! and that it is Love, that God is Love, truth is love and life is a journey to unveil and discover what love really is and become it. It is the Theory of Non-Relativity, Love is the one thing that exists on its own and that no one and no thing can take away from us, it is the Faith and meaning and purpose that we can have and give to others no matter what 'happens.' That's what Jesus proved, that there is nothing you can do to him to make him stop loving you. That is the Glory of God. That is worth living for.

You can't argue someone into being a better artist or into having faith, or into believing something. You can't condescend, disrespect, judge and condemn someone into being a better lover or a better man. Instead of trying to fix what you think is wrong with them, you can inspire them with the faith of your love. You can give advice and speak truth, but only love gives the inspiration that can really heal someone, and help someone be a better artist or lover or man or woman. It's your faith, love and cherishing for your lovers soul that raises them up and enables them to be who they are created to be and I think it's what we are all looking for, wanting for and from each other. When I was sick it was the love in people that still loved me that healed me and gave me hope a hundred times more than advice and it was the love in me, the love that is faith.

The only way I can see to actually be a Soulguardian and to find mine is to live and breathe my faith and to share it. I think whatever your faith is, you need to find out and live it, prove it's real, in that way we are authentic artists. Inspire me don't just argue with me and tell me I'm wrong and you're right, or point out liars and wannabe's among my ancestors, their everywhere in every group. When you do use reason, give me something real. Give me something meaning-Full and beautiful. The truth is true no matter what is happening around it or it's not true. You can have any opinion about it you want, but truth either actually exists or it doesn't, that was the meaning that needed a word and the word is truth.

I want to laugh, I love to make someone laugh really hard! and that laughter is love, but life is so incredibly precious, like that baby with galaxies in his eyes I held in a dream, and I want to prove the truth is love and it's true. I want to share my faith with my woman and love each other for it and in it, there is nothing more passionate. I want to live for each others souls and looking back in a way I've tried all my life, but it's like art, 'God' I was so bad at it in the beginning and maybe I still am, but we do learn slowly and grow, it's an endless reaching for perfection, the kind of beauty I see in the wilderness and in an animal. I saw it in my buffalo bull Chester, we were soul guardians of each other, we really were. I saved his life in the world and he saved my life in dreams, he was sent for my soul.

Saint Francis was a wealthy, gifted young man everybody loved. He gave away everything, put on an old wool robe, and started collecting rocks to rebuild a broken Church. Everybody thought he was crazy and I'll bet he wondered himself at first too, but he saw visions, miracles and he believed, he kissed a leper that turned into Jesus, he bled from the wounds of Christ, and animals that were afraid of everybody else loved him. He was a real man that worked real miracles, he proved it's all real, really real. It's what's behind everything, what we think is real is a dream and we can dream it with faith in love. There have been thousands more among my ancestors and some are on Earth today. You don't hear about them very much unless you search for them, but if you do, you'll find them, you'll see mountains of proof you can't deny. The world can't really comprehend them and there is a strong incentive not to believe in them because then a person has to make an authentic free-choice, and I think almost everybody knows it in their heart.

Saint Francis and Saint Claire loved each other, they were Soulguardians. I think to find your Soulguardian you have be called to them, the same way a Medicine Man or a priest is called, you don't ordain yourself. It's not a job or an arrangement. Sometimes people seem to think of love and marriage as an arrangement, almost like a negotiation. To me that seems about as romantic or beautiful or as passionate as a trip to Vegas, but I know I'm kind of weird and impractical, and a lot of people think Vegas is beautiful.

But wouldn't it be worth it to to be Saint Francis or Saint Claire no matter how much it cost you if you could prove your faith was true? Don't you want to prove it to yourself? I do. The love that makes me want to is more beautiful than anything else. I look around at the people I know and I think, wow, if any of these people, my friends, wanted to be a true saint, I know they could and I know they could be one so much better than I ever could, I'm so self absorbed and selfish, I lack their virtue and will, but they inspire me and I think, these people are saints but don't know it. There is something different that happens in a person, it's rare, but it happens when a person loves love with their whole being, where they become channels of Grace, channels of miracles, they don't point at themselves they point at the truth. I believe in it, all of it. But God doesn't do it all for you, he asks for something, he asks for you to be one with him, part of it, like he asked Mary and like he asked Jesus. The evidence among my ancestors is not little stuff, it's not Mary on a piece of toast. I know, especially for someone like me to say these things, I must appear ridiculous, but I feel like it's worth it, and I want to keep trying.

'Another Kind of Ecstasy'

To give a woman, you, and everyone else what I want to give, and believe my Creator can give through me, when I am loyal to his presence in me, I have to respect myself as I respect him. The way my Creator never compromises himself to be in me; I also, want to be, with myself and with those I'm in relationship with.

There's a degree of autonomy and sovereignty required in that. I see how I have looked for the soul of the women I've loved, and gradually discovered how 'marriage' is what it is because of what it does. A man and a woman become priests. This is the reality of what a priest is, not a name someone gives themselves, but the real presence of the living fruit they offer, to each other and the world and to souls, destined to walk Earth for heaven.

What makes a priest a priest is that what they give is not a symbol or an idea and not just words. I want the most beautiful thing I can find, that's the only reason I believe in anything. For me that is the secret of 'holy matrimony' what a man and woman create in their flesh when they become one. I'm not speaking in regard to definitions of the word marriage, everyone is free to believe in whatever they want the most, in fact, we're obligated to. I'm speaking personally as a man and an artist, of what the meaning of 'marriage' is for me and how it pertains to my intimate sexual relationship with a woman; to become one flesh, in the Life that proceeds from our love and in a laying down of my life for her while living it. If I don't love her that way, and hear that call like a vision, to give her all that I am till death, for me, being with her sexually is kind of like eating Eve's apple, I can eat it if I want to, but I don't taste the fullness of its beauty.

A woman is such a beautiful song, in some the body and soul seem like one, as a creature, there is an overwhelming urge to sing her and hear her heavenly harmonies whispered in my ear. But she is art, and so am I. I can't do it ninety-nine percent, almost is not enough, I'd rather not sing than sing if it's not with everything I am, everything forever. Transforming that overwhelming power and attraction into another kind of creativity becomes art. It is not a cutting off or a repressing at all, it's actually an arousing, it's open to the call, like feeling angels, it's like being the crest of a wave, and balancing there, free, moving, almost breaking forever. It takes faith in a love so beautiful, that being true to it becomes another kind of ecstasy.

'Tough'

SUMMER 2013

My friend Floyd blew his nose off with a shotgun. He lost both his parents in a car crash, he survived Canadian winters with no electricity, he squished his head between two trees that fell on him logging. I think I should think I'm tougher than I am cause when a person does they usually are, but I don't think I'm that tough. I think most people are a lot tougher than me. My friend Floyd just got out of the hospital and was running around like a squirrel with a chainsaw when we were logging the other day, he's sixty seven years old. My back was sore, I wanted to sit down, I did. He sat on my deck and read something I wrote about him one day, I'd described him as a, "Big old tree of a man." He said, "Who's that, not me!?" I looked at him... I'd never seen him that way before, I realized, Floyd's not that big, he's no bigger than me. But he's a big old tree of a man! I've been telling you about being alone in the wilderness, eating rattlesnakes, stalking up on mountain lions and looking into their eyes, how to stand a buffalo down. I used to think all the survival skill stuff was really important to try and teach people, then I'd get them back there and realize they were surviving in civilization, that's a hundred times harder than living out here like I am, this is easy, this is natural, what we're made for. I found that all I had to do was help a person be alone for a while out there and pray for them, I'd tell them a little of my story and listen to theirs carefully, I'd try and help them be sincere. People's whole life would change on many levels and in many ways, always for the good. Like me they'd say what am I so worried about? Here I am alone with nothing and I am happier than I have ever been in my life. This whole place is speaking to me. I think they're all tougher than me. I'd spend a lot of my time out there sprawled out on the hot sandstone sleeping like a snake soaking in the sun. I'd think about what I was going to eat when I walked out and I'd miss my friends. Then also, life has taken every atom of my being. If I hadn't prayed the way I have I'd be dead a couple of times, I'm not just saying that, I would, I prayed and things happened and it happens for anybody that's sincere, but it's not, not being dead that amazes me, it's who it is I pray too that amazes me, the meaning a Sacred Heart brings to life, I ponder the love and I reflect in it and somehow it turns everything, my own weakness and the weakness of others, into something beautiful and strong.

No matter what religion you are, every person has a cross to bear and it's hard, maybe they're sick, addicted like I was, maybe they're jealous, maybe they've been betrayed, molested. I look at people and I see the sign of the cross over them, every single one of us has to pick ours up one day. I picked mine up when I was sixteen. Gail was my piano teacher, she played till her fingers bled, she was Jewish, she was intense, she said, "Leo, you have to respond to your ability, that's, 'Responsibility' and you have to commit yourself to the Truth!" I thought about it. I didn't know what the truth was, but I knew I'd have to choose it if I found it over what I might prefer. It seemed kind of pathetic for me not to so I did. All you have to do is want it more than anything else and it reveals itself, 'seek and you shall find, knock and the door will be opened.'

It's a big commitment, once you do it you can't look back or you turn to stone, you stop growing. The last time I saw Gail was about thirty years ago, I still had my band, I had on skin tight jeans I knew she wouldn't like and was holding a bottle of Wild Turkey in my hand. I pretended I didn't see her and hoped she didn't see me. How tough is that? Anyone at anytime they finally decide, can commit themselves to the truth. It's got nothing to do with you being tough or good. The truth doesn't need you to help it be true. All you have to do is want it more than anything and Wander in the Spirit, the Prayer. The truth will take care of you before you do. No matter how far away you fall the truth is always right there, waiting for you, to hold you and set you free.

I want to be tough but my souls got a thin-skinned hide. My brother called me crummy and I cried. I'm real sensitive. I dropped it. I got so weak. You know that thing about God doesn't make your cross any heavier than you can bear? It's true, just look at Christ, look what they did to Him, look what He took, that's tough. I used to think when I was losing my family and fighting through all of what addiction was; "Is this what You mean by not making our cross heavier than we can bear? Your burden is easy and your yoke is light!? It feels like hard-time in Hell to me." Then I looked at Christ, He died on His, while they spit on the Mother who was his Daughter, He said, "Father, why have you forsaken me?" and then He died, and he went to Hell, how tough do you have to be to do that?

But everything He did, His whole life, like those old Indians with that look in their eyes; was to fulfill His Vision, a Holy Prophecy, and He did it. He said He'd rise again and He did and hundreds of years before there was facebook or virtually any books, we learned from each other and we were picking ours up. We learned from ancestors that didn't just say it, they proved it and passed it on. That's what it means, that it won't be more than you can bear, it will be all you can bear, to the last drop, but you'll do it with this incredible hope that is light and love. "Why?" There are as many why's as there are people, but you know what my why has become? My why's who, an actual real live living human being that I allow myself to believe is Perfect, absolutely perfect, because of what he has done, and how he has done it, and who he is, his beauty, his love, his faith, his passion, and then I let that perfection I see in him, change me. He didn't want to, he picked up and carried the one thing nobody and nothing could take away from him unless he let them take it, Love.

I feel tough, I've got hope, I've got another last breath to love and I'm doing it right now, it feels good, I feel like a man. He was a man. He came to show us who we are. He did it for us to show us we could do it too, for Him and for each other, not for an idea, not for a symbol, bleed God's blood and you'll be tough.

To be committed to the truth I've had to be willing to let everything else go. I remember since the time I was a kid, I'd dream of coming to this dusty crossroad, not knowing what it meant or which way to go, but it felt good. It's a point you come to, where the truth has to be true, God has to be God, not your idea of Him. Like every sacred mystery it's the opposite of how it appears, in weakness we are made tough.

I don't know how to pray, but I love that He left me obedience. I'm not tough, I'm telling you a lot of things that happened, that I've done, that I'm doing; 'For what they mean.' If you feel lost or stuck, or scared, or feel weak or hopeless, if I can do it you can do it and if you can do it I can do it and so can everybody else. I walked on fire once, 5 hours of burned birch, embers and flame. There's nothing to it, it was all about fear, I just had to see the teacher do it and I knew I could do it. The only guy that really had to be tough was the first guy that ever did it. That's what Christ does for me.

Are you getting tired of looking in the mirror and telling yourself how great you are? What kind a car you're gonna have? Do you know how to be sincere? and say, "God, who are you? show me, I'm committed to the truth!" and then be humble, and instead of making God your idea, be willing to find out what God is, if God is, who God is, and why God is Love. Tell whoever is telling you you're no good including yourself to shut up. Fight back. Get your tail out from between your legs and live your own life, help somebody be tough by loving them, that's how my friends helped me remember I was tough. Love when people you love hate you and when you hate yourself, that's tough. Fall down and cry out for help, but don't be a damn fake, that's tough.

LIVE AT THE HARBOR RESTAURANT
SANTA BARBARA
LEO DOWNEY

'The Beauty of It'

It was 1968, I was 8 years old in Monterey, California. It was night. My sister Jean and I were home alone. There was a knock at the front door. I answered it. Three bloody Hells Angels stood there, blood was running down one of the guys tattooed arms and dripping on the slate. In the moonlight behind them were three of the coolest things I could imagine, Choppers. The dripping guy said, "We got in a knife fight with some Greasers in Seaside, is your sister home?" I think I just stood there. My sister walked up behind me. They came in. The next thing I remember we were in the bathroom, the light was bright and the blood was red. It seemed like it was getting all over. My sister was tending these guy's wounds real gently and she was so beautiful, we all just looked at her. She liked these guys. They were talking and even laughing. I don't remember anything else about that night except that beautiful girls liked tough wild guys. They must have known my dad was gone. I wonder today if they cut and beat each other up just to impress and see my sister. I'm not kidding, she was a beauty and she wasn't the least bit afraid.

Then I remember a big party in our house. My parents were gone again. My sister had my Dad's big Telefunken Stereo turned up real loud playing her cool records, Jimi Hendrix, the Doors, Iron Butterfly, Jefferson Airplane, Quick Silver Messenger Service. I used to try and play her folk guitar along with them. There were more choppers outside and those guys were back and a whole bunch of people with interesting waists. I put on my brothers Richard Nixon mask and started introducing myself. I put my hand up and said, "Hi, my name is Joe Schlabotkin." I remember getting a real nice response and even some introductions. Somebody said, "Joe Schlabotkin, who's Joe Schlabotkin?" I said, "He invented the flush toilet, he's got a girlfriend named Bertha Quagmire and they have a big glass toilet in Las Vegas you can put a quarter in and watch flush" That was the first of many good times I had at parties.

I always wanted to be tough, but I never wanted to be mean. I kissed Kristin Nale when I was 9, it lasted a split second and a lifetime. Then we moved to Singapore, I turned 12. All the kids were ex-pats and it was kind of like Lord of the Flies, we all said no kids did this stuff where we came from. Girls were the sources of this incredible energy. They were so beautiful, so soft, so alive, so amazing and they smelled so good. There was this beautiful blond Swedish girl, Katia. I sat behind her in the last row in English class. I would unzip the back of her uniform and slip my hand into her dress and she would squirm. We couldn't wait for English class. I felt no guilt around any of this and it was kind of, inspiring. I wonder if that's what's meant by 'first comes the natural man, then comes the spiritual man'. I began to seriously study the Spanish or 'Classical' guitar when I was ten and I wanted to express beauty and passion on it like Andres Segovia. I didn't need words or want them. There was something about the whole thing that was much like the girls, like the energy and beauty I felt from them.

I must have been about six when I remember crawling on my hands and knees in the chaparral that bordered our property in Monterey. Sunlight flickered through the bushes and was warm, it smelled good and was almost vibrating. I felt like I was doing something dangerous, like an Indian, and I wanted to be one.

There were these beautiful mysterious sounding voices singing, everything was old, the priest raised..., I knew him, he taught me catechism privately sometimes cause I whined about the Nun to my Mom. He raised a Golden Chalice and looked up at this bleeding man named Jesus, suffering on a rough wooden cross. Once when he turned around, I remember seeing tears in his eyes. He was so careful and everybody was kneeling and so different then they were the rest of the time, and it smelled good. There was this vibrating energy. The Priest and the people, the Earth and the sky and the Indian, the girls, the Hells Angels, the music and sometimes what I would play on the guitar. It was all about being a man and it was for the beauty of it.

'A Creature'

What I found in the world was the opposite of what I found in the wilderness, everything Earth told me was true. I felt like I could have died out there without really dying, like everything was close already. There is no substitute for Wandering in the Spirit, I loved Earth like a woman. I wandered all over California, but I always came back to the place I began and I got to know those ranges of desert mountains like the veins in my arms and backs of my hands. I wanted to know and love each place I stepped, black oaks and condor caves, weeping walls of sandstone, places where a bear had left his tracks ten years ago, the same way I want to know the neck and the lips of the woman I love and the small of her back and her eyes. I wanted to be a creature, and with no one there to tell me I wasn't, I was.

'Dad'

My Dad is 94, I asked him if he had a Christmas tree last year, he said, "Uh, wait a minute, let me look, oh yeah Lad, I've got a real nice one. I've mentioned that my Dad is a genius. I mean a real genius. He's got an I.Q. of 156, they think Einstein was 160. My dad is humble, he doesn't care about it and says it only tests a certain kind of intelligence. The 999 Club told him he qualified as a member, being in the top 99.999% of world I.Q. level and asked him if he'd like to join. He said okay. They sent him their quarterly magazine with articles written by other geniuses. I asked him what he thought of it? He said with that look and tone of exasperation he gets, "It's really dumb, it's some of the dumbest stuff I've ever read, here, read it." I laughed and read it. He was right. There were these articles written by a bunch of guys that thought they were real smart, but so much of what they said was based on a bunch of assumptions, all relative knowledge with very little wisdom.

That takes me into the story of a big orb weaver spider I saw in the center of his web in the center of a full moon when I rolled over on the ground the night before I entered a monastery on the Big Sur coast. I was going to live there till I died, you know what happened there is as amazing as anything I might have to say, but right now I want to tell you about my Dad. Some stuff that makes me laugh so hard I cry.

He got lost with my sister in Maui. The police brought him home. He's always driven like a bat out a hell. He was a Naval pilot in World War II, he flew the first canvas biplanes to the first jet fighters. The only way you can get him to slow down is if he thinks you're gonna puke in his car. He really likes my friend Jim here in Canada, Jim told him, "The wars over Dick, you can turn your after burners off now!" Old ladies run for cover in the Church parking lot.

He and my sister Mary, take care of my sister Jean who everybody calls Kood. She was struck with MS in 1980 and went from this amazing, funny, beautiful dancing blond, six months away from her Ph.D. in bio-chemistry, to severely brain damaged in a wheel chair. It was so, so sad, but you know she's taught me some of the most beautiful things in my life…she hardly speaks but she still has her sense of humor.

I looked in on her and one of her wonderful Hawaiian helpers, Bernadette. I said "What ya watchin Kood" she looked up and Bernadett said, "It's a show on extreme cakes Mr. Downeeey." I said, "Extreme cakes!?" and she said, "Yeaaah, man it's da'kine bra." We went to mass where my mom is buried in Makawao and then dinner. I said, "Hey Kood, what's an Extreme Cake anyway?" She said, "I don't know, I guess it's a cake that makes you puke!" 'Oh God' we laughed so hard. I used to think she was a burden.

Anyway, my niece Seana who I call, "Child" and used to be a Montecito Rat took my dad to the neurologist to see what was happening with his memory. He's in good health and good spirits otherwise, he just can't remember much anymore. He felt weird about it and he didn't want to go. The neurologist began looking at his file and speaking to him kind of like he was talking to a child and dad got that exasperated look. The doctor asked him, "What season is it?" Seana tells me he answered with a sigh "What season is it…"(with these funny grumbling sounds he makes) "Well, due to the fact we live at the far southern ebb of the Pacific anti-cyclonic flow 23 degrees North latitude and 124 degrees West longitude, we don't really have seasons, but I suppose you're referring to winter." The doctor read a little more and then said, "Oh, it says here you were a Naval pilot and oh, you're a genius." Seana said dad shrugged kind of sheepishly and said, "uhhh, ohh, yeah I guessss so" I wish you could hear Seana doing my dad cause it is so funny you'd roll out of your chair. So anyway finally Seana is walking fast down the hallway with all these kind of comatose people lining the walls and my dad shuffling along with his hands in his pockets trying to catch up and he says, "Seana-Child, where are we going?" and she says loudly, "We're gettin the hell outa here that's where we're goin!" and dad says, "Oh, good!"

Seana says, "So dad wanted to drive and I felt kind of sorry for him and thought okay." He's flying out of the parking lot and this old man is running for his life and dad says, "My he's a speedy little fella isn't he" and Seana says, "Yeah, and he's gonna be a flat little fella if you don't slow down!" They're almost home and dad says, "Ya know Seana-Child, I don't want to do that again, that was a real waste of time… I think I'm just gonna forget about the whole thing!"

'Montecito Rats'

Montecito is one of the most beautiful places in California, but there's these big ugly Norwegian rats that come out of the ivy at night. I slept outside in my back yard with snares around my head and would wake up with just theirs lying around. They'd crunch, munch and chew on the snared ones all night, but even they wouldn't eat their own heads.

I rolled over on the ground to rest in perfect alignment with a big orb weaver in the middle of her web in the middle of the full moon the night before I entered the Monastery. I was ready to die there and thought I would and I knew that Spider was saying something to me. It felt good to know and I was fine not knowing.

How do you listen to a spider? He tells you. I don't listen to tons of spiders. Most of them are minding their own business and I try to mind mine. I knew this one was there to tell me something, sometimes spiders, and also lizards, are there to witness something, for a reason, it's always important. God speaks through His creation of symbols to man; God's symbol.

Things that happen on the path as I wander in the Spirit, become stories with a purpose. The first time I went to the Immaculate Heart Hermitage, a Catholic Monastery on the Big Sur Coast, it was 1986, long before that spider spoke and I left the world and entered it. I was taking, "Carmel," a second edition of my first CD of original instrumentals on the Spanish/Classical guitar to dozens of places along the coast between Santa Barbara and San Francisco that were selling it. In those days there were lots of coffee houses and galleries and bookstores that would play your CD for their customers to hear and buy. Carmel was selling very well. People would hear it and buy it and the stores wanted it. I was so happy and felt so good about that accomplishment. I was able to get national distribution for it through Narada Records and also full rotation on the Wave, one of the biggest F.M. radio stations, syndicated out of L.A.

At the time I was also recording my first rock record, "Heaven and Hell" with my band. A year earlier and shortly after the night I saw Elan in another guys arms kissing him and kicked his door in, Kimberley Herrin came into the Harbor Restaurant where I was playing and asked me if I wanted to be her Valentine.

She was a very beautiful Playboy Bunny and budding actress. She'd been in Ghostbusters, Romancing the Stone and a ZZ Top video for their song, 'She's Got Legs' and she did! She was gifted in many ways and very giving. I remember a classic photograph of her, John Belushi and Bill Murray playing pool. She said Bill picked her up in the Blues Brother's car for a date in New York and had to kick her door open.

This was when the band started to take off and we were playing more in L.A. the Whiskey and other places I can't remember on Sunset Strip and Hollywood Boulevard. I had an affinity with Jim Morrison since I was a kid and first heard Light My Fire in the back of my dad's car. Recently I read Ray Manzarek's description of Jim and it was uncanny. I'd heard about the dead Indian's spirit going into him as a kid when he drove by the car accident. Ray described him as a shaman and in a way, as I would have described myself in those days. I was drinking and there was other stuff floating around the people around me. The whole dream pulled me in and repulsed me at the same time.

The dark side usually has nothing to do with a conscious choice for evil, or to hurt anyone. In fact, it's often the opposite. I thought all that rocker bohemian stuff was earthy and good, a sign and source of some kind of authenticity, of being a man full of life, but it sucked Jim Morison down into its throat the same way it almost did to me. It turns into a self centered and unquenchable seeking of pleasure. As you allow yourself to be sucked into it's throat, you begin to become filled with its spirit. You begin to possess each other. This was just beginning to happen around then, but it wasn't until twenty-five years or so later that I became addicted to alcohol. That's another part of the story.

'Confession'

I drove up Highway One in my convertible Fiat Spider. Every curve is a new horizon, a thousand feet above the Pacific Ocean on the most romantic and powerful coastline in my world, the place of my birth, I saw a sign. It was hidden back in the bushes and I'd never noticed it all those many times I'd driven past it before. It said, "Immaculate Heart Hermitage." I'd been praying a prayer out of a book I'd been reading called, "A Course in Miracles" It was a good book and a track on the way. It reminded me of the illusion I'd find in a body, my own or someone else's. I had no idea I was about to find reality in Christ's.

I drove another thousand feet up the pampas grass ridge of a redwood canyon and walked into a dark and quiet octagonal Catholic Church, empty but for an altar in the Center. A priest named father Francis asked me if I would like to talk to him. I explained my journey and it became an organic confession. The Course in Miracles stressed the power of the, "Holy Relationship" and as I spoke and he listened and as he spoke and I listened I realized that was what this was.

There is so much to tell you that bears meaning if you 'want' to know, so much, but I can only play and you can only hear so many notes at a time. This one is played on the Angelus; bells that call angels. If I play you one can I play you more? Because once is not enough, each step forms a chain and breaks a path, like the path of the buffalo, from the beginning to the end when I believe we will start over and love each other again, new.

He listened, it was hard for me, as I tried to tell him, he said, "Tell me everything, it's not because I want to know, but because then you begin to know the Mercy of Christ, who will forgive you and me for everything." And as every sacred mystery that has ever revealed itself to me, everything was the opposite of what I thought it would be. As I took responsibility for my actions, I found the worst thing I thought I had done had been done to me. That wasn't what really mattered to me though, what mattered was being able to be honest, to be reconciled and aligned with the truth. Confession is a sacrament, a sacred prayer and channel of God's grace that Jesus gave to His apostles when he sent them in an unending line of succession, a blood tribe of the Lion. He 'breathed' on them and said, "I send you as the Father has sent me, who's sins you forgive are forgiven, who's you retain are retained." It seems like only a few people today believe he could do that, what he said, but for some reason, all the ones I track for their beauty did. Think about somebody breathing on you and saying that, somebody you believed had been killed and come back to life. The only other time God breathed on anyone, he created them.

Then he gave me the Body of Christ, this is one of the beliefs that makes the Catholic faith different from all the rest. It also makes matter sacred. We believe the bread and wine actually do become the body and blood of Christ, for infinite reasons, one being because Christ said they did.

Obviously if I believe this, it's a different experience for me than if I don't, but whether I do or not, if it is, it's, "Something else." Kind of like bringing forth a song, it's an act of faith and an act of love, it's a creative act to believe it and I want to for an infinite number of reasons that are meaningful and are more notes to play you on the chord. The notes on the chord form harmonies and reveal more the fullness, like tracks on the path. If you look at one track and then start looking for what left it, it's difficult to find it, but when you want to enough, you find all the tracks, even partial little pressure releases and they begin to tell a fascinating story. It's very easy to want to believe that you don't believe it though and I try to sincerely respect the wish of anyone that wants to not believe it.

I ate the mystical body and blood of Christ, and like the whole unbelievable story of Christ, I believed it. Me telling you I believe something doesn't mean much, but me telling you what I read in the tracks and hear in the bells of the chord is beautiful. If you don't want to look at it or see it, you probably won't, whether it's true or not, until you do, or you don't. But next I'll begin tell you things that happened when I did.

'The Bells'

Conversion, revelation, insight, even the effect of visions and miracles, doesn't happen all at once. It takes the gift of time to respond and harmonize. It's like tracking the trail of an animal up a mountain and seeing more, looking out over the horizon as you both rise, finding your way. Sincerity and intention are the most important thing, a sincere heart becomes a passionate heart. God says he spits the lukewarm out of his mouth. The communion of the politically correct will say that's not fair, kind of like a brat that says everyone has to keep loving and liking me even if I keep acting like a little pill to everybody. Jesus said to come to God and enter the Kingdom of Heaven we must be childlike, not childish. To do something 'you have to do it', I've learned that from music. Grace is something I have to cooperate with and it takes faith; hope in what is unseen. As I get older I see more and more how every second of time is an infinitely precious gift, one more breath I can breathe in and breath out closer to the way God does, where instead of our breath being a 'using' it is a giving.

I walked into Our Lady of Mount Carmel Church when I got home from my first visit to the Monastery and time with Father Francis. It was empty and I knelt to light a candle and say a prayer. The exact moment I lit the candle, the bells on top of the church went off. It happened to be twelve o'clock when they always went off. A few days later I stopped on my motorcycle at the stop sign in front of the church and the bells went off, I was just noticing. Then I called my girlfriend and asked her to meet me at the Santa Barbara Mission, and that I had to talk with her about something. We met standing at the back of the Church and mass was just starting. I have a really, really hard time with ninety percent of modern Church music, most of the time it's mild torture for me. I guess it's a matter of taste and an aesthetic sense, and I often feel kind of guilty about my negative view of it. I look around and see how the people singing it seem to be enjoying it and getting something out of it, but my feeling of it is that it is so poorly composed and usually performed also, that it grates on me like fingers down a chalkboard. It always feels like the wrong music for the picture, I don't feel that way at all about Gregorian Chant, which is the type of music we have sung for almost 1,500 years until everything got modernized and westernized and the Catholic church more or less decided to be like the rest of the churches. Gregorian chant is a seven note scale instead of eight, its nature is to quiet the mind and emotions instead of rouse them the way our modern eight note scale does. I couldn't take the music, so we went outside onto the grass in front of the mission. I was beating around the bush trying to tell her we had to end the relationship. Finally she said, "Are you saying it's over?" and I said, "Yes!" and as I did I simultaneously stood up and turned around and all the bells went off on top of the Mission. I thought, hmm, that's kind of poignant.

A few weeks later it was time to drive up the coast again with my CD's. I stopped at the monastery and asked if I could see Father Francis. the secretary reached him and I asked if I could talk with him for a few minutes, we walked down the driveway to a bench that overlooked a deep redwood canyon and I began to tell him how the bells seemed to keep going off synchronistically. He was listening with interest and then all the bells went off on top of the Monastery. He smiled, looked at his watch, and said, "Leo I've been here for six months and the bells have never gone off at 3:30, he laughed and said, "I guess that was a powerful transubstantiation". We walked back up to the bookstore, the secretary said some of the monks had asked her to ring the bells at 3:30 so they could meet to pray for one of the old monks that was dying. I had no idea I'd be entering that monastery one day.

'Our Lady of Love'

In 1989 my mom went to a village in Croatia called Medgugorje. Since 1981 six children, now grown with their own children, claim the Virgin Mary has been appearing to them giving them messages of prayer and calling us back to the love of her Son. She has revealed secrets about the future to each of the six visionaries. Three days before they happen, they will reveal them to the world. Some are difficult involving man made and natural calamities, but because nothing else seems to work, they are to help us believe in God and have faith again. The lack of love and peace in human beings manifests itself in nature. The third secret has been partially revealed as an indestructible miraculous sign that will be on Earth till the end of time. It has been described in different ways as accompanied by a worldwide 'Illumination of Conscience' where every person on Earth, at the same time, will see themselves as they really are, in the light of love, they will see all the unloving things they have done and all the good they have not done, they will see the state of their soul.

All who pray now from the heart will be eternally grateful. Everything is coming together to show us that God is real. Fifty million people have been to this remote village, and the vast majority of them experience profound phenomena. My mother saw the sun spinning and throwing out colors along with many others, there have been numerous miraculous healing's, but the biggest miracle that happens is an interior transformation, a glimpse into the heart and through the eyes of Christ and of the Virgin Mary, at each other and at ourselves. What makes what is happening in Medgugorje even more amazing is that it is happening in places all over the world and has been in an increasingly accelerated way over the last one hundred years. Search the links at the end of my book and you'll see. I promise you, if you will take just a little time to look at what is happening, and consider the evidence, you will see a new reality and gradually be astounded by it. It takes a while to sink in, but all it really asks of you is sincerity.

A period of unprecedented prophecy began with Fatima, Portugal in 1913 and continued with Garabandal Spain, Betania Venezuela, Zeituon Egypt, Akita Japan, Lourdes and La Sallette France, and dozens more, but I don't want to just tell you about them, I want to tell you about what they mean to me, as we Wander forward in the Spirit I will. If you explore the links I include at the end of this book, you will discover a world only a small percentage of the worlds population are aware of. Like me, you will be confronted with evidence and proof of miracles unlike any others on earth, nothing even comes close. The Virgin Mary, the Woman Clothed with the Sun, is telling us secrets about a future that is here. She is helping us prepare for a heavenly dawn, the Triumph of her Immaculate Heart, the heart that loves her Son. If all you do is take the time to listen with your heart, carefully and prayerfully to the links I've listed at the end of this book, it will change your whole life. The rest becomes pale in comparison. If you enter into these mysteries sincerely, they will change the way you see everything, yourself, your life, the nature of your soul and spirits, the nature of earth and creatures and even the nature of God.

'My First Bad Review'

When somebody talks about God, they set themselves up to be judged, like all of a sudden they are supposed to be fixed or perfect and if they aren't then it's like they're a hypocrite. But that's not what it's about, it's about being sincere and humble enough to learn something. I don't get mad at somebody because they can't play the guitar or write a song or stand still when a buffalos charging them, I appreciate and admire that they can build a house and be successful or organize and run the details of a business. We have different gifts, I'm trying to do the only things I think I'm any good at and what I can with what I have and I'm praying with all my heart that somehow it's valuable to you, so I'm going to keep trying and tell you this story.

When my mom came back from Medgugorje, she brought back the grace of her journey and she shared it with me. She told me about the Virgin Mary, someone I had never really thought about before. She has had an effect on me more profound than any woman. She showed me what a woman was and then I began to see what a man was and both were so much more than I had ever thought before, that I too began to go through an inner transformation. But this was happening at the height of everything I had worked for in my music career, as I mentioned before, right when my band was offered a record contract with Sony and a promotional contract with Budweiser. I'd been in a relationship with a new actress and Playboy bunny and then with Bonnie Raitt, a woman I respected and admired deeply. Everything I had worked for and wanted was being offered to me on a silver platter. I don't know how to describe how hard it was to be going through this transformation and illumination of my conscience in the middle of all these things being offered to me that I had thought I wanted and worked so hard for.

Since I was a kid I wanted to 'live like an Indian.' I'd been going alone into the wilderness since I was a teenager and having 'mystical' experiences there. I continued to go back there alone regularly throughout my adult life in breaks between work of a few weeks at a time. My experiences there anchored all these things. Things happened that aren't supposed to happen, miracles, and when they do your whole experience of the seen world and of yourself changes. The unseen world and the things of the soul became more and more important and real to me and the things of the 'world' became more and more meaningless to me except in relation to how they could be aligned with what felt like a much greater purpose, this is what a 'vision' is. At first I thought a vision was some visual thing like a ghostly Indian dancing around a fire and beating a drum or an apparition, but usually they are simply a 'miracle.' Miracles come in an infinite gradient of majesty.

This Truth, God, wasn't a vague energy or ideal and wasn't a tool to get what I thought I 'Wanted', it was the love of a 'Person' that stood near me, and a holy ghost, angels and ancestors in an ancient Communion, an eternal tribe, with each member as individual and as real as you and me, but keeping a distance out of a kind of respect for my sovereignty, miracles are withheld for the same reason. Each of these persons had the same quality, Greatness, and it seemed like somehow they saw this in every single person on earth. They were calling me to see it in myself and every single person on earth too and the only way to do it was through Faith in Love.

But I was grinding my jeans against my mic stand and unknowingly using the power and gifts of my soul to illuminate my carnality. I think I've always had a certain kind of spirit or innocence of a little boy and this only added to something I can't explain but that women seemed to find very attractive. I was kind of innocent about it, I was a friendly dog, I loved everybody. A girl that stuck by me through all of it said, 'Yeah, they just all happen to be leggy blondes.' There were some dark haired ones too! Anyways…, I began to see myself and all I was doing, my life, artistically, professionally and personally in the light of these holy beings around me that were calling me to be 'holy' too. I'd felt this calling since I was a teenager and first began to go into the wilderness alone and experienced my first 'vision' quest or miracle, but I remember thinking, yes, I do want to be 'holy', but I'm a man, a musician, a Californian, God can't expect me to give up girls and sex and romance and I don't feel ready at all for marriage. I didn't grow up with a clear 'code' the way many Protestants friends I met later in my life did. I was a Catholic and like many of us I didn't know what that meant or have any idea of the ocean of miracles and holy wisdom my ancestors had carried in their souls and bodies all the way to me. But when the Virgin Mary entered into my life and my heart, all of this treasure of beauty and knowledge, history, mystery and truth and real Love, began to open up and reveal itself. She shows me her heart and her vision and her vision is her Son. She not only interprets her Sons word, she embodies it.

I've said how I committed myself to the truth when I was about 16 years old, not knowing what the truth was but knowing that it was a life changing commitment and that it meant whenever I recognized anything as true I would have to chose it over what I might prefer. Recognizing Truth is a never ending journey, sometimes I can't tell the difference between truth and a pile of crud, but it wasn't so much about 'virtue' thankfully as I don't think I have much of that, but more about awareness. For me recognizing and expressing the beauty of truth is the main work an artist does.

Years earlier, when I'd read, 'A Course in Miracles.' Its main effect was to help me recognize that I couldn't find any lasting satisfaction in a body, mine or a woman's, or ultimately in matter, and this slowly began to awaken a sense that 'sin' was desire born from a lack of love. Though Mary's love is beyond the body, she is a human being, a woman, and she showed me what Love was, she showed me what passion was, what a woman was, she loved me like she loved her Son, who loved her so much he created her. Love between a man and a woman is the foundation of our experience in a body on earth and everything I'm talking about has a correlation to that relationship.

One night after I said some old fashioned prayers, some my ancestors have repeated and taught others for two thousand years, she spoke to me. I awoke to a 'voice.' This voice had a beautiful tone and I recognized it the way I would yours if I knew you and you were on the phone, but it was beautiful like no other. I've never heard a 'voice' before or since. She was speaking and I didn't want to move or I thought it would stop, I only remember the last thing she said, "If you want to be like Jesus, you have to be my son." I sighed, moved with a kind of love and beauty that makes everything less seem worthless, meaningless, and worse; sinful, an act born out of a lack of love. But what was I supposed to do? Leave the world? How could I be true to this kind of real love they were calling me to, the love Christ gave and had told me to give years before when I was so lost I was hopeless.

I tried to integrate all of it into my music and my professional life but I couldn't do it. The conviction alone, that I had to stop sleeping with these beautiful wonderful women that wanted me and wanted me to love them and wanted to love me was overwhelming and seemed impossible. Now each time it happened I was torn apart by this inner conflict and deep concern for them and for me and also for the possibility that I might get a woman pregnant and have the life of an innocent baby on my hands. The word Transformation conjures up wonder and gifts, but when you ask to walk with God and for miracles and God grants them, it's the hardest thing a human being can do to respond, it's difficult and confusing. There's a modern pervasive idea that spirituality and 'God' are tools or ways to get 'what you think you want' to create abundance and prosperity. It is abundance and prosperity but it isn't carnal. The riches or lack of riches and granting of passing desires become like dust a car kicks up. Driving the car and why and where become your focus, not the car. Becoming an instrument of the unseen world becomes your desire, the abundance and riches have been a 100 x more than I ever could have even dreamed up to wish for or 'want' and each time they have been a 'Gift.' That giftedness is an intrinsic part of why they are experienced as such treasure. Because they are a gift, a miracle, you are able to enjoy them 100 x more than anything you ever got that you 'wanted.' It's hard to explain but it's the way it's been for me.

I had been experiencing 'Forgiveness' on many levels in many ways. I had experienced it sacramentally with the priest I confessed to at the monastery. I had experienced it alone in the wilderness and other ways, but one day I spoke to Jesus in prayer and I said, "Lord, I know you've forgiven me and I believe it, but can I please 'feel' it, can I please feel your forgiveness."

About a week later I got my first bad review. It was written by an English guy that had moved to Santa Barbara and wrote for the Independent. I think he wanted to be a singer ~songwriter, but couldn't get any good gigs. He was the classic English 'journalist' that would write these scathing reviews of other musicians and everybody, but I hardly read anything he wrote until I saw he'd written one about me. I had never met or seen him, but in the review he said he stood in front of me with my 'American cheese smile' while I played and he said, "You're shit" and that I was 'visibly shaken.' I'd never seen or heard this guy say anything and if he had have said that to me I'm afraid I'd have been thrown in jail. I'd been a bouncer in bars, I'd had to deal with drunks forcibly, I'd been taking full contact karate for three years and when I read this I was like a volcano. The other guys in the band were looking at me and trying to calm me down because I had this urge to walk a block up State Street and into his office and beat the shit out of him. I was so pissed! I really wanted to punch this guy out and make him apologize and all that, but thankfully I got a hold of myself and drove home. As I sat in traffic, I began to laugh at the whole thing and it was kind of surreal, I was thinking hah, here I am with this guy yanking on me in the paper and it all seemed kind of funny momentarily, but then I thought, wait, what if my mother has to reads this! and then I got all pissed off again.

When I got home I took a shower and tried to center myself for the show that night. I sat down and prayed and I decided to randomly open the book called a 'Course in Miracles' and put my finger down. I opened it up to, 'Forgiveness is the Key to Happiness'…and then the light went on and I sighed and realized the prayer I'd asked for a week earlier had been answered. I'd asked Jesus to let me 'Feel' his forgiveness and he was, by letting me feel what he feels like…having to forgive, me, and so I sat there, shaking my head, thinking of Jesus and then me, realizing, brother, I have to forgive this jerk, ugh, but it's nothing compared to what Jesus had to forgive and forgives in me over and over…

'Grizzly'

FALL 2013

The buffalo were spooked yesterday and I dreamed of a big grizzly last night. My neighbor was walking down to the river this morning and saw him by my Tipi. I've built my fences so the wild creatures can cross over, under and through them following the path of their ancestors. The buffalo stay because they're happy. I figured where he'd cross for the river, they're coming back with the eagles for the salmon. The buffalo thundered for the upper corridor and there he was where I knew he'd be, awesome and beautiful, thick with muscle like rope rolling under his fur. They have the power of an angel.

In the dream there were people I felt responsible for, they weren't listening to me and he was coming for them. They are here every year in the fall and they've never bothered anyone. I take my rifle when I know there's Grizzlies around. I would hate to have to shoot one, or a mountain lion. I've been face to face with mountain lion, seen them hunting numerous times, and had them around me at night with the hair standing up on the back of my neck. I stalked up on one I'd watched in the Sierra Madre's for three years. We came eye to eye twice that day. Two hundred and fifty pounds is not unusual for a male and they can kill a horse, but if you face them they almost always back down. They are so beautiful they're breathtaking. I'm not sure what I would have done if I had seen the one that attacked two of my buffalo last fall. It's kids we have to watch out for. Buffalo are so tough and hard to kill, I've let them take care of themselves. Chester could knock any predator out and the wolves have forgotten how to hunt buffalo here, it takes them about seven years of living with wild ones to learn to get them to run instead of fight. My whole life I've wanted to be another creature, true to my nature like they are, humans can be so lame, God wants to give us a power we're too dumb to take, or maybe it's cowardice, most don't think it's worth it.

I see the predators like angels, that swing their swords. For some reason, I think I might win, but if I went out by one of them, a lion or a bear, it would be a great fight. I would so much rather go as a creature with a creature that had the intelligence and passion and honor to take what God gave it, instead of at the hands of some dumb, lame, human that lies to himself and wants the world to say evil is good, so he can get what he thinks he wants instead. Then I think, oh, that's me, I've been that lame human, hmmm, I wish I'd known then what I know now. I see a whole bunch of people fooling themselves and being attacked like I was. They're personalizing everything but God. They don't know the nature of the predators, they don't know how to fight, and they hate it when anybody tells them the truth. It would feel so good to help someone, I know I can because I could have helped me, but most of us have to get desperate before we will actually listen.

This land and life is amazing, with animals and humans I thank God for, they helped me when I lost a fight. But I didn't a lose the war, I survived, a battle, I've come out strong. I can feel myself taking the power. Chester tried to give his to me, I was too weak to take it then, God has tried all my life. It's not about being strong in the way we think of it, it's about being totally honest, that is where all our strength is. It takes guts to be honest because it means we have to start over. The world builds on lies. People construct themselves on them until that's all they have left to take or give, they become the source of their ideas and desires, their ideas are dishonest because the source of them is.

If you want something good, something beautiful and powerful beyond your dreams, find a creature that has it, and ask them to give it to you, not just their thoughts and ideas, themselves, That's what Christ gave in his humanity. His thoughts became extensions of himself. He gave us his word and he kept it, by becoming it, the way an artist becomes his art. He is a completely different kind of 'teacher' the first one to become what he teaches, that is why he can say, "I am the way the truth and the life" The Holy Spirit is the spirit that enters and transforms each of us from the inside into the image of God, who is Christ, Gods living Son. The Holy Spirit allows those that love to see through the eyes, and feel through the 'Sacred Heart' of Christ. Our flesh becomes Christ's flesh, one body, the way Christ becomes Man. It's all art and an artist does whatever it takes, an artist cares, an artist learns from artists and becomes one. Following your own path sounds good but it's impossible, it's why the world goes in circles.

Nothing in nature and no tribe close to earth forsakes its ancestors, it's like resenting your parents, it makes no sense and keeps doing it until you make no sense. Spirituality is about creatures, they make wanting obsolete. That's what I've learned. I asked God on my first vision quest and he gave me a living oracle, his word, perfect but not enough, without God himself, his creatures, that is where his Spirit, his life and his wisdom lives, in his blood, and the only way to know what his word means, his ideas mean, what he means, what we mean. Ideas separate from their source are meaningless.

Love, passion, beauty, music, the smokey essence of all the earthy good in our culture, the women I've loved gave it to me on Earth. They had it, I saw it in their eyes and I gave it back, I wanted to with everything I had. I turned it into art. A native man gave me his fire, it took him three days in the snow and rain. I want to give my friends something good, something real. They know who they are, I wish the whole world knew, each one is an amazing story. I feel it right on the cusp, somehow they pulled me through all this so I can give something back.

How am I going to do it? I'm like a desert manzanita, a tarantula hawk wasp, an idiot savant, I thrive in my element, I can give what I'm good at, but I wither up and crumble without the beauty of angels, without the Communion of Holy Creatures. They say you can be one of us if you're willing to give everything, everything, your life and your breaths and your thoughts and your will, and even your body. If you'll do it for the beauty, we'll give you ours and then you'll discover you're one of us. I'm not much good at doing something so I can do something else, so I've done something else. I think we all can, you can, all the different ways we give go together, your gift is perfect like the notes in a song, the chords, the harmonies, the eyes and the lips and the fingers, we are being created to do this together, sovereign and one. It is not our bodies that separate us, or limit us. That's why God became lower than the angels, to give us his, to show us what we are, to show us what Love is, it's not a contest, it's an art. Instead of whining about what he asks, some people actually do it. One person at a time is changing everything, and no one else can.

All I do is work, but I'm an artist, we're kinda weird. We only see the invisible clearly, what's visible is unreal to us until we bring it inside and make it invisible for a while. Sifting through the papers, categorizing the linear plan, organizing, 'doing.' I've done it, but it's not my nature, I'm much better and more useful for other things. It might not seem like it, but the invisible things are important, they're why we're doing something or something else. This place is a vision, this country is a treasure, this land is so beautiful and blessed. All the potential I see, it's ripening, it's like it's right here ready to pick. It's taken everything I have to bring it this far, and it's waiting to give a hundred times more.

'She Showed Me What a Woman Was'

I couldn't explain to anybody what I was going through. I tried but I didn't even know myself except that I had met this woman my Mom introduced me to, that was so breathtaking, so full of heart and soul, she was so beautiful that when I looked at her I couldn't see anything but what she saw. I think Bonnie thought it was about a playboy bunny I'd been dating, she said, "I must seem like a rare squash next to her!" I laughed so hard, a rare squash! I've had many times in my life where I could have gained the world and lost my soul, but I thought the world with no soul would be hell. No, this woman looked at me with this beautiful gentleness, the purist femininity, such love, that she showed me what a woman was.

Earlier that afternoon I'd decided to pray these old prayers of my ancestors and I'd decided for some reason to feel how I would feel if the story of the Virgin was true…if she believed it, what if it all really happened and she knew it, how would she feel? Gabriel speaking to her, the Holy Spirit wedding her and putting the seed of Himself in her. God must have been so in love with her too. How would she feel if she looked at her baby and her son as he nursed and grew into a man, and saw her Creator? If she saw the savior of our wounded world and her soul and if when he looked at her he saw his mother, his daughter and his creation… and everything began to change. What kind of love passed between their eyes? I wanted it. It was like I'd never known what a man or a woman was and how could I be her son if I was sleeping with her daughters all over the place? What did it all mean? I'd been deeply in love. Even my critics said I had a romantic streak a mile wide. Years before, I fell in love at first site with Elan. She's wonderful, she'd surrender, she listened like it mattered and it did. I kicked in a door one night. I was so in love with her and we'd been together a few years, but I wasn't ready to get married and it was driving her away. I saw her in another guys arms! I kicked in his door and all of a sudden I was in his kitchen punching him out till he ducked under my arm and ran away. I stood there in disbelief and after that night I was never jealous again. That's the only time I have ever fought when it wasn't to protect myself or someone else. Everybody felt bad, but Later Elan said, "I have never seen you look so handsome." I think a woman wants to know a man will fight for her. Earth is a sacred drama, each person a snowflake. Sometimes two fit together and melt into one and sometimes they just melt. I've got a lot more to say and I pray it will matter, and help

'I Fall in Love With Her'

FALL 2013

There is a way to experience a moment
As if I'm standing beside it
A little outside myself
As if it was a time that already happened
And now I'm looking back on it
Like an intimate memory

I can step into the best of our culture
And become part of it
The collective consciousness
I've felt this way
About the Big Sur Coast and Monterey
The Pacific and on the Mojave
The San Joaquin and Sierra Madre
Mountains I've wandered to pray
And Red Chief
The one that called me to stay

I don't sleep with Earth casually
I want to know her intimately
Like a woman
Sometimes it's a few square inches
Sometimes it's a few hundred thousand acres
It takes time, sweat, devotion, prayer and faithfulness
Earth shows me her body in such a subtle way
Her power is erotic
Because of its holiness

It's beautiful
Because she is humbled by her beauty too
She isn't proud, she doesn't lie
She tests me but never judges me
Most of all
She wants the Truth
She commits me to it
None of the worlds lies
She pleads for me to be honest
I fall in love with her

'Two Mothers'

WINTER 2014

They floated in mercy
Two mothers holding hands
Both my own
Gods daughters
Both loved me when they were here
As the son in their arms
And both love me now
I want to tell you
How they taught me mercy
By showing me what it is

I'd taken a friend in the wilderness
She'd been hurt and grown strong
And it made her weak

It was my first rosary
My mother received it from a child
And gave it to me
I'd never prayed a sacred mystery
The Joyful Annunciation, Visitation, the Birth....
The Sorrowful Agony, the Crowning of Thorns and Crucifixion...
The Glorious Resurrection, the Ascension...
The Crowning of Gods Bride with the stars
My friend said the words while I prayed
And after a while I heard the voice of a little girl

Sweet, innocent, before she was hurt
It brought tears to my eyes
To hear my poor friend pray

Then in the meadow
Of Indian Sage
I saw 'in a way' my two mothers
The two Mary's
Floating just above the grass
Holding hands, smiling on us
And I thought
My God, while I've been out here
My mother has died
And now she's here
Showing Gods Mother her life
Her son
And I'm praying
Loves sacred mystery
And they're smiling!
I wept in a joyful sorrow of glory
I was praying
When My Mother
Showed Gods Mother
Her son

That's when I first felt the mercy
That's when I saw what it is
How heaven wouldn't be heaven for a mother
If her son wasn't there
How our love for God in each other
Is the bond
That saves and brings us there

Have mercy on me
And on yourself
Don't be afraid
She doesn't betray her children
But she has mercy on those that have
She loves them

Mercy in her eyes
Sees her Son rise
On an Earth that kneels
And prays
Like a child for a child

'Everything's Alive'

I held a baby in a dream, with eyes like Galaxies, looking back and beholding me, in eternal wonder, so holy, he brought me to my knees, and then I looked around. I was in a public restroom with filth all over everything, even written on the walls. I thought, how did I get in here, I have to get him out, to even think a thing unlike him in his presence would be to reach into his peace and rip it out, and I looked on my own son the same way.

I had all the joy I've ever had. I loved his mother like a lover and a daughter, and a sister and a mother and a friend. I couldn't dream our love could end. I'd given up everything and been given a hundred times more. I have never been so happy. As a young man, I'd faced the world, and said no, I'd faced the flesh, and said no, but who I faced next, I didn't know. He told me he was me and I believed him.

I was a marked man, a consecrated soul, it was another wilderness. I got scared. Instead of making myself a prayer, I made myself a man. I personalized all the wrong things, losing what they mean. I thought they were ideas, thoughts that didn't seem my own, but who else's could they be? They came at me, through generations, through my senses, and through the words and actions of others. A stalker left his tracks, poisoning my buffalo, I stood with my herd through the nights, he hated, threatened, envied, to destroy me and my family, and then he tried to kill me, and I not knowing who I was, took it all personally. I wanted to fight like Jeremiah Johnson, but they don't let a man do that today, and in the end that was a good thing. It wasn't really him, he was up against the same one I was, like Earth against the world, but neither of us knew.

I entered a new wilderness, a dark night of the soul, where the creatures leave an unseen track, and through, is the only way back. I think Judas fell because he stopped praying. So did I. The cost was betraying, the most beautiful thing I ever had, breaking. I was a walking dead man, I was the writing on the wall, my soul a stall, I flushed with alcohol. I was afraid. I let this thing in, he said he'd go away, if I stopped fighting him.

No one teaches more than an enemy, I learned things from the devil I thank God for, have faith or be afraid and know who you're obeying. Nothing dead can take your life, and what's real is alive.

A Soultracker learns the nature of creatures, the way an artist learns the nature of beauty, the way a man learns the nature of a woman, and of God. The only thought not obsolete is a prayer. Everything here is an expression of a living being, moving in the unfathomable God becoming his creature. I go beyond to be here, the way I'd Wander in the Spirit, to learn the nature of creature's seen, track the unseen footprints. They walk through your life to your soul.

If someone or something comes at you, from out of the black and the blue, lying and dividing, destroying beauty, bribing you for peace, hidden but naked, temptation, ruining reputation, track the prints on your soul. The path that lets them in, is not up or down a gradient of thoughts, but a gradient of sin, face the creature like a lion, by offering yourself to God as a prayer.

To do something real, first I had to feel how I feel. What I was afraid of, I gave my Lifeforce too, it will take it till there's nothing left of you. Don't change it, embrace it, feel it, face it, and it changes you, this is the Sacrament of Confession, compared to it, positive thoughts are repression, forgive everyone but let God forgive you, sincerity is all we hang on to, and watch it set us free, to see, what matters is alive, and just like in the wilderness, I had to say, I can have faith or be afraid, and I choose faith, I offer myself to you now, in every form you take, whatever happens; as a Prayer. If we want the truth, the beauty, the glory of love, the peace the hope the wonder of, eyes of galaxies, this is where.

I've never hurt anyone on purpose in my life, but I hurt my friends, my son and my wife, by being afraid of evil.

'Pope in the Box'

Did I dream
There was a Drive-in Confessional
You had to tell your sins
To a 'Pope in the Box'
The kid that took your request
Would yell them back
"Was that 1 adultery, 2 white lies
and a remark with bad intent, sir!?"
"Shuushhhhh!"
"That will be 1 Our Father, 1 Hail Mary
and an act of contrition at the window please"

I drove across the street to 'Fast Advice'
The girl at the window said,
"Nothing's a sin, that's just some dumb idea
and anyway, you can forgive yourself"
"Oh, I wish I came here first,
you could have saved me two dumb prayers
and a meaningless act of contrition"

Next to the adult bookstore
They were working on a combination
'Drive-in Marriage, Divorce
Assisted Suicide and Used Car lot'

At the corner I saw a billboard
Coming Soon too a city near you
A 'Don't Get Born in the First Place'
"We save a world of trouble"

I walked into 'Truth Bank & Trust'
I tried to deposit some truth
They said they only accepted
My truth or your truth
So it couldn't work for anybody else
But they offered me a line
Of credit with no interest

In the traffic jam
I thought about it all
A homeless guy held a sign
'Will work for Peace'
Somebody yelled 'Get a job!"
"I had one at the Drive-in confessional,
but nobody goes there anymore"

'For A Woman'

I think He did it for a woman and I think he's going to do it for her again. When he did it for her, he did it for everyone because she gave God birth. I think He did it for a woman, each one that would ever live. I think when He walked by they looked into His eyes and were born again, they became little girls again when they are still full of flowers and wonder and gentleness.

More and more I live for the invisible things, the things I can 'see' aren't as real anymore; except in relation to each other, they exist without meaning. True love isn't like that, if the two of you love each other for your relationship to each other, if that's where you are looking for the meaning of your love for each other, it won't last. It's not enough to inspire the kind of Love Christ died for, the kind that makes men great. If you find a woman that will love you for who created you and who calls you back, a woman that will give you birth, that will love you for God, she will become a perfect creation in your eyes. You will be her Christ, her savior and she will give you birth, but all that will happen because you put your faith in your faith and not you or your woman. If you take twenty minutes somewhere quiet where you can let go and just want it, just be humble and sincere for twenty minutes out of all the ones that went before and ask Her to show you, to let you feel as much as your heart can bear of how She loved Her Son, She will, She might make you wait a little while so you can feel her faith and her hope too, but she will show you if you ask Her.

Where I used to tend more to objectify a woman I now sanctify her. To sanctify is to make sacred. This is what Christ did to all matter through the veil of His Body, His person, His flesh. Maybe this seems kind of academic, or esoteric, it's not, it's as practical as gravity and as meaningful as light.

Between three and five hundred years ago the world went through the opposite of what they named it, it suffered a profound dis-enlightenment. The point is, by relying on relative knowledge and empirical evidence only, the world and matter began to lose its sense of the sacred, and matter became a thing instead of a meaning. More and more people focused on the symbol instead of what the symbol symbolizes and the place where this screws everything the worst is religion. It's like the engine falls out. Like God leaves His House and when He comes back the doors locked, it's like a bad cartoon.

The faith of my ancestors isn't about do this and don't do that, that's just tying your shoes. It's pumping a mystery through your veins, the passion of love. It is meaning that is erotic, but not carnal, the subtleties of meaning are those of beauty, I don't know how to describe the heightened joy every physical 'thing' here on earth brings when its meaning is derived in relation to its source, God. I think that's why Christ can say, "If you give up everything for me you will get 100x more in this world and the next." It's true.

When you Enter the Heart of All Things, you Approach from the Center, like the Spider in the Center of her Web in the Center of the Moon; the symbol of Our Mother, God's reflection that is creation, the Mother of Christ bears the Body of Christ who is the, "Eucharist". It is exactly what Christ said it is over and over. It is the symbol that is what it symbolizes. It is to Christ as Christ is to God. It is connected physically to everything, the Center of Divine knowledge, truth that needs nothing else to gain meaning and is true all by itself; You begin to understand and recognize the subtle beauty revealed in the meaning each thing and idea gains and gives in relation to God, Love, The Creator, the one 'Thing' that is not relative is the Center that gives every-thing else its true meaning and it becomes you when you fall in love with it and consume it and let it consume you.

http://miracle-witness.blogspot.ca/2010/10/explain-this.html

'A Coyote Story'

I think the angelic kingdoms are a symphony, an unending hierarchy like the hierarchies of the insect and animal kingdoms, but without material separation, and nobody whining about where they are on the ladder, except for the ones that, 'Fall'. It must be why those that have heard and seen them call the angels 'Choirs.'

At the end of a wrenching examination of conscience, came an Illumination of Conscience, and a Coyote that tricked me into my 'vision.' I watched his family grow up. Then that night with mice running down my shirt and bats flying around my head in Lamar Johnston's old shack at Black Willow Springs in the Sierra Madre Mountains in a wilderness named after an Arch-angel in a place the Native people consider their Garden of Eden, the House of the Sun, where the Great Spirit put them on earth, where the last Condors lived and ones I love and touched and got bitten by live again, in the sky and painted in caves, to carry the souls of the dead to heaven; I had this 'dream' where I built the 'Angelus' out of old fairground parts, with these huge bells, and a big teeter-totter you rose up into with faith, when they rang you could see the music, it became light and matter, like a glorified body, and I didn't only hear the music or play it, I became it.

Forlorn, hopeless, depressed, lost, desperately sad, suffering, people, men, women and children, came out of the fog and the trees to see this old fairground ride. It was rusty and greasy and broken, but I'd been working on it out there alone in the wilderness. A few days after the dream, when I walked out of the mountains later, an old priest I know asked me to climb high up on top of Our Lady of Mount Carmel Church, and fix the broken mounts and greasy old chains that had stopped ringing the big bells, in an ancient prayer that calls the angels; the 'Angelus.'

My friend, Leslie Lembo, had dreamed of me building this old fairground ride and she described it to me and some friends before I told her about it. In the dream, it seemed like we, the Earth, had come through something or maybe we were in something still, everyone had lost their faith. No one had any faith! Like we existed, but there was no God, like he was gone and just left us here alone, maybe because the whole world had been whining for him to leave us alone in every way and everything we thought, taught and wanted, and so finally, he gave us what we asked for, and did.

The culture and the people, the tribe, had all forgotten how infinitely holy we are and the beauty and the price of that holiness. The price of a thing is its value. The price of holiness, of the Sacred, is blood, Life. That 'Life' is what makes it real. Every idea the world believed and didn't believe, was teaching us we had become things or ideas, everything was symbolic, things weren't allowed to be real anymore, because then they would be 'Sacred', and beyond our dumb opinions about them and imagined control. They were people but they didn't think they had souls. They were so sad, it was heartbreaking and brings tears to my eyes above all to remember the look on the children....there is no joy for children or their parents in a world without innocence. How can we give the children, a child, a world like that? But we are, the ones that make it here alive. We'd rather fight for the right for porn and stuff like that. We're so proud and it's so lame. We don't want to sing in the Angels choirs anymore.

Some of the angels said they wouldn't serve us, they are jealous of human love and hate us, especially the Woman that crushed their princes head with her heel. They are the ones that inspire us to hate each other, they are not ideas, they are creatures, and now it's like we are saying we won't serve with the Angels of Heaven, we don't want our souls anymore, they stop us from doing what we think we want with our bodies, we're asking God to leave us alone, what if he does? But maybe because I'd been out there with the Earth, away from this unnatural culture and the world, and maybe because miracles, mine and others, keep convincing me, I still believed in my tribe and the 'Sacred' and real Medicine Men, the Communion of the truly holy, and the angels I feel and sometimes I think I see, I felt I had something, 'different' to give.

They all stood around so sad looking at the Angelus. I wiped the grease off my hands on the old overalls the previous guy that worked the bells had left there and I got into the bottom of it, it was a kind of see through tower. I stood there and then I raised my hand up over my head and I believed, I loved God, I prayed, but not just for me, for everybody there, and the kids, and I rose, I started to rise slowly up off the ground and all the poor people sighed this incredible sigh of relief and joy and hope and life. They smiled and looked at each other, the kids were suddenly happy cause their moms and dads were happy, they could see it and feel it, they were Overjoyed! and started holding and hugging each other laughing. It was like all we needed was for some of us to have some faith and then everybody would. We just needed a few people to prove God is real.

I rose up into the middle of the teeter-totter and then the huge high crystal bells rang. The music mixed with my material body and my soul, I became it, the energy was like pure undiluted, un-symbolic, God. If I had not spent the previous years and that month out there purgating myself of this 'impurity', like a pupating insect, this false desire for something so beneath myself, 'sin' I'd been able to say I was sorry for, I would have been incinerated, but the light-music-matter was able to go through me without getting hot and transform…the way the Eucharist does in a body, heart and soul, that hides nothing, and surrenders like a woman to a man she loves and longs for. She doesn't receive him in vain.

I came out of the dream very slowly with my heart pounding out of my chest and my whole body vooooming. The Body of Christ, is our glorified body. The body of the New Adam. It is real, that is the entire, the whole, the total Point of why, and how, and what, God did the night before he was betrayed, and when he chose Mary and filled her with himself, 'Full of Grace', and became flesh, a creature of Earth; Us. He expressed heavenly beauty with his whole self, he glorified his body and gave it to us, nobody has to believe it, some think, 'well okay, as long as I can be in control of it, keep it just an idea, a symbol', but we all have to believe and not believe something. Christ without the sacred is like God without Mary, it's like man without woman, instead of love and a family, real people and beings, it slowly turns into a bunch of ideas, maybe the ideas are good enough to save us, the way the intention to love someone is good, but becoming One flesh, like a groom and a bride is a million times better. If I were a woman, I'd want to be Gods bride.

The ones that believed and believe what I'm talking about often manifest something awesome, something different from anything else on earth in human flesh. Hardly anybody knows about it. Some spend incredible care and effort carefully documenting it and letting scientists try to disprove or explain it, but they can't. You'd think they'd advertise it, but they keep kind of quiet about it, maybe too quiet.

You might look into it and ask yourself if you believe you don't believe it or not. And then you could ask yourself, if any of these things are real, how does that alter my view of reality? When Jesus spoke about his body, what if he knew what he meant, when he said what he said, and believed it? You could ask yourself, why do I believe it's better not to believe it? What do I gain by believing I don't believe it? What's more beautiful about not believing it? What would it mean to me if I believed it? Would I want to touch it? Would I want to spit on it? Would I want to kiss it? Would I want Gods blood in my veins…? Or would I want to fight for the right to kill it? The only unforgivable sin is the one you won't ask forgiveness for. I'm not very courageous, I don't like to suffer, I give in to temptation more easily than I wish, but if I was courageous, if I could be every good thing a human being is capable of being, I'd lay my life down to prove he believed it. That would be a good way to die, because I believe it, and because that's what he did for me.

Everything I'm trying to express isn't a molecule of it. When I went out there, I thought, I don't know what I am, who I am, or what this is or who this is, I don't know a damn thing, so I said, 'I don't know, please show me' and I didn't care about what I might have to change or do if he did. I ate snakes and found water, I made my bed in the dirt, I wanted to be another creature. I thought if God is real, God is what matters, and I want to find out, really, not symbolically. I didn't have to know what 'I am" any more than I have to know what a song is going to be before I write it. How can I 'know' anything except through a faith that proves it's real? Earth humbled me and I live on Earth. I am grateful for the holy honor to live on Earth. To me that's an aspect of what Baptism is, it's like a gate, it's a huge accomplishment. For a soul to come here and be sincere, takes tons of courage, even if they blow it. Millions of innocent souls lose their lives trying every year and our numbers are not in our hands, they can change in an instant. For me, my life and your life is so much more beautiful when I let it be Gods life, and approach it on my knees. It's not a virtue contest, I'm proof.

The word humility comes from the word, humus, or Earth. I had her, she had me, that was a great gift, I have her again here in Canada with the buffalo and I'm trying to share what she gives me, and even if it's an encore or a finale, live on Earth in the 'world'. I realized I was never lost in the wilderness, because I was with me and I was with God, I was with creatures that are true to their nature and I listened to them. What they whisper is always beautiful, like the angels. It was in the 'world' that I became lost.

Everybody's living in the "world' today, further and further from their Creators creation and closer and closer to their own, but it doesn't have to be this way. It may be a difficult time, but we are promised something ecstatically beautiful if we are humble; Heaven and Earth. We don't achieve that by having idea's about it, dialoguing, and building some kind of social utopia, we achieve it by loving God on Earth, really, not symbolically. By all kneeling and saying, 'I don't know, please show me." What the hell am I gonna live for? For some passing achievement? For money? For my body? To be able to do what I think I want with my wiener?! When I can live for the Angels, for heaven, for heavens creatures on Earth, for God, for beauty, for salvation, even if I'm no stronger than a child...

The most important thing I might have done was to admit and allow myself to, 'not know,' not as an excuse but as a way to know. There were times when that was extremely scary, especially back in the world, even paralyzing, but it's been the only way I've been able to know anything with a kind of certainty that is infinitely more certain than anything else I know, a kind of certainty called faith. What I come to know, not every moment, but more and more beautifully, like the pursuit of music, of art, is this profound thing; 'I am', 'I Exist.' This is the ultimate miracle that is happening for you and me every second, Life. But only when looked on with Love. Without Love, to exist is hell, and we can have it if we want it. To exist with Love is Heaven. I want to find out what Love is and express it on Earth.

'The Monastery'

I'd been wandering alone in the Ventana Wilderness. It's a steep, hot landscape. Something stopped me drinking from a creek, I found a horse dead in the water about half a mile upstream. There are wild boar there that get over five hundred pounds. Their tusks, two to three inch thick hide, intelligence, fearlessness and the destruction they cause is legendary. I'd spent several nights with them grunting and rooting around real close, but not had any problems. I have a friend from high school, her dad Bill Richardson, hunted them with a long knife and trained dogs. He'd have to sew up his dogs on the run when the pigs would gore them with their tusks. He passed on recently and I had the honor of writing something for him.

I slept with my Dad's old Navy survival knife under my head. one night something kept tugging on it and pulling it away. It was too dark to see what it was, but the third time it was almost out of arms reach before I grabbed it back. Whatever it was smelled the rattlesnake I cleaned earlier on it, I went back to sleep laughing to myself.

It was 1993, I was 33, I'd officially quit the music business a year before and been living alone in the desert mountains of California as much as I could, but eventually I'd have to come out each time because I couldn't get enough to eat. I loved to see my friends and tell them about my experiences there, but my experiences were taking me down a path so different from most of my friends, I was following a spiritual bloodline of a communion of ancestral mystics. What they believed was backed up by signs, theirs and my own too, signs available to anyone that wants them more than anything else, but signs that lead us down a different path. It is a path where we step out of the world in order to help save the Earth, and where we step out of our society in order to help the human beings that live in it. I decided I wanted to talk to the monks at the monastery about joining them.

I climbed down into the canyon the Monastery bordered, cool, dark and mossy under the Redwoods. Perched on a ridge overlooking the Big Sur Coast, I sat with a monk and told him a little bit of my story. I went back to Santa Barbara and talked to the priest that had helped me and heard my confessions over the last

3 years as I tried to align my life with the truth of the love I was discovering. He wrote them a letter. It unfolded and they accepted me to enter as a postulant. The night before I left, I was sleeping on the ground and I rolled over on my back. Above my head, perfectly aligned and centered with my vision was a big orb weaver spider in the center of her web in the exact center of the full moon with the moons circumference aligned with the outer circumference of the web. It was a remarkable sight and I said to myself, 'I don't know what that means but I know I'll find out.' Spiders speak and they will speak more as we go.

The first two or three months at the Monastery were filled with the grace of God, I entered believing that as long as God kept calling me I wanted to live there until I died and I believed that is what I was going to do. The monks accepted me. The world, especially the western world, looks at the idea of men and women spending their life in solitude and prayer and thinks they're wasting it, that they should be out doing something useful, but the western mind and modern mind has neither the experience or the tradition of the 'Sacred'. My ancestors have carried that wisdom and handed it on for thousands of years going all the way back to the Ancients. The Native Americans passed on a tradition similar in many ways. The sacred and the miracle, or vision, was a central and real part of their experience and I am just being honest when I say it has been at the core of mine, it is our 'normal' un-diseased state.

I encountered something I did not expect and would not learn how to recognize the tracks of until a fight for my life with it in my late forties, evil. Telling you what happened is easy, anybody could do it, it's like reading the bible, what matters is what it means and if there is a way to know instead of guess. I will tell you the best way I can, which is to take you with me Wandering in the Spirit, that takes some time and trust, but I promise you your time and mine is precious to me, every word I say and story I tell is for the most important reason I know, our heart and soul.

'Who You Want To Be Is Who You Are'

WINTER 2014

If I had stayed in the Monastery
I'd have a new name
Given to me for a person I loved
That lived on Earth before
Like they lived in heaven now
It doesn't have to be a man
I could even chose an angel
Or a woman
An ancestor of my Communion
Someone that believed
They could change the world
And did
By the way they loved and lived
For God

They're strange and inexplicable
Even to themselves
They walk out on the edge
And jump off
Mine was this old priest that was a monk
He was Italian and funny
If I told you the miracles
That happened in his presence
You wouldn't believe me
So I won't
You can find out for yourself
The same way you find out for you

And I find out for me
It's not what we think
But who we truly want to be
Is who we are
We all live in a name
His was Padre Pio
He wanted to be a child like Jesus
He wanted to love like he did
What if we all did
Then that's who we'd be
Ourselves
Happy
Innocent
Friendly and faithful
Like our dogs
Arf, Arf Wag, Wag
It's all who we follow
I've got a million miles to go
Before my name is Leo Pio

'The Orchestra'

I'll begin this way. There was this guy in the audience. They were there for the most beautiful orchestra on Earth. It had been around forever and you could only play for life. He saw the people around him moved to tears, he was thrilled by the chill of the strings, the pomp, the grandeur, and the humble silence between each note, the way they trail off and never end, each one as perfect as a perfect kiss.

He thought it looked like such fun, the grand theatre and the stage, the handsome men dressed in tuxedos, the women divine in black, the way the audience rose, rapt in applause and clapped. He wanted to be one of them for all the wrong reasons. When the Conductor left the podium he was at the side door waiting and he asked if he could join? The Conductor made the gravity clear, "Do you know the weight of the music we play here? Heaven and Earth hang on each nuance, for me and for us. We give up our life and our death for the music. We are what we are because of who we are here for, one living breathing body, we are blood brothers of the one who wrote the music and sang the song. Are you willing to listen to me, listen to the Conductors that came before me, and the Conductors that come after me like… they do!?…" He looked out over their heads. "The first one was given this wand, a new name, a sacred promise and a sacred authority, the gift is a cross to bear son." The guy said, "Yes…"

"Pardon me John, could I come over tonight and discuss my feelings about the second movement with you?" "I've got some issues with it, I'll bring a bottle of wine." The guy continued, "I don't like the way the Conductor is conducting, he's too heavy here and too light there and these notes, lets write them into a Major key, something more happy." John replied, "Well, I don't know, I feel that way sometimes too, but this orchestra is God's body to me, I'd rather be part of it than take it apart." The guy quickly replied, "Oh, I don't want to take it apart or make a new one, it could never be as nice as this one, I just want to change some things, you know, give the audience what they want, I think they're getting bored and all these minor keys are too hard for them to bear, think how much more they'd like it if it we made it sound happy and fun!" The guy turned to the piccolo player, "What are you doing tonight?"

Gradually the orchestra lost its breath. The guy knelt with others but they didn't pray and the audience couldn't tell the difference, they weren't musicians, it was still all music and most of them thought it was what they wanted. It wasn't great like it used to be, it wasn't even good enough to be bad. John listened to the Conductor with appreciation for what he heard. The orchestra was coming to a crescendo.

I want to tell you secrets of a Monastery, how evil defines itself in the presence of the holy, how it hides its difference by appearing the same, how a real Priest is a Medicine Man an Artist and a Soldier by a different name, why I left and why I came, how a spider weaves a web and what happens in the Center.

'God Thinks'

WINTER 2014

For a long time I thought thoughts were the way
To get what I thought I wanted
And I usually did
But it never turned out to be what I thought it was

Thoughts to my life
Are like notes to my music
I don't think them
My mind is a kind of instrument
And so am I
Sometimes a living being plays it
I've found it in a woman, in creatures
In the Earth, the sky, the sea
A living beauty
My self in the presence of God
And God in the presence of me

When I've needed help
When I've been in a fight for my life
When I've longed to create beauty
To touch something true
I've held you
I've loved you
I wandered for a Spirit
I tracked creatures for their eyes
And then there were angels
And saints prayed for me

I can't describe how wonderful and good they are
You don't need intentions with tears in your eyes
I think they just want us to love them
And each other
Enough to care how they feel
I think that's what God thinks

'Medicine Man'

After three days of trying the way human beings have from the beginning, I made fire. Making fire is a skill of intrinsic value, but the skill is not what I'm hoping to illuminate tonight, I want to illuminate the, "fire." Fire has lived in human beings since the beginning of time as knowledge and wisdom and it burned in every member of the tribe from the woman's womb to the dying elder. Until a few hundred years ago fire had to live in each one of us because there was virtually no other way for it to be passed on. Fire can be written about in a book and a lot can be learned there with a guide that has the fire in him, but the fire can't be passed on without a teacher that actually has it and virtually no one had a book or could read until the historic blink of a few hundred years ago. To interpret the symbols without honoring the interpretation and the fire that burned in the ancestors that brought the meaning of the book alive, is to dishonor them and your self and the purpose and meaning of the book. The Fire of Wisdom and every other real power can only live in people and be passed from one person to another. The fuel is love. Except for a relative few, we have continued to walk further and further from the fire, but it's going to change, it's changing, it must, because we are getting cold.

The spark came to me the moment I breathed a tiny struggling coal into a flame in the snow and rain on a winter survival course in Mount Shasta a long time ago. It's easy to make smoke, but not fire unless you do every little thing just right, and it took a man who had learned from another man who had learned from another man all the way back to the first man to teach me. That's what the light of my first flame illuminated in me, that I am connected to fire and that fire burns in men. We have never had more knowledge and more books at our fingertips and less wisdom and fire than we do today. Something is ending, almost everybody feels it, a flame is burning out, we are like dying coals, but I believe God is going to breathe on us. He is breathing life into our flame right now in a remarkable way for a remarkable time.

'A long time ago, the time of the thundering buffalo, rivers ran and the north lights glowed, the heart of Earth beat so slow, then out of the north on two legs walked a teller of stories a thinker of thoughts.' Those two legs and the tracks they have left are ours, our tribe. I want mine back, so I'm going to tell the truth the way I see it with as much love as I possibly can, love is both the fuel and the fire, the reason and the way, and if somebody doesn't like it or doesn't like me for telling it, that is going to have be and stay their problem. Sometimes I feel like when I'm writing I'm yelling at people. I'm a very gentle man, I never yell at anybody! "AaaarrrggghhhhRRaaaaahhhhh!" But sometimes I think everything I think is the opposite of what the world thinks and it takes more guts than I feel I always have to say it. Life has always been such a big deal to me. It's like a woman I'm in love with, all that that is, that's what life is like, intense. She takes every drop of your self you can give her and when you do, she is exquisite. I have this sneaky suspicion though that almost all of us are much wiser and more sensitive and more thoughtful and care more than we let anybody else know, that we don't really believe an awful lot of what we are being told and say we do, dumb slogans, partial truths and clichés, a lot of us just haven't thought them through.

There are men with usurped authority and no wisdom, big fire with no light, their love is lust. They are the one kind of man that made Jesus lose His temper and they've made me lose mine. I met some at the Monastery, but they are all over and in every group. They were trying to take over while the majority of real priests and monks who were compassionate and profoundly thoughtful men, were trying to shut up, listen and pray. They're called a hypocrite and they are the 'guy in the orchestra.' Again, why do they make me burn so? Because they ruin the reputation of men that tell the truth to the tribe and that live to keep the tribes fire alive. They lie and their lie is believed by almost everyone, it is malicious, a lie told to poison a Medicine Man. They have to poison the Medicine Man because he tells truth to their lie. He's real and their fake and they hate him for it.

The fire the life and the lie have lived in man for a long time. It's the mystery of iniquity, we can't explain the intrinsic essence of imperfection perfectly, but every sacred mystery reveals itself to be the opposite of what it appears, it happens every time and it's going to happen this time too. Man has had to be a killer and predator, a hunter, a provider through toil, a dominator, a fighter, a soldier, an aggressor and often a dutiful and justified defender. Woman holds all his life in her womb, she gives him birth and he fights to keep and protect her. The tracks make a path. I have my tribes symbols of symbols that are more meaningful, more amazing than any other I have found so I believed them, and then I found that they were true, because they are what they symbolize, that's how miracles work.

Meaning and truth must be equals. Our first Medicine Man was Melchizadek, a real man who lived and never died, a mystical prefigurement of Christ without beginning or end, he was the first priest and still is, Christ was and is a priest of the Order of Melchizadek and every priest that came after Christ, doing what Christ told them to do the night before he was betrayed, to, "Do this." Do what I am doing, offer yourself eternally with me in me and through me. That's what a priest does, instead of killing, he offers himself and it has to be life giving or he's not a priest, he's just a symbolic idea, blood is the test, life is the answer. Don't be afraid of blood, find out what blood is instead. We are not ideas! I don't want to love, live and die for an idea, I want to love live and die for a person, a woman I love and all the fruit that will come through our love if she will believe too. We bleed and if we do what Jesus tells us to we bleed Gods blood. It's not an idea, it's really and truly His flesh and blood exactly like He said it was over and over and was later recorded in His sacred word, the Holy Bible, but if you think you are somehow qualified to limit it to the opposite of what He said it was and make it just a symbolic idea of course you're free to, or you can believe you don't believe any of it too, but like I've said before, unless you enter into it first, you'll never even know what it is you believe you don't believe and teach others not to believe with you, that's your faith.

My faith is the only place I can secure my confidence. From the time I was eight years old in that earthquake, I thought it was my, 'self', but it is through my faith that I find and get to know my true self. I think part of being a man is knowing your faith, what you believe and why. Then come miracles and you realize, my faith is a sacred treasure I have to give my woman and the world. My faith is what she can rely on and what her true love helps me be faithful to. My faith is the meaning I give to her. The fact is, I haven't found that confidence in any faith but my own, where else could I find it? You've got a religion even if you think you hate religion, it's just a word for what you believe and don't believe, and if you think the solution is to avoid thinking about it, that's just another act of your faith.

Many Native Americans knew profound wisdom and honor, they didn't have books, they passed it on to one another by keeping it alive in themselves. You can't fake that by saying words with tears in your eyes. All that is holy in any sincere religion is worthy of respect. If you think someone is sincerely reading and playing the music wrong, don't get mad at them, don't be offended by them, show them and me how your way is more meaningful, more coherent in relation to the words, explain your way and why precisely and if it's true, and you're committed to the truth instead of to being right, no matter what the cost, truth will reveal itself. Explain it so that you can know what you believe and don't believe and why, yourself.

All of this beating around the bush was to light it on fire. The women, the children and the men; they made a conscious illuminated, 'free choice', to say to the man, "We need You!" "To do something for us only You! Can do." We give you this role and this throne of fire to offer yourself for us instead of to be an aggressor for us and we say out of love and illumination, "We need You, a 'Man' to do it for us." And men did and they became Medicine Men not because it was an idea, but because they gave life to their tribe by offering their life instead of taking life. The Medicine Man was not an authority to be grasped for, it was a sacred duty and a throne a Man was called to and the people gave to him out of love, because they had true wisdom. Anybody that wants to can get and up talk, they can say and believe anything they want, maybe good ideas, maybe not so good ideas. But a man is a baby if he resents a woman because he can't have one and only a woman that doesn't understand how her love is the best thing she can give a man would miss why it's good for him and for her and for the Earth to tell him we need him for something only he can do.

The women didn't resent it, their love was confidence. They changed the identity of what it means to be a man and in doing so they change the identity of every man, women and child in the tribe and of life itself. They raise the identity and desire and honor of the tribe and of Men to one of holiness and healing instead of fighting and avenging. Those women, the ones that gave the Medicine Man birth, nursed him and played with him and brought him up until he was twelve and then let him go through the fire with the men, they didn't whine because they couldn't be the Medicine Man. They didn't say why does he get to have all the fun? They didn't take his fire and his wisdom and sit in his tipi and tell him he should bow down to them now and that all the ancestors before him were stupid men and wrong. I think that if women like those that lived close to the Earth and to their man and helped him and relied on him to fight and hunt, didn't like the Medicine Man and what he and their ancestors believed, that they would have had the honor and honesty to go off and start their own tribe where they could pass on any idea they wanted to and call themselves anything they wanted to instead of conspire to subvert their tribe because it was ancient and powerful and had the flame they wanted to take.

And if the guy in the orchestra and his allies would do that they wouldn't be hypocrites, they might be wrong but we all are wrong many times along our way, it's fine to be wrong, but it's trying to make wrong right to lie. If they don't like the music and the conductor go start their own crummy orchestra and play anything they want but don't try and wreck my ancestors tribe! Instead those women became holy themselves often more saintly than the Medicine Man and he knew it and did everything he could to serve the woman's need of him, both of them, man and woman, out of love instead of childish greed. They made holy relationships and transformed each other.

I leap ahead on the path to Easter of 2010, my friend, Pat Milliken died, I was losing everything, my purpose, my family, maybe my buffalo and now my best friend and I felt like my dignity had been taken away, or worse, I'd given it away. I sat there with my tail between my legs going through a divorce, feeling to blame and also feeling totally misunderstood, but I started to feel the thing I had been using all my life force to resist feeling, "How I felt." That is the first step, that was the first thing I had to do. The week before Easter has been filled with miracles in my life ever since I looked at what it meant about twenty years ago, amazing things happen that week on earth and in heaven. I said to myself, "Pat's dead and I'm alive, look at what he faced…" I felt like how can I possibly try and tell anybody anything? Why on earth would anybody listen to someone like me, I just got out a jail! I let myself get addicted to alcohol, I have not been faithful to my faith, I've been afraid to live my vision and it's killing me, I dug my own hole, maybe I don't have it in me…" and on like that. That was part of what I realized when I finally was shocked into, "Feeling how I felt." My God, no wonder I'm in such anguish, listen to these thoughts, these can't be all my thoughts can they? I wouldn't talk to anybody like this. Again, a long and deep story, not the same old stuff I kept reading at all…but this was the answer, where the direction changed from down to up, 'I exist, I'm alive.' I asked myself what would I do if I had a week to live, and thought, I want to live like I have a week to live and began to. It was hard and I had to be patient, but it was working, there was a lot more going on than I knew yet and there was a long way to go.

I'd gotten so far off the path, instead of Wandering in the Spirit, I'd thought, well, now I guess I'm supposed to be a rancher, build up a business get more land get more buffalo, make more money, be a guy. Brother, that doesn't work, it's just doing something so you can do something else and dying while you never get to do it. I turned back to my Medicine Men, the ones that offer themselves eternally with the First One, it's real, Christ sanctified flesh and blood and made matter sacred, it's not an idea, it's not figuring things out, it's pulling predators off and you can't always do it yourself. Medicine Men can do it, they wield invisible weapons. The real priest is a man like me, he needs me as much as I need him, sometimes more. It's not the man and his personality, it's a throne of blood he sits on as a mystic soldier. A real women lets him help her because she's knows what it is to love instead of want, and she teaches him that way and lets him sit on a throne with her flame and the flame of her children watching her love him and honor him, not because she's less than him, because he needs her and she knows it! She doesn't want to be a Medicine Man, she wants to love one so he can be one for her and for the whole tribe.

'Religious'

WINTER 2013

I'm an extreme introvert
Everything I see on the outside
Is inside in reverse
Not better or worse
But the opposite

There's nothing more opposite than 'Religion'
What people believe
Its fullness is the revelation of the opposite
To describe it to someone
Is like describing music
It's better to play something beautiful

There's a bunch of different 'religions'
Whatever is holy in any is good
But everybody's got one
Even if theirs is that they don't
I can believe in a myth
And become one
I can believe in a God that is Love
And become One
I can believe in a God that doesn't exist
And become an atheist
I can believe whatever I want
But believe it or not I believe it

Most people today believe a priest
Follows a line of ancestors
Who's motive isn't the mystery
Of doing what Christ does
And told them to do
For love
But to gain 'Control' over everybody
I look inside and ask myself really?
Why?
So he can sleep alone on a cot in a cell
In silence except for the prayers of dawn
And dusk alone with God
Holding the universe in his heart
In a vow of poverty, celibate
Examining his conscience in confession on his knees
To be true to Who he receives
Or make all he says he lives for a lie
What the hell is it I have he wants?
My sins...
Except for my love
That's all I've got
To get his own he could leave
Or hide with the liars in every group
I've met them everywhere and there too
Standing next to the real thing
They're pathetic
But the world doesn't enter mysteries
It explains them from the outside
The way it explains you

Christ is meaningless to the passionless
Christ the anti Life-Coach
Christ the anti Motivational-Speaker
'Listen to my voice'
Do what I did
When you are betrayed
Offer your being
Turn your blood into wine
For love to consume you

Become who I am
Forgive
Teach the truth
Feed the poor
Cherish the unwanted
Pray for your enemies
Heal the sick
Love Love more than pleasure
And look what you'll get
Killed'
Oh boy!
But wait, then you'll Resurrect
For men that explain you're a myth
And it's them that are real
The more they know the less they get
How can
The last be first
The meek be rich
We give to receive
Dying be birth
And a Communion exist
In Heaven on Earth
Is that why He died
Broken like a heart
On a cross forsaken
To give spirits his blood
Instead of opinions

I see this religion
A cathedral of light
Souls in legion
With choirs of angels
The light of the stars
Their hearts are the planets
With heavenly bodies
Incorrupt in the altars
Tears oil and blood
Crying out from the stones
Dripping from Icons
No one can explain
Why demons submit

And testify and levitate
And leave
We don't have a clue
That what is real is living
Beings breathing
Their hate to curse
Their love to bless
Us
Beyond time but real
Hidden to reveal
Like creatures in the wilderness
Sharing the Earth
It's not just Gods spirit
It's Gods blood
That's our species
That's religion
It's claws and a tongue
And a butterfly
It's the story of time
When it happens it does
The history of eternity
The air we share
From birth
With mystical bodies
Where heaven met Earth
Breaking the mirror
The source of the symbol
Not some stupid idea
We wouldn't know a saint
If he slapped us in the face
But he can't when he's crying
Because we believe
We're not
Religious

'What I Want'

WINTER 2013

Is who I am
The purpose of a thing
Is its identity
My purpose is the thing
Each of us
Regardless of what's gone
What is
Or what comes
Can choose
Everything we could ever want
Is ours by the virtue
Of our identity

My purpose is what I want the most;
To think what I think is positive
To get what I think I want
To feel good

Or to be the son of my Creator
To be the lover of Gods daughter
To be One
Gods Soul in us
Our purpose His identity

Most people I know want to love
We want to be sincere
We want to be a 'good' person

We try our best
To be kind and help others
But we don't know who or what we are
A false identity ~ A false purpose
Who am I
What am I
Why am I

From:
Tracks on a path
Left as miracles to follow
Through the wilderness
And as battles to enter
In a world
Where love enters darkness
With sincere and holy men
Priest brother monks
And an eternal Holy Communion
The world has no idea of
A Woman Clothed with the Sun
Appears in Heaven
Giving secrets
To children
For the rest
Oil pours from Icons
Human tears cry the stones
The sun spins
Bilocating levitating
Reading souls
Incorrupt
And Christ their King
Calling
'Wake up'

To:
Pretenders to a Throne
Wolves in sheep's clothing
There to steal
For a temple to a Liar
Seated on a vulvicphallus
I found it in the valley

Opposite of us
We are their offerings
Covered in blood lust
The sacred and living Body of Christ
Desecrated profaned mocked
But unable to be killed
Or made into a symbol
The spiritual is real
You see we want to love
But wolves love sheep
And eat their agony in the garden
When the Shepherds fall asleep

I knelt in adoration
With too much to tell you now
But the last thing
The last thread
Of a heavenly tapestry
Weaved of meaning
With my eyes on the 'Ark'
In answer to my question,
"When will you speak up for yourself!?"
"How can I be there with you!?"
He spoke as forlorn as a God unloved
Can speak;
"Is it any harder for you to believe
I am in this bread as I said
Than for you to believe
I am in you?"

"Yes! The bread is innocent!"
I didn't speak I wept

And then again that night
In the spiders web
Centered in the moon
The Cross of matter and of light
On my forehead
The One who's love
Calls the rest
To be children of light

Or children of death
Said,

"You must enter the Heart of All Things
Go where you are needed most
And remain still
In the end
You will ask and be asked
Were you true to your true self
That self is, I"

I've lived twenty one years since then
Wondering
Who is my true self?
Who is I?

It's like my knowing you
Loving you
I never will enough
I hid my heart
Undiscerning
Coming so far to know so little
Like a beginner
Answering every call
Down a hall full of voices
Like a man who sleeps with women
But never marries one
I could have had Communion
With the ones that never die
To teach me
But I waited
Alone, unaware
Afraid I'd fall
Breaking into pieces
God put back together
With a purpose
His
Identity
My True Self Is
What I want

'The Monastery ~ Predator and Prey'

Perched opposite the Monastery, across a deep valley of redwoods, was a Satanic temple. Its position was not coincidence, evil always apes and mocks. I followed the 'tracks' down into the canyon and up the other side, past perverted paraphernalia, trashed vehicles, a mattress and blood stains, and found it. Evil longs to perfect itself. It is most evil the closer it comes to something holy. Christ, the apostles, his first priests, and his Communion of Saints, exercise the authority he breathed on them over demons.

The apostles were healing people by exorcising demons all the time, everybody seems to ignore this today, but the need for exorcism has risen seven hundred and fifty percent since the 1970's in the North East corner of the United States alone. In the worship of Satan, every loving and holy thing is reversed, instead of love and mercy, cruelty and the infliction of pain on the innocent is a 'virtue.' It's worse than the normal person could ever imagine, and not something to dwell on, but to be aware of. Demonic harassment, obsession and possession are much more common than anyone thinks except for those that know about it. Those that know the most are priests called, 'Exorcists'.

There is a vast creation of angelic beings, they're real, to witness the rite of exorcism is to become convinced. Atheists become incontinent, laws of nature are suspended, things fly around the room, the presence and reality of the demon is more real than anybody needs or wants real to be, but virtually nobody today knows about it, and many priests since 1960 either don't believe they exist either, are afraid of them, or are in league with them. If the priest is not in a State of Grace the demons will reveal their sins and can destroy them. It is more than a healing prayer, it is a confrontation, an interrogation and a battle where one side wins the territory of a soul and the other side loses. According to exorcist priest's that prove what they believe is true, like Father Malachi Martin and many others going all the way back to Christ in an unbroken line of succession, the world doesn't realize a great majority of our dysfunction; addiction, anxiety, depression, murder and worse, and up to seventy percent of what is diagnosed as mental illness, is being caused by demonic attack, and there is a cure. It is the answer to every question and available to every one of us; holiness.

Now I feel I have to tell you some things that are hard to tell. They're hard because they aren't beautiful and because how I feel about their affect can be misunderstood to be how I feel about the people behind them. Hypocrites do exasperate me, but I don't want to judge anybody. I'm an earthy O blood type hunter gatherer, I apologize if my tone or emotion comes through too strongly, but I can't leave this out and also tell you the truth.

There were two camps in the Monastery and over the last fifty years or so, one has gained power and spread through the whole Catholic Chruch. In the last fifty years, one has grown to take control of the institution, its smoke rises from the bottom into the top. It wants the Church to modernize and tell the world the same things the world tells it. The other, much smaller group wants to follow the Communion of Saints, believing and teaching what they believed, died for, lived for, taught and passed down for 2,000 years. The 'modernist' camp is more than seventy percent of the Church, clergy and laity both. In the Monastery some of this group happened to be gay, but this isn't about being gay, it's just part of me describing what happened.

I feel like I have to say again from my heart, I do not judge a gay person any differently than anybody else, especially myself. I want to love a gay person the way Christ loves them and me, and it doesn't work for me to judge the state of anyone's soul. As an artist I must judge ideas and beliefs and actions for their beauty. That's what I'm trying to express and describe here, what was so ugly, dark and exasperating about some of the men I encountered at the Monastery was their intellectual and spiritual dishonesty.

In the midst of sexual advances, I sought the company of the old camp of monks. I was invited to the old monk priest, Father Joseph's 4 a.m. morning mass. My "Postulant master" who was sexually attracted to me, called me to his office.

He said he didn't want me to go to Father Joseph's mass because it would take away from the eleven a.m. mass that was the, "Center of our prayer life and day". The real reason he didn't want me to go to father Josephs mass was because Father Joseph believed the same thing the communion of my holy ancestors have for two thousand years and Father Joseph taught it by living it. My postulant master and the group of modernists that were taking power in the Monastery and through the whole Church didn't believe in any of that. They think that what our ancestors believed was bad, wrong and repressed. They loath my ancestors and priests like Father Joseph, but they like their power.

I could sense his motivation as he moved closer to me on the couch and the bell for the eleven a.m. mass rang. I said I had to go and he said "That's okay, we're talking" and I said, "You just said the eleven a.m. mass is the center of our day and now you're saying it's okay for me to be late to it." The 11 a.m. mass had nothing to do with why he didn't want me to go to Father Joseph's mass. What I feel goes right into my body, it is more a physical and emotional energy than a process of my mind. Father Joseph believed the mass was what the apostles believed it was, and what the disciples they knew and taught wrote that they believed it was, the same thing Jesus believed it was, what it has been since the night before he was betrayed, exactly what he said it was. If you believe you don't believe in what all of them believed in unity, it probably doesn't matter to you and maybe you think it's just dumb religious stuff I shouldn't care about either. But if you decide to believe what Christ said, sincerely, for even a few seconds, your whole reality will begin to change.

It wasn't that I had to put up with his sexual advances, I've been around the block and everybody, including me has their own desires born from a lack of love, but what about some vulnerable young man that thinks the guy is a real priest? I'm not good or virtuous, I confess it and I want to grow in holiness. I feel exasperated by, but also sorry for that priest. I empathize with what seems like a very difficult and challenging orientation, but I also know what it's like for a predator to come after you and I have to put the victims first.

Categorizing people by their sexual desires seems lame to me. Men do things sexually they think is great and the person they do it to thinks is the worst thing that ever happened to them. They also do things they think they want to do they wish they'd never done. There seems to be more and more kinds of sex people are defining themselves by. How many variations are there? How can I really know what kind of sex someone has, why should I want to? I'm not interested, I don't want to know, half the time, the person that's doing it doesn't even know. Who cares, what's important to me is holiness.

According to third party studies, paid for and held up as evidence in court by groups suing the Catholic Church, over a twenty five-year period from 1960 to about 1985, 90% of the predation took place, by only 3% of predatory 'priests.' Approximately 86% of those the 3% abused were teenage males between the ages of 11 and 17. Being homosexual does not mean you're a pedophile, they are two different kinds of sexual orientation. The media never mentions that the same type of sexual abuse, and institutional cover-up, is occurring at a higher rate in almost every other group studied in North America, including non-'celibate' Protestant clergy at 3.5%, in the family at 5%, and in our public school system at 10%. I experienced this kind of abuse, it destroys lives, and I have a right and an obligation to speak up for the victims and do whatever I can to prevent it happening to another young man.

When I first wrote this, I allowed myself to vent about the ass grabbing baloney, but it's a waste of time so I took it out. All I've left of it is a little detour to the Monastery book store. It was a place I could find the writings of saints, not what people write about them although those can be good too, but what they wrote themselves, books very difficult to find anyplace else. Relatively few people have read anything a saint has written, they should. A saint proves what they believe is true. The library within the walls of the Monastery and the book store outside the walls were both treasures in that they offered something rare and the opposite of what you can find everywhere else.

A few years after I left the Monastery, I came back to say hello to the real priests, pray at the Eucharist, and to look in the book store. One of the fake priests had worked his way into taking it over. On the best seller rack at the front, I saw a bunch of dumb books. Basically they preach a gospel the opposite of what every saint for 2,000 years before these authors preached. They follow their own path and say follow me, which is fine, they can write and do whatever they want. The part that isn't fine is that they claim they are of the same tribe as the saints while secretly hating and opposing them. They want their power without their holiness. They want to take over the Church and they almost have. I walked up to the counter and asked the fake priest if there were any writings of the saints left in the bookstore? He said, "Oh yes Leo, over there" pointing with a poised finger at a little shelf in a hallway to the toilet. I was disgusted. It all came flooding back, why I'd had to leave before I clobbered somebody. It reminded me of when Jesus weaved that whip and beat the liars out of his Fathers house. I said something like, "You throw the saints in the toilet, and put the Wickanuns in the front window!" He said, "We have to give the people what they want." Maybe he's got Penthouse and Playboy on the rack now. Brother.

'A Spider in the Center'

After my meeting with the postulant master and mass, I went back to the tabernacle and kneeled in prayer. I could feel the invisible battle going on and how the men taking over were both willing and unwilling pawns in it. I saw how the demonic uses men to dominate other men and submit to a will neither recognize. If they did, they'd run like hell. Looking at the bigger picture, I guess it all has to happen, it's the price of free will, together and individually. Truth is always a process of purification. I felt so bad for the real priests and monks, like Father Joseph and so many others in the Church, being squeezed out by the pawns of a snake. I felt bad for Jesus too, in my heart I was saying, "Lord, why won't you speak up for yourself and stop these liars!?"

I kneeled and waited determined not to leave until God spoke. I was so upset with the evil I saw rising from within the church and with these false priests, wolves in sheep's clothing. I'm describing what I encountered at the Monastery as honestly as I can. I'm still driven by my sexual passions, and even when I try as hard as I can, I still fall. If you're gay and you're reading this I want you to know I love and like you and sincerely care about you just as much as I do everyone else. My problem with what was happening in the Monastery and in Church is with liars and predators of all kinds. In the presence of God I can't judge anybody else as more deserving of judgement than me, because I can't know the journey of their soul and their life, but I think when we see ourself the way God sees us, each one of us will be infinitely humbled.

I waited on my knees with no answer and then focusing on the Eucharist, I said, "Lord, why won't you speak up for yourself and show them that you're real?" I waited and then he spoke to me interiorly in such a forlorn voice and said, "Is it any harder for you to believe that I am in this piece of bread than it is for you to believe I am in you?" Tears filled my eyes and I said, "It's so much harder for me to believe that you are in me than in that innocent piece of bread." I said, "Lord, please tell me a story, tell me a story about you and me" and he said, "That's what your life is, a story I'm telling you about you and me." Then I asked, "How can I get in there with you?" and didn't get an answer until later in a dream.

Our day at the monastery always ended with adoration. This is really a prayer born during the forty days Mary and the Apostles waited in the upper room for the Holy Spirit, doing what Christ said to do, what he did, the prayer of the mass. We kneel and "Adore" Christ present as he said he is, in his body. It is a silent prayer where we reveal ourselves, empty ourselves and listen. It took place right after evening vespers.

I've asked myself, and God, what is it to adore you? What is it to worship you? It's not singing more of those crummy songs is it! (sorry, I couldn't help it) Obviously it is to love you, but what is the difference between worship, adoration and love? How is it Christ is different for me than anyone else? Here is a partial answer. I've decided to believe that Christ is 'Perfect.' I mean that, in every way there is, even in his body, he is absolutely Perfect. I have to lay quiet and still, to listen and feel, it's how you track an animal when you can't see his tracks. To do it, you must become as sensitive as you can in each moment, and this can make the world hard to take. Then I ask with my being, not just my thoughts, 'If Christ is perfect, what does he mean?' How is it changing me to realize that Christ is Perfect? What does it do to reality? Christ is Perfect, absolutely Perfect, he is the presence, even in his body, the body he said he left us, of God, what is that doing to me right now? It allows perfection to exist, and me to experience it, not as an idea, as a living being, God, who is the name of perfection. This is what truth means. Perfection is the truth that sets us free, the truth I speak of that's not mine or yours, but all of ours in unity. That's what truth does, it unifies, because it is One like God, it is God. He says, "I am the way the light and the life" that's why it's shared and not mine or yours. Our relationship with God is the truth. For perfection to exist, it can't be an idea, because then it's up to us to think it, it has to be a living being, a God that is alive like us, the Heart of All Things.

The Heart of All Things is the mystical meaning for me of the Sacred Heart. It is Gods Heart, the Center, it is Perfect, even in its flesh and blood, Christ has glorified it out of his total love. This Perfection of Christ is an endless unfolding I can put myself next to, into the presence of, like putting your feet into his tracks until you leave them, for me, and everyone else to follow.

For me, Christ is the Word of God, he's shown that to me in extraordinary ways since I found the little bible my first time seeking him alone in the wilderness. For the Word of God to be what it has to be to be the Word of God, it has to be exactly what he says it is, never, ever, less. Really, it is a belief in perfection, because he proves it. He puts his whole self into his life, into who and what he is and says and does. The perfection of creation is for the Creator to become the creature and the creature to become the Creator. These are mysteries I'm free not to believe with the rest of the world, but I'm unable to see anything more beautiful or more perfect about not believing in them. I can believe what Christ said, or not believe. The two choices take me down two very different paths. I keep finding one infinitely more beautiful than the other.

The false priests in the Monastery and in the Church, don't like anything that truly honors the Eucharist so they wouldn't attend adoration. One of the excuses they use is to say that they don't want to offend people that don't believe it's what Christ said it is. I love lots of people that don't believe it's what he said it is, and they love me, but for me it was the most powerful prayer and part of the day after mass.

Later that day at adoration I knelt in silence. Most of the time It was kind of an effort to empty my mind and let go of my own thoughts in what the west calls contemplation, similar to what the east calls meditation. I felt quiet and also moved by what I was going through. After a while I had an image of a spider of half metal and half light on my forehead and then it changed to the image of a cross of half metal and half light on my forehead. I wondered what that could mean but didn't know. I trusted the meaning would come.

That night I had a powerful dream. In it there was a giant spider web with the spider in the center all made of half light and half matter. I saw how when the spider was in the center, she was aware of all relative knowledge, through the web. Relative knowledge must be perceived and interpreted through our senses and symbols and to a great extent even our thoughts are symbolic. It seems like I've always plopped myself in the center of what it is I'm addressing, not only in spiritual matters, but in art and in relative matters too. It's hard to explain, like describing music, but it's what approaching from the center is.

Then the full moon appeared behind the web just like how I saw the whole thing months before, the night before I left for the monastery. I saw then in the dream how the moon symbolized the Eucharist and how when we center our selves in the Eucharist we are connected with all Divine knowledge through the body of Christ, God perfect, even in form.

Through the Eucharist we become one with Jesus the way that through Jesus we become one with God.

Then a man's voice spoke in the dream and said this:

"You must enter the heart of all things
Go where you are needed most and remain still
In the end you will ask and be asked
Were you true to your true self
That self is I"

~

I have a lot to say about discovering what that means to me, but one thing I have asked was how can I go where I am needed most and remain still? I tended to think of it as remaining still interiorly while venturing into the world. Especially since I lost my wife, that feels challenging in different ways. Kind and sincere people can distract me from my path, it's easy to follow the wrong tracks, but as I began to write and share my life, heart and soul, I realized were I was needed most was where I could be the most useful. I realized who I was speaking to when I wrote was my friends and that is how I found my voice, a voice that had something true to say because of who I am saying it to. I realized that here with the buffalo on this blessed and consecrated land the wilderness wanders in me, and here in this moment as I write I can go to where I am needed most, and remain still.

'Tunnel Rat'

Those Indian men and the look in their eyes, they believed, with passion, I think their tribe was proud of them for believing and wanted them to. I think whatever we are what's important is to be a real one. What's important to me isn't that you believe in my faith it's that I do, but I wonder if those men worried they might make somebody feel uncomfortable by believing the way they did... until they bled and the buffalo bones tore through the skin from their chest. I've read some of their accounts, there was honor, faith, respect, heartbreak and happiness... and as with every group of humans, there was also rivalry, bullshit and lies. I think the way that affected a man on his first Sundance was like a taste of the Agony in the Garden and the way it made him feel on his second Sundance was to ask the Medicine Man to pierce him with the big bones. It feels good to be around a man that's lost everything and still believes, that's almost given up but finds out he can't, he's got something nobody can take away and he knows it, like a buffalo that's fought for a herd.

When those men went alone into the desert of their hearts asking for their vision and the Great Spirit gave it to them, they always kept part of it a secret. In my book I tell how I let myself get talked out of my first 'vision' and I literally became a 'walking dead man' just like the Native People said a man would, all before I knew anything about them and what they believed. Other than wandering alone in their Garden of Eden and seeing the same things they did and wanting to with all my heart, I knew nothing of their experience. I never wanted to usurp their rituals or their religion or pretend I was one of them, I wanted to learn from them and be myself, I knew who I was out there.

Asking for a vision is like marrying a woman, don't do it unless you're as committed to her is as you are to your own father or mother or child. I've carried something that's hard to share, it used to be my sins, but not for a long time anymore, once you share those they become the opposite of what they appear, it's this, 'vision.' The reason I want to share mine, is for the hope. I hope that you will find and share yours.

There was a paranoid schizophrenic Vietnam Vet that lived in the wilderness sometimes too, I'd always know when he was around, he'd leave weird fake booby traps on the trail and other signs, he had wide feet. The Sheriff came back in on horseback looking for him and left warnings for people in the metal trail boxes. He'd been chasing people out of the woods, he chased a friend of mine that's not afraid of anybody out with an axe. I spent twenty-four hours with him one winter. I saw his tracks and then his smoke before I got to 'Tin Shack' in a storm. He was sharpening his knife and looked up at me with a look I've never seen before, of pure hatred. I'd just gotten out of the Monastery, I felt my, 'vision' called me to be celibate and wander in the woods as long as I could like my idea of a monk until somehow I hoped I'd fulfill it in the world. It's not something you do like fulfilling a dream, like a family and a home and friends, it's something you do in a way alone but not for yourself. I think I was the first person he'd met in a long time and ever back there that wasn't afraid of him, and it wasn't because I thought I'd win for sure in a fight with him, it was because I was wandering alone celibate like a monk, that's why a real priest lives that way, not because they believe there's something wrong with sex or because they're repressed with guilt and don't long for the love of a woman that would really love them, and it really pisses me off when people that don't know anything about it say that. It's to live ready to die all the time, free from anything they have a duty to defend but their vision. It really is, but I wasn't a monk, or a 'holy man', I didn't have any kind of virtue or will power... for the first fifty years of my life I think I was a friendly dog and the only trainers I had were invisible. I'm not a friendly dog anymore, it's like a nice little boy growing up cause somebody beats the crap out of him. I don't have a mean bone in my body and I never will, I don't want to upset or offend anybody, I want nothing but love, beauty, meaning and truth in my life, I love stillness and peace, I want to be a good friend and do what I'm supposed to, but I feel like the only way I can do what I'm 'supposed' to is to ask the Medicine Man to stick the big bones through my skin and bear my teeth.

The best thing about the Vet was his name, it was classic, but I guess it wouldn't be wise for me to use it. When he took off his hat I recognized him from wanted posters that had been all over Santa Barbara in the mid 80's. A young woman had been abducted in the Lazy Acres parking lot, they found her dismembered remains strewn down the side of Camino Cielo close to where he lived in an old hippy commune called Sunburst Farm. As soon as I recognized him, he could tell and asked if I knew about her and he said, "Yeah, they 'tried' to pin that one on me..." And then he went on in a surreal meeting of two souls to confess his sins to me... all accept that one, and that's why I can tell you about it. That man was tortured with his sister from the time he was a baby, he was taken away to an orphanage and then he left at 18 and became a Tunnel Rat in Vietnam. What do you say to that? What do the people my father fought to free from the concentration camps say to God? And what does He say to them? A friendly dog is so innocent, he's a good boy, he's happy and he just wants to love people, but he isn't much good to anybody in a fight.

When I tell you about the Virgin Mary, I want to tell you about her beauty, about the passion of her purity and the love she inspires in a man. I want to tell you about the hope and the goodness and Love that means everything and the ways She and her Son show me, but it's for the same reason He doesn't show Himself to us, it's out of Mercy that he doesn't always work miracles the way we think we want him to, that I don't want to tell you, and have struggled. Miracles are what 'visions' are, they change your reality and then you have to respond to them, they show you God is real and confront you with yourself, that's what they're for. Why do I worry about sharing her message, I think everybody already knows on some level, she says something is coming... Everything, every single molecule of what we are in faith, is Good! Love is going to triumph! Do you see how sin came through the Woman's no and salvation comes through the Woman's yes? Do you see how God is Love and Love without a Woman is meaningless? Do you see how God being and idea, unlike you is meaningless? My ancestors and I do. Jesus Christ is a man, he's one of us, He's real and He's conquered death with Love, with Passion. He enters us from the inside, in every cell, exactly like He said He does, with His Holy Spirit and with His Flesh, His Life Blood. But I remember each year before Christmas holding my son and praying for one more, one more with lights and Santa Clause and snuggles and laughter and it hurts me to think of people afraid. I've been afraid to talk about it, but no one has to be afraid, if they will ask humbly and sincerely for help with one main thing; An, 'Illumination of Conscience.'

What's really happening is that Love is coming into the world from the inside out, and what love does is illuminate everything including everything we try to keep in the dark. Time is for embracing the Light and letting go of the dark. It is so much more satisfying and so much less fearful to let go of it than to have it ripped out of your heart like a god you love and worship. What Mary did and has done and does for me is to so tenderly and gently like a mother, help me become a man, like she did for her Son. She helps me walk by faith, creatively instead of reactively. She does that by loving a man, broken and with all his faults, and seeing her Son in him. She gives her love to a woman to give to a man if she wants it. I don't know why it's so hard for me to say, but I have to, it almost killed me not being true to her and to the 'vision' of love that Her Son gives her and she gives back. She's Real, She's Here, She's the Woman Clothed with the Sun and Crowned with Stars, she is appearing all over the world to call us back to God and the Love that God is, we all know what that Love is in our heart already and as a planet we have to respond to it.

When it's dark and your heads on your pillow, open your heart, the part that doesn't know what to do or how to do it and let her have it, give it to her and say, "Virgin, please, pray for me... ... show me how much you love your Son, God..." I rest my head on mine and whisper, "Queen of the Angels, Blessed humble woman, Mary the little girl, Queen of Heaven and Earth, pray for me, ask God to heal me and to give me the faith and the love of Your Son, Gods Son, Christ, our King." Find a real Medicine Man, a true priest, test them by the tracks they follow. Find a friend to love you and help you believe instead of 'react,' make it a holy relationship, a friendship for God, trust and it happens, real miracles, joy, hope, peace, strength, the whole foundation of your situation changes; Love rewards faith. This Love is so much better than anything I'm afraid of or have had to give up that a Man was willing to go through hell for it.

'The Last Detail'

Winter 2014

To make what is similar the same
Is to make beauty a meaningless detail
Why do you want to distill the living thing
And lose your essence to make it clean

If there were no countries
And no religions too
Then will we all be the same
When your throne is empty
Will you finally be free
Is that mans final solution
Or is freedom the love of light
And holiness the hierarchy
Where every detail is of consequence
Because God really does live in us

The best the world could do was guess
So I left
To learn from creatures
When I was alone with them
I was one of them
I shared their reason
Earth is a teacher the world needs
The mother of myriad breeds
One a butterfly One a lion
They don't want to be the same

They want to be true to their nature
Like a child to its mother

I realize mine
As I realize hers
She teaches me on Earth
The way she taught her Son
She never said my Son be the same
That's how you'll get along
You are You
She said
You are true
To our nature
Our Father is God
He loves every curl on your head
Every word you've ever said
Every detail
To be loved instead
His orbits our rings
His planets our jewels
I am the Bride of His Spirit
Angels kneel before me
And you my Son are my Creator
Nothing will ever be the same
The universe will love you
And Crown me in Your Light
While men fight
Their kings are slaves
Their kingdom's of the world
Where they make a heaven of hell
Each man a religion to himself
Each one the child of his own god
Alone in billions
Lost and too afraid
To see
They didn't come for each other
They didn't come for me
They didn't come for you
My Son
You've come for them

I love you Child
I love your every breath
I suffer your death
For each one of them
My tears will fall for mercy
I will be their last chance
To feel Your love
The last thread of their compassion
Their last glimpse of dignity
I will be the last detail
Of a woman's infinite beauty
And let them pierce my heart
To reveal them to their own
My Faith is You my Son
You
Are my Throne

'Indian Nation'

I'd been Wandering the Sequoia and came down off the west slope of the Sierra Nevada to where I parked my truck weeks before near the Tule Indian Reservation. When I turned on the radio, O.J. Simpson was being chased by the police for something, I turned it off and drove towards the reserve. I'd never been there but something was drawing me so I went. When the soul is in a 'state of grace', a state of honesty with God, which is what Confession is about, you can Wander in the Spirit, something always happens, I don't know how to explain it, so I try to describe it.

About a mile before I reached the gates of the reservation I saw a bird dead on the road, a beautiful big barn owl. They fly into car lights at night. I'd had one hover over me with its silent feathers and the full moon as I lay on the ground in the Sierra Madre a few weeks before. I found the bones and fur it had been coughing up on the ground beneath where it would perch and I went to sleep there hoping I might see him in the night and I did, I woke up with him hovering there about three feet above my head. Owl's feathers are virtually silent so they can catch prey unaware. Barn owls are brindle-brown and gold on top and cloud white on their underwings, breast and belly, he was a breathtaking sight in the full moonlight.

I pulled to the side of the road, got out of my Isuzu, picked up the owl, spread it's big wings and put it in the back under a blanket and I thought, maybe there's an Elder on the reservation that wants this.

On the arch above the entrance was the name of a tribe followed by the word, 'Nation' and I realized I was going into another one. It was Sunday morning and I was hoping there would be a Catholic Church their where I could go to mass. It was by itself in the hot dust weathered and white and I walked inside. A few old Indians were kneeling at the altar in silence and I did too. After a while they left and I sat on a bench. An old nun came in, she looked in her eighties and she smiled. I said, "Hi Sister, my name's Leo, I was hoping I'd be in time for mass." She said, "Well we haven't had a priest out here in a long while, but I bring the Eucharist with me from town and we have communion, I can give you communion if you'd like" we prayed together and she did. Then we walked outside. She said she'd been on the reservation for twenty five years and tomorrow was her last day there. She was going back to South Dakota to the Sisters of the Incarnation she had come from. We talked. I told her a little bit of my story and my wandering alone in the wilderness, how I'd always wanted to 'live like an Indian' and how my experiences there had been so Catholic and so close to the Earth, how I had experienced God speaking to me through creation in ways I thought must have been similar to the people God had put there first.

She told me in a desire for healing between the Church and the Indian people, the priests and the Elders and an old Medicine Man had decided to meet and to focus on the similarities between Catholicism and their ancestors religion and the result had been a book called the Eucharist and the Peace Pipe. She said it wasn't in print anymore but she'd try to mail me a copy when she got back to South Dakota. Some people think the White Buffalo Calf Woman was the Virgin Mary and their is support that she first appeared about 2,000 years ago. She had a profound effect on the Native people and her message is so like that of Mary in many ways that it's remarkable. She appeared miraculously to an Aztec named Juan Diego in 1520 and within a few years 7 million Aztecs loved her and her Son and converted out of their hearts. This happened in spite of Spanish atrocities committed against the Native people and Juan Diego's 'Tilma,' a poncho woven of fibers that should have turned to dust 400 years ago, is still venerated in the Basilica of Our Lady of Guadalupe in Mexico. Her image is miraculously imbued on it and teams of scientists using the most modern and sophisticated equipment and tests that exist still cannot come close to explaining it. It is not pigment or paint, the color and image 'float' above the cells of the fibers, they have undergone no effects of age in five centuries and in the reflection of her eyes under electron microscope appear the people that witnessed the miracle.

Her name was Sister Agnes...she told me she would take me to the artesian springs on the Tule river called Soda Spring where crystal clear water bubbled up like champagne out of a rock and flowed into a beautiful swimming hole where the people had been going for as long as they could remember. I drove very slowly and we passed a couple groups of tired hard worn young men, some with black eyes and broken lips from fighting the night before. They all knew her and would slowly raise their hand and say, 'Hey Sister.' I liked this old woman from the moment I met her, my affection grew to a humbled honor as I thought of her living here alone for so many years among these people so wronged, who obviously felt honor and affection for her too. I wonder what a heart like hers has to say.

She continued to tell me the story about the Elders, the Medicine Man and the priests. The priest told her one day they were driving together somewhere and on the side of the road they saw a dead eagle. They stopped and picked it up and put it in the trunk of the car under a blanket. When they got back in the car it wouldn't start. The priest said the car always started and ran fine. The Medicine Man said the spirit of the eagle didn't want to go with them, the priest didn't think that was why the car wouldn't start, but the other priests agreed with the Medicine Man and so they took the eagle out and put him beside the road back in the grass. They got into the car and it started, but the priest behind the wheel was still incredulous. The Medicine Man wasn't and he said if they put the eagle back in the car he knew it would not start, so they did and it didn't. They left the eagle in the grass again and drove home closer to each other in many ways.

I said, "Sister, that is really beautiful and I have something pretty neat to show you." We got out and walked to the back and I opened the door and I said, "Okay sister get ready." She looked as I pulled the blanket off the owl with it's white wings spread. She laughed and said, "Well, God is blessing us today Leo isn't he" and I said, "Yes Sister he is." Hers was a surprise free of incredulity, she was used to it. I saw it on the face of Father Francis at the Monastery when the bells went off and I saw it in the Sisters face, and I've come to have the same look on mine, it's happened too many times. It's not surprise anymore, it's love that we feel.

Sister took me to find the Chief, a woman, who I was going to give the owl to, but we couldn't find her. So I took the owl home and I spread his wings behind the cross I've had on my altar for 20 years, I cut it out of a burned Manzanita that went through the painted cave fire with me and Jack. And you know it isn't until today, that an old friend mentioned the reservation and I heard of the shooting that happened on the 8th of December, 2012, the day my wife left for California with my son, ten days later I had to shoot my beloved old buffalo friend Chester. God's been knocking, I've been opening my door.

As I write this last paragraph I remember that some years after we had moved here to Canada, a dog had gotten into our porch where I used to keep my altar and torn the owls wings from my cross and chewed them up. I've forgotten all this till now. I was off my path already, not listening, not living for the truth, but for some 'Idea' I had of it, and it was soon after that when this perfect storm started, our herd was attacked by dogs I had to shoot and I thought to myself, these dogs are cursing me. I tried to get them to stop but they wouldn't and their owner was worse than they were, soon after threatening to cut our fences and kill our buffalo one of them was poisoned and I had to put her down, and that was just the beginning of an attack I had no idea until years later, was demonically inspired. Then upstream neighbors diverted a creek I had spent hundreds of hours rehabbing and I'd walk out to fish dying in the mud. The ministries in charge of protecting the environment passed the buck, covered their asses and didn't care. It was one thing after another, trials of the world I didn't know how to deal with, with an added dimension coming through I had virtually no knowledge of; humans under the influence of evil I took personally, until I fell under it's spell too and realized none of us knew what we were dealing with. I don't think any of them had invited it in consciously, but evil doesn't need a formal invitation anymore than death does.

The stem of the pipe and the bowl symbolize Man and Woman. The smoke from the fruit of the earth rises to God as incense in a prayer, and the circle of ancestors breathe in and share, the Holy Spirit, to became one with God and each other, even in our body. The air and the Spirit they breathed was real, not an idea, not a symbol, the air was the life of God and the spirit of Life in them and God loved them into creation like he does each one of us. The Sundance was a repentance and a reconciliation and the life of the buffalo was the Life in them also. They couldn't receive it in vain and live in harmony with the Earth and each other and they knew it, they agreed and submitted themselves to the truth of it and they handed it down. My ancestors have done the same for 2,000 years. We can grow further from or closer to God by our religion, but we can't be judged by our religion, it makes no sense. We can be and we are judged by Love, we judge ourselves by Love because to have the life in us Love is, love is what we must become. Love is the Life. Love is the music of our soul, we have to live for it and make it the absolute most exquisite music we can possibly make it, with precision and detail and passion we each have to care what we believe and then believe it. We each have a religion, there is no way around it, it's what we believe and don't believe and it matters. We have to give it every drop of our blood and our intellect and our soul to become the Tribe of a New Nation.

'An Idea'

WINTER 2014

I can't persuade you to be Native American
Or argue with you till you're Black
I'm not trying to convince you to be me
It's the same with my faith
The worlds faith's are all the same
The way the worlds people are
What's holy in them is good
My faith isn't what I call myself
It's who I actually am
In my Heart
Mind
And Soul

We are, Human ~ Beings
Jesus and Hitler both breathed, ate and slept
But did Hitler believe what Jesus believed?
Were Hitler's beliefs true because he said they were?
Did what he believe matter?
Did his beliefs affect the rest of us?
Do you think he's had to take responsibility?
Or do you think he's gotten away with it
At the final judgment for his final solution
Does he just say
"It Vas Mien Own Truth"
If everybody has their own
Shouldn't Hitler have his too?
Sure he should

And he would
Unless
Something true exists
That is true
No matter what Hitler or anyone else
Thinks about it;
Like you

I was a teenager
The first step I took
To 'Commit myself to the truth'
It was like a woman
I didn't know yet
But she was so beautiful to me
I've loved truth like a woman
That I've married
I've become one flesh with her
And betrayed her
She shames me
Because she never wants to
She's too good to hurt me
I want her
She is so beautiful
I can't help adore her
Nothing comes close to her intellect
She reveals myself to me
Her sensitivity, her grace
Truth gives you everything
Every drop of herself
And remains a virgin
In her heart
All along the way
I'm discovering the love she is
And I am
Her loves is Gods
And so is her forgiveness
She gives it to me
By teaching me what it is
Truth is the song behind everything
Dressed in veils
I undress her with love…

She becomes God
To love truth like this
Takes more than our will
No matter how strong we think we are
It's not enough
Her Son died on my Cross
She looks in my eyes and pleads
I kiss her with prayers
Our love is an exorcise
Of what dies
That never ends
I can't and I must
What the world calls passion
Is lying
With lust

Christ said knock, ask, seek truth
And you will find it
And it will set you free
Every word Christ says is true
The difference between the spirit of the Earth
And the spirit of the world
Is that the spirit of the world
Does not want to confess truth exists
Because it thinks it prefers something else more
And what ever we prefer more becomes our god
It's a shame
Because truth has a pure intellect
Infinitely better than our ideas
It sets us free
Of our opinions
It brings us to our knees
In tears of wonder
It leads us to God
It turns love from a symbol
Into Gods Real Presence
On Earth and in Heaven
The truth of truths
Is God becoming Man
Even in our cells
And transubstantiating

Flesh, Matter, life,
Reality in Time
With eternity
To become One with God
Our will becomes His
The conflict and struggle
Are the pains of our birth
They turn to a joy beyond understanding
To the extent we love Him
And then more and more
His will becomes our joy
And our prayer

I've 'sought' truth
The way I felt when I looked into a mountain range
And wondered, what will I find…
I cherished and embraced it
Every second of existence in it
Became my prayer
Dirt sweat sand flies ticks wasps thirst thorns blood
Sleep resurrection
Waking silent in the tingling mist
Miracles showed me I exist
I heard the sun rise on the wind
In Condors wings
And I knew them
They knew me
We thanked each other
For what God gave

I love the Holy Kingdom
On Earth
But it's hard in the 'world'
The spirit of the 'world' isn't Ours
It is stalked by a creature that divides us
To rule
Like men that went to sea
To worlds yet to discover
A different kind of predator
For a different kind of prey
A spirit that infiltrates

To deceive and betray
It competes
For the strength and weakness in you
With God
For 'Authority'
It lies torments obsesses and bribes
For our will
And all it takes to make it run away
Is to stand up to it
And face it
With everything you have
God gives you

If you make that spirit your idea
It will make you its idea
I can tell you
On a Sacred Oath
That spirit is alive
It doesn't need us to make it real
Like a deer and a lion
It hides
With slaves and allies
It eats souls
And ruins lives
I know
I experienced it
Like a fire I set myself to
And walked through
I didn't want to
I had to
To become my prayer here
The way smoke rises

When I was sick and dying
Every path I searched
All I read and tried and did
Addicted
Were all ways to think to be
Or ways to not think to be
They were all 'ideas'
They deal only with symptoms

I'd been in the world too long
To remember
Earth
How everything real is alive
It is not about thoughts
It is about who thinks them
Who we cling to
Who we listen to
Who we follow
Who we love
Who we become
No true thought is our own
True thought is of a Holy Communion
Gods Mystical Body becomes us
With guts
Who feels
Who loves
Who hurts
And forgives
You
Me

Everybody believes
Whatever they want the most
You have to
You must
You're on your own
You'll do what you want
And we will all either love
Or endure it
I will look for the best in you
Please look for it in me
But everybody knows
The different ideas people hold
The myriad different beliefs
Are not the same at all
Every molecule matters
And it's not because they think they're the same
That they're saying they are
It's because they think God is an idea

'Practical'

I've approached this book mystically, more as a work of art than a manual, cryptically to sneak past prejudice, but I'm thinking, maybe you'd like a chapter that just tells some of what I ''Do' to get into the wilderness, and concisely, how to do it. Here's a bare bones skeleton.

The most important thing about going into the wilderness alone is doing it. The world will tell you to go with bells on in a group and make lots of noise so you scare the animals away before they attack you. What I like is to go alone and silently so that I meet them. Maybe you'll get lost without food or water, maybe you'll get bitten by a rattlesnake, eaten by a bear or a mountain lion, maybe you'll finally be scared of something real, beautiful and alive, and see its beauty and decide to make it a prayer. That's what I did, I didn't ask to be protected and safe, I moved with care, but I asked for every breath to be my prayer, no matter what happened, and it was.

For Wandering in the Spirit, I prefer deserts and semi-arid desert mountains. They are different from a forest the way people or animals are different from each other. The desert is open and empty, and full of hidden life, I can see there. The wilderness is a place to listen instead of talk. Behold instead of think. The less you take the better. Here's a list you can work from. Once you're out there, you can wander with nothing.

Desert & Semi-arid Desert Mountains List:

> Medium to small quiet, narrow, back pack
> Broken in good leather hiking boots
> Two pairs of medium socks with 75% wool in them
> A thin virgin marino wool sleeveless shirt, you might have to make one,
> it wicks the moisture away for warmth in the cold and coolness in the
> heat, isn't itchy and wool doesn't get smelly like cotton and manmade
> fabrics do quickly. Wool is also silent to stalk in.
> Strong lightweight quiet shorts
> Hat or cap, thin balacava for night

Thin foam pad, not the inflatable kind they'll get punctured.

Lightweight down sleeping bag, 1 or 2 lbs.

Gortex bivysack, though I've never had one, they're good when it rains

Lightweight tarp about 8'x9' instead of tent

Strong thin string

Leatherman tool with locking blades and a strong hunting knife

Lightweight leather gloves

Synchilla or wool jacket that zips up around neck, t-shirt

Toque or beanie high in wool

Stainless Steel big cup 1 litre + smaller 1/2 litre stainless steel cup that fits inside if you bend the handle, spoon

Collapsable one gallon water jug, water filter. 25 feet of line with a few fish hooks.

Toothbrush, tweezers, moleskins, tp, bury or burn and poo far from water. Mule hide gators, cut piece that fits loosely around lower leg up to about two inches below your knee. Leave slight overlap, line up and poke holes with a big nail, tie seam together with leather cordage. These protect from rattlesnake bites, help with pushing through thick chaparral and also double as a survival tool for holding a rock heated in your fire and hugged in your bag when you sleep. Make sure the rock is dry so it doesn't explode.

Matches, pen, small notebook, small bible

FOOD:

Rattlesnakes and rabbits are good. Rattlesnakes still strike and bite when they're dead, put a stick behind their neck, step on it hard with your foot and sever the head, put a big rock on it.

Food:

Miso soup packets, nature valley oat bars, dried seaweed, couscous, coffee, nuts

fish, cat-tail shoots and roots, stinging nettle boiled, grubs in rotten logs and grass hoppers, taste better lightly cooked on coals.

Couscous and miso soup can be put in your liter pot of boiling water, taken off the fire and covered and ready in 5 minutes, you don't have to cook it, and the pot is easy to clean when you're done. Clean it with dirt or sand and rinse it with water. You can boil water in your liter steel big cup shaped pot using a stove made from a few dry rocks to create a channel and little pieces of wood and a little fire. Nature valley oat bars are light and not made with corn syrup. Miso soup has salt, you need it when you're sweating. You don't need to wear a pack of water with a straw in your mouth all the time. Carry extra water, but find where the water is, once you get there, drink all you can and fill your collapsable bag for the night. I've learned a lot from being thirsty.

Walk with one foot in front of the other in a single file line, not with your two feet spread out side by side. When going up hill, don't reach way out with your thigh, put your foot in front of you and straighten your leg at the knee like a horse. Pace yourself by your breath, deep, easy and steady, there's nobody to keep up with. Every few hours or so, rest. stop, take off your shoes, jump in the water if its there, make a cup of pine needle tea, it's got lots of vitamin c. If the biting flies are bad, make a smudge of sage, be very very careful with fire. Use a thin branch with some leaves on it to swat and wave away the flies as you walk. In the winter stop and flick ticks off. As soon as you feel any pinchy feeling in your nooks and crannies, stop and pick the tick out of there before it sinks in.

The reason for my journeys is to pray, listen for God and experience what people that lived with and from Earth experienced. They would have been taught everything, including the way, by people that knew. Get good topo maps. It's much easier to get lost up the wrong canyon or valley than you think, even with a map. If you get lost, go back to where you last knew where you were, consider all your options before you proceed, don't keep going blindly, but getting lost is part of finding your way, I never brought electronic devices. Forget the world. Go for at least three nights, but the longer the better. Hike into the wilderness for a few days till you get far away from people, and then Wander in the Spirit, as I've described in other chapters.

You can scoop out a slight depression in the sand or dirt for your bed, but make sure it's level. Don't sleep in a gulch prone to flash floods. The thin balacava will keep insects from crawling in your ear or biting you on the face. If it's going to rain, tie your tarp up at a slant above you a couple feet, it stays pretty dry near the trunk beneath some thicker evergreens like spruce, fir and cedar, or look for a cave.

If I were you, I'd find a real priest and go to confession before I left on my journey. Even if you don't believe in it, demons do, it will help you greatly to heal and open to grace. Old fashioned prayers like the one Christ taught the apostles when they asked him how to pray, and the rosary which comes out of the bible and whose fifteen joyful, sorrowful and glorious mysteries are a meditation on Christ's life, repeated slowly as you walk, will not be said in vain, in fact repeating these prayers from the heart is the opposite of what the world says. I've said thousands of rosaries in my life, not one was in vain, every single one is eternal, and the whole thing grows, deepens and unfolds. Like learning to play music, with practice, you stop thinking and start floating. Besides the fact that your prayers are heard, they also help keep your mind off the world. The rosary is one of the most powerful prayers there is after the prayer Christ left us in his blood the night before he was betrayed. On my first step into the wilderness I stop and say, quietly and humbly, with my heart, something like, "Father, Son, Holy Spirit, Mary, angels and saints, please, look on me with pity, pray for me and with me, and help me please you, I offer you every breath and step and thought as my prayer, I put all my faith in God with you, please speak to me." Every single time I have entered the wilderness as a prayer, they have.

'Get Lost'

If you ever go alone
All by yourself
Out onto the Earth
Like the creatures
You'll get 'Lost'
You won't know which way to go
Where, or how to get there
And if you keep on going
You won't know how to get back

'Follow your own path'
and you will go in circles

But in the world
I had no one to follow
I looked, I loved
But, I asked...
Who do I see that is truly happy?
With something nothing can take away?
Who has something no on else has?
And who can I follow?
Without giving them me?

Let them love you or hate you
But never, ever, let another
Dominate you
Because the spirit they follow
Is dominating them

I realized in the Monastery
The holiest person I would ever meet
Would be the humblest
Because a person becomes holy
By seeing the holiness of God
Our unfathomable holiness as creatures
Is equaled only by our ingratitude
Our 'sinfulness'
A saint is a person who becomes aware
Of what he has to be grateful for

In the wilderness I stopped wanting
To be better, greater, more
I wanted to be quieter, smaller
Innocent like a child
And then I walked into Gods Kingdom
On Earth
I slept with her soul
On her horizons I saw heaven
I Wandered in the Spirit

When we try to be big
We make our world
And everyone in it, small
Everything real, every sacred mystery
Is the opposite
Of what the 'world' believes

Chose something to believe
So you can find out if it's true
If it isn't the highest, most beautiful
Most honorable, glorious thing I can find
I don't want anything to do with it
Because that is what Love is
And that is what God does

He followed his path
Because it was ours
He lost everything
His friends, his life
He became forsaken

To show us what passion is
He said, "follow me"
I don't dominate, I set free
In chains or free you follow
So decide
Who will it be you follow?
I can't fake it
Thats why it's so good
That's why it's true
That's why it's art
Start over, we have to
If you really want to find your path
Get lost

'One Man'

It took a few years when I began going into the mountains alone till I could look across to a distant mountain range and tell how far away it was. It might take two or three days or a week to wind through the chaparral and cross through the river valleys and canyons at the bottom, in the beginning I got lost a lot, the trails there were ancient and faint, the deer and the Indians found them, white men came and cut some of them in, but a lot of the time you have to walk in the creeks and river beds or just find your way cross country, I loved going into canyons with no trails and discovering each next solitary footstep, slowly.

I remember one time crossing back and forth across a creek climbing up out of Don Victor valley, a place I was never too crazy about. When it got too dark to walk anymore I dug a bed in the dirt and I woke up with a bear sniffing my toe, it was still in my sock cause it was cold. The sound of him crunching through the brush woke me, but when I moved he heard me and stood silent and still so I didn't know where he was, or if he was really there. I laid there listening…then I lifted my head and the second I moved he took off crashing away through the bush, he'd been there right at my foot, having a sniff. He probably thought it was something good and dead to eat.

The next day as I worked my way back and forth up the creek, I came on wet momma and baby bear tracks. I could tell they were just ahead of me. I tried to slow down so I wouldn't catch up but I wanted to get over the next range to a cave cause a storm was coming, I don't use tents. Each time I crossed the creek behind her, their tracks were still wet, dried enough to have been there twenty minutes or so, but she was stopping and eating acorns, and berries off the Manzanita, I knew I was too close when I came around a corner and saw the little butt of a bear cub following its mother in front of me. She was really taking her time and it took all day to get up the creek. I've seen 23 different black bears back there, many repeatedly, they come in beautiful colors, black, brown and cinnamon and one was an almost blonde champagne, they never gave me a problem. Blue Jays and Ravens will let you know when predators are around. Everything in the wilderness speaks like ripples in a pond, each thing affecting another and communicating it out, on a tiny scale with insects and bigger with animals. If you listen in the quietness, the peace that engulfs your whole being alone back there when you wander in a prayer, you begin to read the ripples of the spirits of things. It's like music, I don't understand it, but I hear it. It's all part of Soultracking.

When I came out of the Monastery I wanted to take people back and help them learn what it was like to be alone so they could find out they weren't. I am very interested in, but don't feel comfortable usurping other peoples cultures, rituals or religions. What I found I was doing was a kind of combination of what the Native people called the Vision Quest and what I came to recognize as Wandering in the Spirit, but it all just unfolded directly from my experience before I knew about any of those things, I think this is our natural state. Since I was a kid I wanted to 'live like an Indian'.

I wanted to experience their experience, but as myself. If you don't honor your own ancestors, and then try or kind of pretend to be someone else's, it's not what Indians or my own ancestors did. It feels kind of like going into someones house and using their personal things. But I understand, we need the sacred in our lives and people are looking for it in a society that doesn't believe anything is truly sacred anymore, so I don't mean to judge anyones sincere search. I do think it is essential that whatever you are, you're a real one. That the Native people lived on the land I was on and always had, as at home as the plants and animals, inspired a deep love and admiration in me for them. I address this issue because I believe ignoring and dishonoring the Communion of our own holy ancestors is a disconnect of immense consequences among most of western civilization, who for some reason only seem to remember the ones worth forgetting.

One winter it rained and snowed for a month and I couldn't cross the river back to the coast. I built a small shelter out of driftwood with a thatched grass roof and a stone stove. One night I heard an old Indian beating his drum and singing. His voice was so lonely and sincere and holy it echoed in me as if it were my own. I heard this voice clearly, I walked the flooded edges of the river looking and listening and trying to see if his ghost was over there on the other side...I can't explain how I wept with him, for everything, except to say I begin to weep now. Weeping isn't crying, weeping is something that takes strength, weeping is something we do for others more than for ourselves. I feel we are forsaking our greatness, and with exception but in general, that the spirituality we talk about and kind of pretend to isn't really holy, there's no sacrifice in it, it's not really love, it's 'getting along'. Often it's self-seeking, kind of immature, weakly reasoned talk in feathers and robes. There's this new 'personality' that says, 'you're not nice because you won't tell me my crummy performance is beautiful.' I always felt like; there is a music and song that exists, that is so beautiful it will make my heart, your heart and Gods heart weep in love, and I want it, and I don't care what I have to do or how I have to change to get it, and whoever I am as weak and faulted as

I am, I can reach for it. This is not a comparative judgement on anyones sincere effort, it's the thing that makes art, art, the 'Reaching' with our whole being, with everything we are. Art is really the secret of the first commandment. It seems like there's this new religion that's mostly about people instead of about God, about what you think you want and feeling good about yourself and whatever you do, and I think it's making the stones weep tears of blood.

I felt more happy and at home alone in the wilderness than I ever did in civilization, but still, I'd always have to come out eventually because I'd get so hungry and I couldn't get enough to eat, I'd lose ten to twenty five pounds on every journey. I did have opportunities to kill deer but I didn't want to do that if I couldn't use all of it, and I didn't know how to do that back then so I didn't. I ate all the plants I could, my main source of protein was rattlesnakes, I snatched a rabbit from a red tail hawk once. I fell in love with Canada on my honeymoon, here I finally found a place that felt wild and vast enough to be able to feed myself off the land. Predators and herds of wild animals were all around me. It was majestic and clean and the people seemed simpler and less influenced by the media and culture I'd come from. That culture was one I loved deeply, but I felt like it was losing itself in some way. When I was a kid growing up in the 60's and 70's, every town and city was unique like a person. Each one had its own stores and restaurants and bars and burger places and motels and gas stations and personality, from the old Italians of Monterey to choppers flying down the highway, there was this earthy inspiring, quaintness. I am still a Californian, and I am grateful to be, but the whole country is going through a trauma like a broken family. In a new way, I think the whole world is.

When I listen to someone telling me what they think about, reality, faith, religion and God, I listen the way I do to someone playing music. It's not all the same, there is a nuance of thought and emotion that is infinitely subtle, the thought, the beauty, is more important to me than just strumming and singing because we can. Sometimes it's mild torture to listen to, it's a hokey cacophony. Don't listen to me unless I have something to say you think is beautiful, the beauty of thought is my only right and it has to be a kind of obligation. If you think something I say is in error, please, explain it to me, precisely and beautifully so I can learn. I want to learn and I want to know if I am in error about anything, if there is something I'm not seeing, including my own view of myself. I'm trying to express my beliefs with humility and love even though I feel passionate about them.

One man falls and his wife leaves him, another falls and he's humiliated in front of the world. One's responsibility is war, thousands are killed; but what if a man believes that if he goes to hell the whole world goes to hell, if he falls, the whole world falls with him and if he rises the whole world rises with him? What if he really believes that? What if it's true? Just what if? The whole idea of a God-man, of a 'Savior' an At-one-ment and a Sacrifice, or anything at all being

Sacred, is worth the question, 'What the hell for? Why? How?' People come up with different answers, some are more beautiful and passionate than others.

Our skin, our eyes, our fingers, our ears, intellects, language, they are the instruments we use to perceive and express, but they aren't 'Us', we are more than our eyes and our skin and our form. That's why I say to comprehend reality with accuracy, I interpret it symbolically, as if it were a dream. Everything, everything here, is symbolic, everything we are experiencing is an expression of what and who is expressing it, the same way I try to express my heart and soul and humanity and being in a song or in words, the song and the words aren't me, but if art is real it is here to sanctify the air and so are we, we are supposed to be Gods art and at times we're so ugly that we are a living, breathing sacrilege. The obligation to beauty and any real art demands we discern ugliness, we have to perceive the false shadow of things, the ugliness of 'Sin,' anything born from a lack of love, but also the ugliness of wimpy, insincere, false and pathetic Reason.

What a man or woman that overcomes limit does is become what and who they are. His or her symbol becomes what and who it symbolizes. The nature of form is symbolic, there is a perceived 'distance' between everything, It's edge is what gives it form. I look at nature, everything is wanting to join, through love, and the story is being told in this way we are experiencing, with all its imperfections and all its beauty. It is meaningless to fight the way it's told or to judge it by the liars, hypocrites and predators that are in every group. What is important to me is the beauty I can find in it. A thing can be limited but pure and in its purity is its beauty. I think your purpose, my purpose, is to learn to recognize it and express it, the Truth, and the way to discern it is through a kind of beauty that is every beauty at once, every love at once. The joining of lovers is both surrender and conquest at once and it's real, not symbolic. I let my lover be who she is and I adore her for it, finally it is something that is actually real, eternally real right now. It's the difference between lame, hokey, cliched music and music that melts your heart into your soul, love that melts your body and Gods body into our bride, really, not symbolically.

So I look, where is it? Where do I see it, where is it first in the interpretations of words and ideas that posses a logic and reason that is sublime, that truly hold together, not relative, and that breaks through the symbols, drawing them closer and closer to what they symbolize and to each other? This is why I see it as a divine romance between a man and his bride and the art that proceeds from them that is life, not a symbol of it or an idea or even an interpretation of it, but really it. What makes it Treasure is that it is Real. What makes what's real good is that it isn't fake. Ideas and symbols are tracks on the trail, I want to read them with my whole being but they are for following who is leaving them. I'm laying the tracks too, by following them, for me, finding God and his creatures, his offspring, finding me, has been the same as finding a mountain lion and him finding me,

I didn't decide what was there and then keep pointing at the tracks to convince myself and others, I followed the tracks not knowing what I'd find and they found me, that is being committed to the truth and Wandering in the Spirit. It's being in love with a Woman who you want to make your Bride and 'making' love with her, holy love, with your whole being, giving your whole life, this is why we are called to a reaching for the Highest love, the Most beautiful love, and not reaching purposely for something less, that is passion, that is holiness, just the way we are in a song, not just any song we can get people to go along with, only the most beautiful song we can discover. It takes Respect that is Undeserved, love that is faith in your lovers Creator.

Anybody can strum and sing and write anything they want, and have sex with whoever they want, they can believe and believe they don't believe in any idea they want, and call things whatever they want, but what's the point? The New Adam and Eve somehow in every way, prove it, they tell me with everything they are, not only with ideas and words; that they follow the tracks for the beauty of what they reveal instead of for themselves, and they do it no matter what the cost, because it's all they want, their love never ends because it is for each other, really, not symbolically. All of God is found in everything real, in the tiniest sub atomic speck, and in each one of us. Though I've never found another, or a way that comes close to the beauty and the passion, I could say, if somebody else did it better I'd follow them, but it's not about thoughts, it's about beings, God who is love, it's like loving you, am I going to forsake you for somebody better? Is that love? I can't, because God makes you real, and that's the reason I want it, the way I want to want and love and be loved by a woman, in every way there is to love at once. That joining is the 'Oneness' that is more than just another idea.

Life on Earth is Wandering in the Spirit and looking across toward the next mountain range. I don't know what is there and getting there has meant a willingness to become lost, even to the point of losing my faith if that's what it takes to find out if it's real, and losing the truth to find out if it's true. The Son himself cried out, "Father why have you forsaken me…..?" You have to be willing to lose everything to go beyond pretending, and beyond symbols and ideas to find what is Real. It has been such a treasure of beauty because it is what God creates, not my 'ideas' not my 'wanting. Life here is not the End but the Means, putting our foot into the tracks on the path until we experience the same thing the being that left them experienced. For me that being is both the creature and the Creator. He has told me that story like a King and Spirit. He has painted it with his life, His-story, more beautifully and meaningfully than anyone else I've met. A Father and a Son, a God and a Man, that died asking his friends to pray for him so he could do it for them, to love him. Do you ever think what it would mean if you believed it was real and God asked you to pray for him? Why does God ask us to pray for him? Because the Creator wants to become his creation and he wants his creation to become him, really not symbolically. He wants us to create with his faith, the man wants to become one with the woman, one Flesh one Body, and the art they produce, the beauty they express is Life, that is how and why they are 'priests', because their sacrament gives Life, it is alive, it exists, really not only a symbolic memory and not only an idea. The offering being real, Life giving Life, is what makes a priest a priest, not because they decide to call themselves one, calling yourself a musician doesn't make you one. We remember who and what we are by what we offer, when we believe it is Real, because our lover said it was, that's all I need, it's all I want, her whisper is enough to make us One.

God gives us pieces of himself in space, time and form, and weapons not ideas, instruments to play his memory, a Kings Will, God's Will and Testament, the blood of a Medicine Man, a Priest that never died, and warriors that fight in his tribe against evil, the force of death you can't think or vote away, the force that lies and steals. He leaves us symbols that are what they symbolize, Signs that are unexplainable, unmistakable miracles for any sincere person that looks, authority that is real, on Earth and in Heaven, Keys, a tribe, offspring that are more than people claiming things or thinking they believe they don't believe things, limiting things to the symbolic we have no way of knowing aren't real. Recognizing they are is what a miracle is. This is a story, His-tory, your story, mine, right here, now, it's as real as real gets. It's not real because I'm a 'believer' in something and you're a believer in something else, it's real because I'm a creature and your a creature and we exist, like a mountain lion and a buffalo and a rattlesnake and a spider.

I am as much a member of a tribe with holy ancestors who's spirits and angels walk beside me as the Indian brothers and children of the same Great Spirit that sat in the same sand and sang and wept the same song. The tracks and the weapons and the ancestors and the flesh and the blood being real, really, is the whole point! to make you and me the 'image' we are created in, really, now, here, but we are each sovereign, we each are called and we're not only free, we're obligated whether we like it or not, to do and believe and not believe whatever we want the most.

Christ knew what he meant when he said what he said and he believed it. God's words do what they say. When God says, 'This is my body, this is my blood' 'Have faith my son' he is instructing but he is also creating the condition by virtue of saying it. If he isn't then I'm just listening to some guys words and ideas, not Gods. This is the transubstantiation of matter, or reality, of mortal bodies into glorified bodies, bodies of the material of light. That's how one man's falling can mean the whole world falls and one man's rising can mean the whole world rises. This is the beautiful part and the hard part, he is creating each of us to be that One Man.

The Path of the Buffalo ~ Part I

A few days after we took possession of our land, another buffalo rancher called me, his herd had gotten out. They went north for four days with us tracking and losing them repeatedly. They would fly through stuff so thick and steep I could hardly crawl or climb through it. It's nothing but hundreds and hundreds of miles of wilderness and they can survive out there on their own fine, they don't lose their wild instincts, wild public herds have started that way. He had buffalo he paid over twenty-five thousand dollars each for but it's so much more than the money. On the fourth day a friend of ours spotted them from his plane and called us. Another friend, an old hunter, climbed a ridge and howled like a wolf, they got up and turned around and they ran all the way back in about five hours. Mine got out a couple years later, crossed the river and headed north too. I tracked and found them but I had to leave them overnight and come back the next morning, I was beside myself with my stomach in a knot. My wife said a prayer and looked in the little bible I had found on my first vision quest and put her finger down, she came in and told me, it said, 'Do not worry about tomorrow, for your Father in heaven knows your needs...' That really helped me, I calmed down and I trusted. Thirteen friends and neighbors helped me get them back the next day. Chester charged my friends Gary and Shane on horseback, but they got away. They took some photos of that day I hope I'll get into this book.

I won't go into the details of what happened, everybody is stretched for time these days, but if you ever find yourself in the Canadian Rockies tracking buffalo among all the other tracks you come across out there, you'd probably find the details of interest. Horse people are usually familiar with all the gates from a walk to a gallop. When you learn to identify gates by the grouping of footfalls, it helps because you know where to look for the next track even when you can't see it. It might be the slightest little mark on hard ground. My hunting partner grew up here on a trapping line, he has hunted his meat his whole life. I have other friends here that have grown up like that and I'll never match their ability, but I don't have to, to soultrack and to love it.

Last year a mountain lion attacked two of my buffalo. It left its claw marks down their backs when they kicked it off. Then he killed a cow elk and then a big Grizzly crawled through the fence and cached what the mountain lion had left under a thousand pounds plus of dirt. He came back for the next few nights to eat it. That went on a hundred yards or so from my music cabin while a smaller grizzly belched Ash berries on my deck. I love that.

It makes me feel happy, alive and grateful, to live in a place where life is still happening the way God creates it all around me and to be able to share it with people. It's natural to feel scared if you're not used to that and thinking about coming here, but you don't have to feel scared. You just have to get used to it. Nobody that lives out here in the wild worries much about it, you deal with it the way a person that lives in the city deals with danger, the difference is, this is a beautiful danger, a 'beautiful fear', from animals being true to their nature, in the world it's man, betraying his nature and being ugly. Living in the wilderness tends to make people trust each other instead of fear each other. I love to visit cities and man can shape beautiful moods and environments. There's often a vibrant creative energy and most of the people are warm and loving. I think and feel how beautiful it will be when everyone knows that God exists and is Love and they let Him become them. When we all realize that all we want is love and that it is the answer to every question and every need and every desire. Down to the molecules of His flesh and blood I believe that day is coming.

'The Path of the Buffalo' ~ Part II

I fell in love with her the moment I baptized her in the Sisquoc River. I took her into the San Raphael Wilderness to Wander in the Spirit with me and we did. I don't run around baptizing people, it just happened, although I did baptize a kid who then changed his name from Casey to Augustine John and makes John the Baptist look lukewarm! I'd known my wife for several months before I saw her physical beauty, a 'veil' like this has been drawn over my eyes in other situations a few times before, it's an interesting thing, it allowed me to become her friend without wanting to 'impress' her or wanting anything from her. I'd been living alone in the woods as much as could like a monk. Celibacy, when its chosen out of love, as a way of giving yourself, allows a man to give himself to others, especially women, in a beautiful and unique way the world doesn't know a thing about. But you might laugh cause a few years earlier the veil came down under very different circumstances.

A Playboy Bunny brought Michael Douglass in to see me play in a club on Coast Village Road in Montecito one night. I'd met him before and he had my Carmel CD. She was trying to help us make a connection and it's hard to explain, but I knew if we had, we would have become friends and it would have changed the course of my life. For the first ten years of my life that's what I wanted, to be the best singer-songwriter I could be, a musician, a rock star, and it was beginning to happen, but then my Mom went to Medgugorje, and brought Mary back with her. I'd never thought much about Mary, slowly, she came into my life, she changed everything. Michael and the Bunny (not my girlfriend Bunny, but a Bunny friend of hers) sat down right in front of me at a small table to watch my first set. It was like I saw them there, but I didn't recognize them. I had no idea who they were even though I knew them both, until the moment they walked out the door, and then suddenly it was as clear as it should have been when they sat down. I never said hi or even acknowledged them and they must have thought it was really weird. But later the same kind of connections and doors opened for me to walk down that path, it was all laid out in front of me, all I had to do was take it, but I knew in my heart, down in my soul, somehow, in this strong and subtle way, it wasn't the path I came here to follow. I came to follow the path of the buffalo, The White Buffalo Calf Woman, Mary and her Son and their tribe, the first born of the dead and the Medicine Man that never died.

My wife was one of the most beautiful women anybody has ever ever seen and for as long as I was in love with her she was to me too. Columbian, Russian and Native American, she was my Pocahontas and I never dreamed it could end, choosing that would be like ending my relationship with my father, mother, sister, brother or child, but it happened sixteen years later, I didn't choose it but I can't blame anyone for not being able to bare the anguish of what I went through, I mean that, I am as sorry as I can be, I couldn't bare it myself and it almost killed me.

Sixteen years prior to now I had just crossed the border into Canada and I was telling everybody, 'Hi, my name's Leo, we're on our honeymoon!' After a whole bunch of this she reminded me what people do a whole lot of on their honeymoon and pointed out that other people knew that too so I toned it down a little. I was like a big friendly dog for the first ten years of our marriage, but then I rolled over a couple times and got kicked. I didn't understand it. I had a dog that was real sensitive like that, you had to be real gentle when you reprimanded her or she would really get her feelings hurt. Friendly dog's are so nice, but they're not much good in a fight, I've been in a fight and I've had to turn back into Leo, a friendly Lion! 'Hear me Rooaaaar!' It's been hard to be true to my nature but not anywhere near as hard as not being true to it. It's kind of weird because in a way all my life I think I've been kinda like a cat that thought he was a dog.

I was looking for a big hot Espresso in a town called 'Medicine Hat' which is about the best name I can think of for a town out on the Prairies, but not a good place to look for an Espresso. I went into a place full of cowboys and cowgirls, the lady behind the counter took the pencil out of her mouth and called out, 'Heeaay Shaaaaayyne, do yuuu know how ta make an Eeeeeexxxxsssspresssoooo?!' Everybody turned around from their bacon 'n' eggs and looked at me real funny. Lol! Wag, wag.

We followed the path of the buffalo into the Gardens of Eden North, and I fell in love with Canada too, I still am. I knew that first day this was real wilderness, the stuff I'd been looking for all my life. Our second day in Canada we saw grizzlies, black bear, deer, elk, moose, mountain goats, mountain sheep and a wolf. As we dropped into the Banff Valley I caught my breath and said, 'This place feels like it has three big angels looking over it.' It might seem like the kind of thing I'd say because of what I write about, but it's not. Then somebody told me these three big mountains were called the Three Sisters and I still feel like that about Banff and Canmore, Alberta. You know the movie Legends of the Fall, it was filmed south of here in the Canadian Rockies of the Kananaskis. There's a wild kind of majesty and the animals bring the peace with them.

I was led to this land. It looked just like a place I had drawn since I was a little boy. I'd explored for a week, it was the first place I looked at, it wasn't advertised, I Wandered in the Spirit to it. I knew I was going to win this big old stuffed buffalo head and robe in a raffle at the Mountain Man Museum in Pine Dale Wyoming, a year and nine months before on our honeymoon, but I didn't and was surprised. I've never won anything but a crummy lawnmower, but I knew I was going to win that stuffed buffalo, my wife looked at Chester when I brought the family back with me to take possession of our land and said, 'Hey, look you won!' I didn't think it would be a live one, but from the moment I saw Chester I was filled with a Spirit of hope and a kind of strength that has carried me when I couldn't carry myself. He is the most beautiful and powerful creature I have ever known and I consider myself blessed in a way that will take the 'Rest of My Life' to express for having him in it, still true to his nature and wild enough to kill me, and my friend. I had to put him down Christmas 2012. He has left me a son and since the day he was born, I see his Fathers spirit in him everyday more and more.

'Buffalo & Horses'

Winter 2014

I was looking for a place that still felt wild, when I found Canada. There was peace and space I could walk into and feed myself. Since I was a child I wanted to 'live like an Indian.' I remember crawling through the chaparral when I was five or six, shafts of sunlight illuminated the ground and earthy smells came out of it. It was the first of many times I Wandered in the Spirit. I felt like I was doing something dangerous and I liked how it felt, like I was another one of the creatures. I think they were the kind that were just out of sight, illuminating me.

But I wanted to tell you about the first time I worked with buffalo on horseback. I made friends with a man from Saskatchewan. He had a black mustache and cowboy hat and he'd lived with buffalo his whole life. His horses and his buffalo have worked out a truce kind of like those ones in the middle east. He had three hundred and fifty head of beautiful rolling hills and deep draws, and all those humps and rumps going over them was something I wanted to follow forever.

I was newly married with a one year old son I'd carry on long walks while I prayed for us and waved to the engineers that rolled by the home we'd come here from in Mt. Shasta, California. I was the first rancher to represent the Canadian Bison Association in the United States and I was building a market to supply families and high end restaurants with organic buffalo. I eat it almost raw and I don't think you can know what it means to me, because you've probably never been graced with the prayer of what it is, to starve or kill and eat another creature. That is the background, like music, of what going into the wilderness alone became for me, a kind of Sundance. If I couldn't feed myself, it felt like pretend, like a lot of life seemed back in the world. A coyote showed me at the end of a long journey, what my body was for, to carry my soul around. That's my why for keeping it alive. I was a prayer back there.

My friend had some huge bulls like my bull Chester, but even a little longer. The dominant bulls are the only buffalo that don't mind being alone, they kind of like it, they aren't scared of anything. They've won every fight they've ever had. That whole thing, the life of one of those bulls, gives me shivers when I talk about it. They know what greatness is, it's in their blood because of their hearts. We were very lightly pressuring them, trying to get them to join the rest of the herd and move to new grass.

It was early summer just before the rut, and the bulls were growling that deep roar you hear all the way in the ground beneath you. Buffalo are real touchy about their comfort zone, they might not charge from a few feet or so if you know each other and if they're in a good mood, or they might charge you from six hundred yards. I've been charged many times on foot, I'd have to tell about that in another chapter, but this time I got charged on horseback. A dry cow came out of the herd at us and me and the horse took off. I can't remember if was I thinking 'woohoooooo or uh oh', probably both, but my horse knew what to do, run! Buffalo can run faster than a horse for the first four hundred yards. She turned around and ran back when we were a few hundred yards from the herd.

You've got to watch out for dry cows, because they don't have their own calf, they become guards of the rest and will leave the herd to face a threat. Instead of running as an initial response like most ungulates, buffalo charge and face predators. Last year I was charged by one of my cows who had lost her calf to ravens that spring. The rest of the herd had left and she ended up giving birth alone, the ravens know they can peck a newborns eyes when there aren't other cows standing guard. I was picking up wool far away from the fences and she came galloping, thrrump, thrrump, thrrump. If it's a female, you just have to stand there and face them and usually they'll stop. Don't get charged by an adult bull cause they will rarely stop. Anyway, she ran up and stopped about ten feet from me like they usually do, but then she put her tail up and her head down and did a combination with her horns and jumped another five feet, and then she did it again. Her horns were twisting back and forth kind of like hooks and upper cuts just a few inches from my crotch. I've never had one do that before. I moved my upper body forward, stomped my foot under her nose, and yelled, 'Geeeeeet outa here you....' and she backed off and around all pissed off with her tail up. I still couldn't back away, they'll take it as a sign of submission or fear, but too much pressure will cause them to come for you too. It's a real funny balance, each buffalo and each time is different. You get a feel for each other.

I called my friend a few weeks ago and told him about what happened. He told me he got charged on his horse by a dry cow just a few days before. They were riled up about something and he pressured them a little bit. She charged and gored his horse in the side. She backed off came back and gored the horse again. Then she did it a third time, her horn went all the way through his boot between the inside of the sole and the bottom of his foot. She ran back to the herd. He got his horse away, her lungs weren't punctured and she survived with two holes in her side he could put his fingers in through the ribs. I like living in the unseen world and writing about it, but I thought you might like to hear about me 'doing' something.

'Down the Alley'

This morning I have to run the buffalo through the handling system, worm them and give them a Selenium shot. The Rocky Mountain Trench is low in that mineral. I get them hungry enough to go into the corral for some hay and then sneak around and close the crash gate on the squeeze before they all run out, that's the plan, but somehow they know before I even go up there that I'm up to something.

A couple years ago I had them closed in and Chester walked down the back of the alley and smashed through a 350 lb. 7 foot high chained door, he just put his head down and kept going! My friend Chad was standing up on the side of the corral next to him when he did it and we both just stood there with this funny look on our face, kind of chuckling, all the rest of the buffalo ran out the hole after him, then I've got to start all over and it takes me days because I don't force them, but it didn't matter. We were both so impressed with Chester.

It always takes a determination to stay calm, because they hate to be handled and separated from each other and they can get hurt. I used to get so pissed off when they got hurt. I don't even put ear tags in them anymore, they never leave the ranch. Once in the old days before I knew better, I took this big beautiful son of Chester to a show and sale. Bulls were going for $50,000 dollars and more sometimes. The organizers said I had to put their special ear tags in him. They sent me the wrong applicator. I kept squeezing this tag into his ear as hard as I could and it wouldn't stay, his head and horns were crashing up and down and they'll crush your hands. Each time I'd squeeze it hurt him and blood was all over his ear, I was so angry, pissed off and upset for hurting him like that. I stopped taking bulls to shows, it's too far away and too much stress on them.

These animals are creatures, with an animating soul, life, they carry the blood of their ancestors just like you and me, I love them, people don't know what they mean to me, kind of like they don't know what my 'religion' is, but I'd like them too. My love for them is full of emotion and affection, but I've had to learn to grab hold of myself. I wanted to live from the Earth and I do. These animals are medicine. They consume beauty, everything they see and feel is innocent and true. God turns into light and light turns into grass and grass turn into their flesh and their flesh turns into mine. I consume beauty.

For me there is no food more beautiful or more mystical than the mystical body of Christ. It is my souls food and I pray with the heat that swells in my heart that I'd die for it. Just the way they do. They are stoic, with wolves and with men, they accept death the way we should. What's tragic is to be dead before we die.

I have to reconcile what I eat, what is sacrificed for me to live; with who I am. That's what the Sundance was. That's what Christ gave the night before he was betrayed, but we're like cattle on a big feedlot, we've lost our meaning and it's made us mean. I get a little pissed off when people that don't know what the hell they're talking about, talk about it like they do. But I know it's up to me to prove I do, to prove it's true. The fruit is the sign. It's hard but I love it. It's all going to become one, the veil is getting very thin.

'Conception Sky'

The night before my son was conceived and the sky turned a liquid gold and blue, I saw eyes I've never seen before. These weren't eyes I've looked into when I pray for a woman I could love to heaven, these were the eyes of Men. They had something in them, I've never seen before or again. They were the eyes of an Indian looking out from each man I looked into. Years later, I saw tired and forlorn oncs in jail with Sundance scars across his chest, he told me his tribe was lost and the worst he could do was his best.

The eyes I saw the night before the sky turned liquid gold and blue were the last eyes to live while their tribes were still alive. Now they were left only to look out from the pages of a book at Saint Mary's Lake, Montana. I've never forgotten them and that's why I saw their memory in that great big forlorn Indian man I met in jail and I told him. He cried and so did I. Every time I tell the story of the buffalo and how the United States government put a bounty on them in order to starve the great tribes of the plains, I cannot hold back my tears, and I swear I don't try to conjure them, I don't feel good about them, I hate those tears, they are so sad, so tragic, such a waste of everything good. Men can be the ugliest animals on Earth when they are possessed by animals without bodies, hellhounds.

The eyes I looked into on the pages that night, just shortly before we crossed the border into Canada the same way they did to escape the trail of tears, were filled with an honor, a dignity, a confidence I've looked for and dreamed about ever since. Why? I've asked and I think it's why I start to choke every time I think of the last ones closing and never looking out again on the beauty of an Earth they knew was being created for them, before their eyes, every moment of their lives. They were Animists and in a most holy and mystical way their faith is very close to mine. Everything those eyes looked on was Sacred, everything was One Thing, speaking to them through messengers of meaning, messengers of God. That's what they were to me alone in the wilderness too, angels with bodies and they'll speak to anyone humble enough to listen.

The path of the buffalo, the trail of tears and the eyes of those men led me to Canada and to this moment. They keep me here still. Through my own trail of tears I believe I have a chance to look out with them, I believe I've found Who it was they saw and Who they saw looking back. I really do. I don't think my eyes have it yet but I pray one day they will, and I'm convinced by the evidence I have seen with my own of the unseen, it's all True.

'Elk Spirit Woman'

Len and I reached the Columbia River a few hours before sunrise. It took us an hour to haul the boat and gear down from Spillimachene Bridge to the water's edge. It was Fall our breath was on the air and our faces stung as we motored by moonlight up stream. Len had grown up here on the river, hunting and fishing and running away from home. For him safety was in the bush, life at home was more dangerous than the grizzlies.

Except for a black tail buck deer I bow hunted for two weeks straight in northern California, hunting was new to me until I moved to Canada. We had been hunting every day and night since elk season opened, waking up at four or five a.m., working in the middle of the day and then hunting again till dusk. In the early season, the elk are still up in the alpine. We had bugled in several elk in the higher mountain reaches framed by breathtakingly beautiful glaciers. I have spent months at a time alone in the wilderness, fasting, praying and, "Wandering in the Spirit." I always felt like I was faking it partly though because I wasn't able to provide all my own food. I'd eat wild plants and rattlesnake and the rare fish, but eventually I would lose too much weight and get so hungry I'd have to come back to civilization so I could, "Buy" my food. The longest I had ever gone with almost no food at all was 18 days. I lost 24 pounds and covered over 100 hard miles. I've been hungry and I've learned lessons in the process, the most basic of which is that when you're really hungry food becomes everything and almost all you think about. If your willing to give up food and go alone into the wilderness, honest and sincere, and offer each step and breath as a prayer, you will experience miracles, even if you think your troubles are hopeless. In different forms, this is what the Native Americans called the Vision Quest, Jesus and the prophets practiced this also. I'd been doing it since I was a teenager. In later years I found out the hard way there is no substitute for it.

We had glassed a six-point bull the previous evening and Len had a plan. We were to beach at a small inlet to a slough and as quietly as possible position ourselves and bugle. We share half of all our hunted meat and do our best to share half of all the work. Len relies on his hunting and fishing for his food. Ever since

I could remember that was something I wanted to experience and be able to do. Being dependant on others, especially the "System" for something as essential and immediate as my food seemed wrong to me. I remember seeing a book of old photographs of Indian men before the slaughter of the buffalo and the time of reservations. In each photograph I saw a look in their eyes that I have never seen before or since. It was a look of holy confidence, complete self-assuredness but somehow without Ego. I am convinced that much of this quality was due to their self-reliance and their mystical attunement with the spiritual side of nature.

As we paddled up to the beach a bull bugled close. We stalked up and saw him there in the mist. Len glassed to assure he was a six point (called a 12 point in the States) the only elk legal to hunt. It was still dawn and our lenses were fogging up in the cold. He motioned for me to crawl forward about twenty feet to a mound of dirt to rest my aim. When we reached it, I aimed, but I couldn't see the elk in my fogged scope. He whispered, "Take him, take him!" I said, "I can't see him in my scope"! A shot from Len's rifle flashed and rang out.

We searched for hours but could not find one drop of blood. The bull was trotting away when Len took the shot. The light was still low, he had no rest and was expecting me to shoot. I asked him if he had ever hit an animal and then not scene any blood at all left behind? He answered no. It was so close, but he got away. We heard a bull bugle from just across the river and figured our bull had crossed and was heading for the mountains. Elk posses a tremendous endurance and will often travel great distances when spooked or pushed.

The morning and evening continued, glassing, dragging the boat and gear from place to place, slugging through the mud, pushing through the willows, crawling over black and grizzly bear tracks and spending the nights out on many occasions...

Yesterday we returned to Spillimachene Bridge and set out for the area where we missed the bull a couple weeks earlier. We hunted opposite sides of the river. There was abundant elk and moose activity and we had bulls bugling us. Len spooked a bull but it only retreated a little ways and we bugled it back and forth till dark. We camped in an old tarpaper roofed hunting cabin built in the 1930's by a group of men from Kimberely B.C. that hunted and fished together, we ate elk steak for dinner from last year's hunt, it was very good. As usual we talked about all kinds of personal and interesting things. Through a series of synchronistic events, Len humbly carries a Sioux Peace Pipe. We both do our best to approach hunting prayerfully, and find wisdom in the old ways. Len blew out one last bugle and a big throaty bugle came back from the same place where we had missed the bull two weeks before!

I had a powerful dream that night:

In it, Len flushed a beautiful six-point bull into my sight. It walked towards me. I wasn't absolutely sure if it had six points and I was trying hard to count and handle my rifle, which was still an unfamiliar process in those days. The bull came up right in front of me with Len flushing it from behind. I shot and wounded it in the shoulder. It fell over and wasn't running away, but was suffering and I wanted to shoot again to kill it quickly.

Slowly the bull began to change into a Native or Metis woman. She too was shot in the shoulder and suffering, I was distraught and couldn't shoot again. She said, "It is alright." She was suffering but that it was alright and then she either crept away or disappeared. It was still hard to see. I saw an elk skull with antlers in the river and fished it out. It was somehow filled with canoes, one inside the other, progressively smaller. I had the feeling of the passage of time.

We heard drumming in the distance and soft native singing and we walked towards it. There were four very old native women sitting on the ground and preparing food, I remember their faces. As I came to the fifth younger woman it was the same woman that had been the bull elk. She was sitting under the trees in the grass wounded in the shoulder. She looked at me prayerfully saying again, "It is alright." I woke up feeling very moved knowing it was somehow a sign about our hunt the next morning.

Before daybreak I told Len the dream and we agreed that it was powerful, but had no idea yet what it meant. Len hunted the west side of the river and I paddled across to the east side where we had heard the big throaty bull bugle us after dinner the night before and where we had missed the bull weeks earlier.

I crept around the willows following lots of tracks, but seeing no elk. About 30 minutes later, I heard a bunch of Ravens and saw several of them in the distance. I approached carefully ready for a bear on a kill. There under the trees was our six-point bull, the one we thought we missed, mostly consumed. My first reaction was of shame and disappointment in myself for failing to find him and wasting his gift of meat. What a waste, but then I remembered the dream, and how I had walked up to the women and now the elk carcass in just the same setting. The powerful meaning of the dream began to reveal itself as I crossed the river to find Len. I told him what I found and reminded him of the dream and the parallels.

As we walked towards the elk he said that he had been so close to that spot and both of us talked about not finding the slightest drop of blood. We sat down and talked. He asked me what I wanted to do, what I thought the dream meant. I said I felt very sorry that we didn't find the bull and wasted the gift of his food, but that I felt we had been given a great gift. Those women in the dream felt like the spirits of Native women that lived here, I called them the Elk Spirit Women and they had visited us and led us here. I talked about how the old warriors and hunters must have felt, the relationships they must have had living this kind of thing as reality everyday. Len and I both believe in that and try to honor it, but we were both experiencing it now as hunting partners and it tied us together more. The hunter used to be the true provider of food, especially in the north and this was a great gift, ask anybody who has ever been really hungry, his hunt meant life and death for him and his family and tribe, it wasn't for trophies. The beauty and power of the animals gifts were treasured and so were the stories, but the animals flesh was life giving. Even today, those tribes of isolated people that still follow their native hunter-gatherer diet are almost totally free of chronic disease.

Together we valued the story and its power to share what we believe hunting was, is, and should continue to be. I filled out my tag for the remains of our bull. I felt the skull and antlers held a kind of, "Medicine". We carefully inspected the bull and found that Len's bullet had entered the gut, gone through one lung and come to rest in the shoulder… We loaded the skull in the boat, broke camp and headed home.

I believe these Elk Spirit Women were real and that they will always be with Len and I on our hunts if we ask them to pray for us. Like saints or angels, keeping us humble and prayerful and grateful to be able to live and hunt and honor the ancestors that have gone before us here in Canada.

'Canadian Winter Account'

"Breathe, relax, let go"
~ Wise Old Sage
"Run Around, Pant, Barf"
~ Crusty the Ranch Hand

Minus thirty, five a.m. black, I woke up hot! The stove pipe chimney goes up through the floor by my bed. Usually it's cold by 5 a.m. and I have to get up to put more wood in the stove. I went down stairs and it was really cold down there and I opened the stove to put more wood in and WWWHHHOOOOOOOSSSHHH, it sounds like a jet engine and suddenly the whole snowy meadow around my cabin lights up cause there must have been a 15 foot flame shooting out of the top of the chimney. I closed the stove but it kept going and the chimney was glowing red hot, I shot a fire extinguisher in the stove and closed it again and the big flame went out but the chimney was still burning with creosote. So I'm running around putting on my clothes and boots and running through the snow to get the ladder and it doesn't reach the roof two story's up until I find a pile of snow from where it slid off the roof and put the ladder on top of it and it just barely reaches the icy edge of snow that's still hanging down off the roof. I have to throw a rope up on the roof on the opposite side from the ladder so when I get up there there's something to hang onto. There's nothing to tie the rope too so I'm trying to start the old farm truck so I can back it up and tie the rope to it but it won't start cause it's so dang cold! Minus 30 makes your whole body hurt.

Meanwhile all this time I'm scared my cabin is going to burn down! The chimney is starting to melt inside the house. I remembered a friend down the road that had to smash his burning kitchen off his house with his skidder, water won't work cause it freezes. Finally I get up on the roof holding the rope so I don't slide off and I shoot the fire extinguisher down the chimney and slowly the fire starts dying down. We go through so much wood and the wood stove is going 24/7 for about 6 months and sometimes I end up having to use wood that hasn't dried out as much as it should which builds up the creosote. So because we're now running out of wood I'm having to log in the snow which means dragging choker cable for a 100 yards or so in snow shoes cause the old front loader has to work too hard to push through that much snow that far....and then I'm cutting the tree down and my chainsaw gets pinched in the back cut and I just barely get it out yanking on it and fall backwards in my snowshoes throwing the chainsaw away from me and flailing around on my back in the snow like a turtle while the tree starts to go over, and you can't back up cause your hands and arms just go down through the snow....and I'm plowing with the loader but it runs out of gas in the driveway so I cant get the car around it to get out to town and get more gas so I have to take gas out of the chainsaw and other stuff to get enough into the front loader to move it..........and the whole time your breathing really hard and wearing about 20 pounds of clothes, like when my tractor got stuck in a big burn pile and I had to run from the river back to the house and get the old loader to pull it out and the tractor front tires were on fire and I barfed, Sumpum!

Yesterday I went with Floyd to his ranch to get more firewood, which reminds me of when he hired me to help him log a satellite tower cut block way up on a peak and he drove his big skidder up onto my 30 foot gooseneck and it lifted the back of my one ton dually off the ground and then the truck and trailer and Floyd inside the skidder with his foot stomping on the breaks went rolling down the road with me trying to get back in the truck before it jackknifed...oh I don't want to remember that right now, but later following his finger through the woods I'm pulling his seven ton skidder up a very steep narrow logging road with three hundred feet of cliff on one side and the truck starts spinning out. I'm thinking the clutch is slipping as we're sliding backwards down the hill and I slam the clutch in and hit the breaks, but the engine is redlined and sucks the air filter half way down the turbo charger with a great big Bang that sounds like a gun going off in the truck. I loved that Cummins one ton dually diesel. Just the other day there were a few of us sitting in my cabin for some morning prayers and one of the guys actually had these big tears in his eyes talking about how much he loved to hear his big old 550 horsepower 10 wheel drive Cat purr! We thought it was pretty cute to see a logger crying about how much he loved his truck.

Anyway, we were running out of wood and there's too much snow to get my equipment down to the river woods on the lower part of our property and get more. Floyd had a hernia operation so he's just running the skidder and instructing me. I thought we'd just cut a big snag Aspen or something on the side of his logging roads, but there was too much snow to get get down those roads unless we took his snowmobile in to where his bulldozer is back in the woods and tried to get that out. There's these big old bulldozers around here that have another engine on top you have to start by pulling a rope and then that engine starts the bulldozer engine. There's this guy we call Brutus that is great to have around to start the engine that starts the engine, but he wasn't around so we had to log up the side of this double black diamond steep mountainside in five feet of snow. I have to carry the big chainsaw and drag a long choker cable behind me and your falling in the snow up to your crotch and snow goes down your boots and you have to try and take your next step out of the snow and up the hill and you slide backwards and all around. Then you have to dig out the tree and fall it so it lands in a way that you can skid it out without it hanging up on other trees. I've done a lot of that on flat ground without snow, but when you do it in the snow on a mountainside it's a whole different ball of wax. The tree hits the bank of snow around where you dug it out on the hill side and bounces around like a teeter totter, then it slides down the hill, you have to try and get out of the way when it starts to fall and your falling all over in the snow. One broke in half as it fell, so the top half is falling back down on top of you...and they're around 100 feet tall. It's hard to believe people do this for a living.

Floyd's my dear friend that shot his nose off with a shotgun climbing over a fence. A few years ago he scraped the top of his head off when two trees fell on him and pinched it. They checked and actually his head scrapped the bark off the tree which doesn't really surprise me with Floyd. He lost both his parents when he was 19 in a head on car crash and was left alone with his younger sister to run the farm and survive, because of this he saves every piece of binder twine over five inches long and ties them together in big balls in case he ever needs more string. He works so hard that when I was teaching him to make fire with friction the Native way, we were all laughing that he didn't need wood, he could start a fire with friction the way he shovels buffalo dung! He's a "Big old tree of a man" but when he read this he said, "Who the heck are you talking about?" and I looked at him and realized for the first time he's just a normal sized guy. It was -39 yesterday! I was real happy we got a load of firewood.

'Freedom to Choose What We Eat'

After four years of public outcry and the bankruptcy of most of the few remaining family farms that thrived in this valley and across Canada and the United States until the last couple decades, the government backed off on another law lobbied and marshaled by a few giant food monopolies that prohibited on farm slaughter and local direct sale of meat grown on family farms like ours. So this year with a lot of qualifications, I am allowed to do what people have done since the beginning of time again, without getting fined or thrown in jail.

Being able to choose what we eat and refuse to eat, and in the case of animals, how they are raised and slaughtered, is a basic human right and freedom. I'd like to tell you first hand, a little bit about this issue of the family farm, what you and I eat and corrupt corporately lobbied laws presented under the guise of, 'Food safety.' It's about our health and our food, but it's also about our culture and our most basic freedoms.

School children, local families and tourists from all around the world visit our ranch. I see them moved by the same beauty and culture that made me want to move to Canada. I was helped and in real ways, taught how to survive here and farm by the local people who grew up here doing the same thing. Every person that visits the ranch is moved by the way, "People in Canada live close to the land and each other". The family farm and process of growing and providing our own food ties us to the land and to nature intrinsically. This bond fosters an honorable respect and appreciation for life. Plants, animals, water, weather, people and the earth itself are all experienced as life giving. This local, meaningful way of life together with our growing awareness of the finite resources of the earth is the answer to a sustainable future, economy and truly safe food supply. Global food monopolies and the lawmakers in bed with them destroy family farms and Canadian culture, it's not just bureaucratic ineptitude, it is a corrupt agenda that turns everything, even people, into commodities. It is a basic human right to provide and insure our food supply. It is a basic human right to choose and to refuse what we will eat.

The ongoing and recent deadly E-Coli poisonings are a product of commodity driven, industrial agricultural practices and laws exactly like these. Outbreaks of deadly anti biotic and acid resistant e-coli contaminated meat all originate from modern inspected large plants and from the very way this new law would require us to operate. This industrially produced meat has poisoned and seriously injured thousands of people, sometimes resulting in death. Contamination spreads to 100's of thousands of pounds of meat as the processing plants mix the meat of many animals together. One lot of meat all processed at the same plant is then packaged and sold under as many as 12 different names and trucked to multiple states and provinces and multiple retail stores.

Because of laws like these, large plants are able to dictate price to farmers. With this power they monopolize the entire process of farming from seed to packaged meat. Farmers then have no choice but to quit farming or sell their young animals to the plant where they are raised on feedlots. Trucking animals, in our case buffalo, over avalanche threatened mountain passes and under the stress of being handled and separated from their herd and then lining them up for hours in an alley head to tail while they wait to be killed is just plain sad in every way. They have lived a happy life here in their natural social order. The end is always hard, but it can come with almost no stress or fear to the animal when you just do it the same way a good predator can, instantly.

On the feedlots they are fed an unnatural mixture of feed laced with antibiotics so that they are able to survive under feedlot induced stress and gain weight as rapidly as possible. This high protein and carbohydrate feed causes unnaturally high acidity of the rumen. Bacteria in the rumen then become acid resistant and the acid in a person's stomach that has killed e-coli and other harmful bacteria for hundreds of thousands of years can no longer do so, once the person is poisoned by the acid-resistant bacteria, antibiotics are not able to save them because the bacteria have also become antibiotic resistant from the feedlot process.

Food safety is obsolete if you don't have any food! Allowing the government and big corporate interests and lobbyists to control and monopolize our food results in the loss of local infrastructure and reliance on centralized infrastructure. That infrastructure is inherently and unavoidably vulnerable to disruption. The food you buy in the grocery store has traveled an average of 2,400 km. From bird flu to all kinds of natural and man made disasters, this centralized, industrialized, mechanized, unnatural, closed system of food production, processing and distribution can be disrupted or shut down very possibly for months at a time. All leading authorities state that these kinds of disasters and disruptions "Will" happen. Local food production and economy solve this problem.

In the extremely unlikely event that a person were to become poisoned by e-coli bacteria from an animal killed on my farm, they would know exactly where it came from and it would not go beyond their immediate family or circle. The e-coli would not be acid or anti biotic resistant. I know each of my customers and their families personally and consider their well being as important as my famiies. We are all members of the same community. My animals are harvested as humanely as possible one at a time on fresh clean snow. The chance of any person being poisoned by meat raised and harvested this way are virtually non existent and the last thing on earth I would want is to poison my neighbors. This real bond between people is the way to insure trust, honesty and safe food.

When I moved to Canada and to this community of Golden B.C., 16 years ago, I found a thriving local economy and culture of family farming. Much of life still revolved around the growing of food. That process is intrinsically cultural and involves all kinds of local and extended professions, small businesses and resources. Land was valued intrinsically for its ability to produce food and not only for real estate speculation, sub development and recreation. In the 16 years I have lived here I have watched this local culture and economy begin to vanish. This law threatens to put me out of business as a viable supplier of meat. Of the hundreds of people I have spoken to about this on the educational buffalo tours I give, I have heard unanimous and often vociferous disagreement with this law. Any politician looking to gain or keep a job needs to consider this. There is virtually no public support for this law and any perceived support is reliant on ignorance of the issue. Reading this letter from a simple farmer should help convince anyone that the position of the government and the big plants they are in cooperation with is utterly indefensible in a public debate. Serious politicians should consider the risk they run if they are forced to try and defend this law publicly.

I wrote a letter to the minister of health at the time this law was first introduced. He wrote back with a letter I found condescending stating that the people of B.C. "Deserved" to have a "Safe food supply" and not answering or addressing even one of the same issues I have brought up in this letter to you. I have news for him, the people of B.C. don't want the food he says they "Deserve." In creating new laws and regulations in order to fix something that isn't broken, the government not only destroys family farms and the small businesses they support, they waist tax payer money. If you work for the government it is your legal, personal and moral responsibility to act in accordance with the truth. Constitutionally, those in authority in Canada are mandated to "Good governance", instead through laws like these they gradually destroy the beautiful fabric of this awesome country. They destroy families. They are given the public's trust. My family has experienced the blatant breaking of that trust by government. When they break that trust they hurt people and the environment they have been elected to protect.

If you appreciate what an important freedom, choice and civil right you are relinquishing to big corporate interests when you allow them to usurp such a basic human right as being able to choose what you eat; I urge you to take positive actions toward protecting those rights and along with them, your food supply, the family farm and our shared Canadian culture and heritage.

Sincerely,
Leo Downey
Rocky Mountain Buffalo Ranch
Golden B.C.

'InSpiration'

One of the most beautiful mysteries I have entered
Is the mystery of the buffalo
As creatures they are a 'people'
A buffalo nation
Of a Great Spirit
On my land I have a vein of Red Clay
It stains their robes like blood
They are a chain linked by ancient love
The kind legends are made of
And I knew one

I saw him kill bulls and lick calves
To be in his presence was always an encounter
It took about six years for him
To say, 'Okay, you can come closer'
I saw him in my dreams
They're the only ones that wander alone
Because they aren't afraid, of anything
They win every fight they ever have
For as long as they live they won't give up
The first one they lose is the last
He did more than inspire
He was a living InSpiration

As he died I breathed his last breath
He closed his eyes and cried one tear
Mine felt like a sea
In dreams he'd tried
To give me his strength

But I was afraid
I didn't have the guts to take
What I long to give
I'm learning
It's the same with God
His strength is his InSpiration

There are two worlds and it's okay
Spirit in form is art
But one world believes in what it doesn't believe
It takes a lot of its kind of faith
To believe in a God that doesn't exist
To give up meaning-more
For meaning-less
To see but be visionless
Is what the 'world' does
But not the Earth
And not her creatures

We have something holy to give
To take it
Our body grows wings
And our soul grows guts
We have to stain our robes with blood
Just to live here
I want mine to be sacred
And it is
Every drop I've shed to live
Brings a sadness
And a gratitude
Life is something every creature
Dies for

What we perceive as separation
Is more than an illusion
It is our own Oneness
Our likeness to God
In Christ I find Man
I don't lose myself
And either does he
He's not afraid of anything

To believe in him, really
...Takes guts
It is so unbelievable to believe
It is his breath I breathe
And that it's not wasted in me
The Creator and the creatures
Teach me that Beings
Mean more than ideas
And that God above all
Is a Being like me and like you
Who's soul I want to give a home
He fills with his art
His guts
And His InSpiration

For me
To be an Artist
Is to become a prayer

'Chester'

CHRISTMAS 2012

He went the way a wave too big for its depth walls out. I couldn't get outside of him. He held for the last moments and came down on himself, and me. I put my hand on his head, one tear came out when he closed his eye and then all mine came out for my old friend, my buffalo king. I put my face right close to his. He breathed his last breathe and so did I, he breathed it out and I breathed it in. It was minus twelve and he came out on the air the way the mist blows out the end of a wave. I prayed I could save his great spirit in me. I cried for my friend, not a drop of false sentiment, but the way you love someone innocent, how they give you honor you don't deserve. I felt it from the Condors too, they say they carry the souls of the dead to heaven, I hope they carry his and mine there. Nobody blames them for the things they can't do and they don't know how to live in the world of man any better than I do.

Brothers came to help me. His hide was two inches thick in places. Life is graphic and there is this kind of unavoidable violence that stains everything. My friends blood was on my hands. He couldn't get up, I had to kill him and I will eat him, and then I have to live the way he did or I receive him in vain. But how do I do it, I don't even come close. I tried to feel his spirit but I feel empty. For the same reason I wouldn't give the job to someone else, I have to believe in him, whether others do or not, whether they judge me or think I'm not good enough, even when I begin to believe them. Consuming his beauty is very hard, it's finding life in death. In a way the only thing I have to give anybody is what they don't believe in. I want to love them the way I loved him.

He left me a beautiful son, how could a King ever have been that small and how could I ever have been that innocent? Life takes it out of you and love puts it back in. When your world ends it takes a long time again, like those great Pacific swells no one forgets. The Universe was once a baby and soon it will be again.

'The Voice of Creation'

When I wandered in the wilderness in a prayer, I felt I belonged perfectly, alone, like Adam before Eve, I remember feeling, my God… I am just as much a part of Earth and creation as these creatures around me and I remember being struck to my soul at how everything, was 'Listening.'

Animals, insects, plants, stones, sand through my fingers, even the sky, they were listening in a State of Innocence. There is power like a giant sacred spiritual generator I find in the prayer of the wilderness I find nowhere else. I could say it's like the few times I have been in love, I'll never find what a man found in a woman in anyone else. It's the same way I feel about my ancestors, my ancestors are exactly who they are and no one else, no more anyone else than you are. I've tried to quiet my mind, I've felt like the only thing that gets me 'quiet' is passion. Music and its performance, to be in love and Wandering in the Spirit, faith in the meaning of what I believe and the unbelievable realization that it's actually true, miracles I can't deny, bring me into passion, a place where I give everything I have to give, for some surfers it takes the face of a giant, then I'm quiet.

Listening as if your life depends on it is a way to become quiet, so quiet it's almost like you listen beyond everything for that One thing your life depends on. Your motivation to meditate or visualize or to actually pray isn't to somehow 'progress,' it's a desire to live… in the fullness of what life is. First all thoughts of the world of man fade away as relatively meaningless, then even your own highest thoughts become kind of like distraction, it's not that they aren't good it's that they are like noise obscuring a Voice that speaks beyond you and everything; you begin to hear it. I remember a priest at the Monastery a long time ago, my very first time there, told me that if I listened God would really speak, and I remember I trusted him and I listened, and then this sequence of bells going off, what we call the Angelus and how I brought the story of them back to him and the bells went off as we spoke and things like this. I am finally getting to know what he meant and that he heard the Voice of Creation. It speaks to every living thing individually and as one with a love that I believe is our very existence. The deer and the tarantula and mountain lion and the condor, the oak alone on the savannah and the grass swaying across the high meadow portreros, they are all 'listening' with this innocent but incredible intensity, and it makes them so quiet…they open themselves and become vast and you enter into the vastness, with them. They listen to each other and their voices travel in circles as from a pebble in a pool, out far beyond them and I would hear them too and I'd know. It was so beautiful to know from these seemingly unrelated sounds and flourishes that pretty soon I was going to see people, even a certain person, or a bear and then, there he would be and sometimes I had others with me and I could tell them it was going to happen and it would. There was nothing special about it, I was just listening to the Voice of Creation like creation was. You become one of them and one with them and in a way all you have to 'do' is 'be' quiet; and Behold.

There are practical ways and examples to enter into this listening, like every sacred mystery it is where the spiritual and physical meet. Animals do listen as if their life depends on it and listening that way works as a vehicle to get past the noise, but there is no fear in it because fear is loud. You let go of every other voice except the One that's whispering because even the loftiest become noise, that is the Voice of Creation, its whisper is deafening for the volume of its Meaning, the same way that to see an eyelash of the Virgin Mary's beauty is to be blinded by love. Is that religion? I don't care what it is, I care that it is, and the unbelievably amazing thing is, that it is, all of it is and that She is, I'm not talking about an idea, I'm talking about someone that is Real with a real voice. That's the point, I'm not believing or forsaking an idea, I'm believing and loving a human being, like you. How could I forsake you after you showed me the Heart of All Things? Why do we stop listening and get scared? Because as we did from the very beginning until Mary, we listen to a Lie and I think we actually know it's a lie, at least on some level, but we believe it, we believe it's our voice and then we act on it and perform its tragedy, the way the young gunman did in New Town Connecticut, he listened to the voices of destruction and thought they were his, the way they want all of us to.

I used to think the thoughts of others were mine, that their voice was my voice. I guess sometimes I still do, but now I catch it and let it go. I couldn't tell the difference between the Voice of Creation and the voices of destruction, I've learned painfully, but gratefully, that when people are mean or disrespectful to me they are under the same spell and they can't tell the difference either. It's not their weakness, we can make room for all the weakness in the world through love and all someone has to do is ask. This voice condemns and does all it can to make you believe you are not good enough for God or His creatures to love you. It tells you you're stupid, there's something wrong with you and that you will fail. But Love loves the least of us, like a child; sometimes this has been and still is my only comfort. I feel and believe something that seems so beautiful to me that I have to share it, even if it turns out I am what the voices of destruction and his minions tell me I am. I used to hear that voice and think it was my own, it wants you to give up to prove it is right, to let go of greatness, of your vision and your faith. It rarely comes from within anymore, but I recognize it now in the conjuring's of other people that think it's their own and I do all I can to have faith instead.

The Voice of Creation speaks the invisible beauty of love into the visible and audible realm of form. This Voice Creates through you and me, its own creation, its Self, the Soul of the Earth and our flesh and blood, I believe that is who Jesus was and is, God becoming His Creation. Speaking his Word his Voice; Jesus does the same thing God did with Him… with us. He's returning from the inside and the world is getting ready without knowing it, but we'd all know if we'd listen.

Sometimes I think people hear it but they're scared and don't know how to get quiet enough to listen. I know what that's like, at one point I turned to alcohol, I listened to its spirit, its voice and it tried to kill me, but the Voice of Creation overcame it with me. When a man overcomes spirits he learns amazing and beautiful things about himself and them. They're real and they don't want us to know because once we do they can't fool us into thinking their voice is ours or anybody else's. I've said the world needs more artists, I hope it does because it's the only thing I seem to know how to be and because I think a true artist helps express the beauty and meaning of truth, but I couldn't be being an artist if it weren't for people that love me and that know how to be other things that are just as much if not more important. The world would be on a giant turd-hunt if all we had was a bunch of artists running around!

The most important gift and skill an artist develops is the discernment of beauty. If I look deeply enough I find beauty is one with meaning. If as an artist you 'love' then you 'care,' you learn to 'listen' in a way and with a will that discerns beauty. It instills passion and makes you care even more because beauty is filled with hope, it says the truth is actually true. It's not just music, it exists in more or less meaningfulness in everything, every-thing, every idea, every religion, every thought…the depth of their meaning becomes the illumination of their beauty. Their meaning becomes their holiness. Beauty, Meaning and Truth live as One in a Trinity of Love and the Voice of Creation speaks with these three in perfect Harmony. If you want to, you begin to be able to distinguish voices like a three part harmony, whenever one is off you can tell, it causes an ugly stress, its affect is always the opposite of the LifeForce we long to be filled with. A "Voice" doesn't have to have an audible tone for you to be able to 'hear' it and discern its origin and authenticity, but it's, 'Deceptive' and difficult, art takes everything you have and that is what makes art what it is. As a singer/songwriter I'm constantly discerning, I'm making choices between good and better and whether what I am singing is authentic, both the word and the voice make me ask myself am I authentic? It's an eternal journey and honestly I don't know, in the background of my every breath I pray with all my heart that I am, but it still takes all the belief and faith I have to hope in the end that I will be. I think the ultimate purpose of art both for the artist and for those that experience his or her art, is to recognize the Beauty of Truth and that that Truth is alive, a Person, like you and me, and a God who is Love.

When I hear the Voice of Creation, I create with it. I often use the relationship of man and woman as an analogy, my relationship with this Voice is like being in love. It's an inspiration like falling at first site, even through tears it is always creative and from the Heart of Love. It doesn't condemn, it calls, and sees through everything ugly, weak and deceived about us. It looks on all things, on myself and on all people and all thoughts and even death with Love, nothing can make it stop loving, God I want that love. It is the Voice of the Spirit of Love. It discerns light from dark, truth from ugliness and it shows me, me, inside and outside myself, but it doesn't criticize, it loves. It is exactly the way Earth has spoken to me all my life. She's tested me to where all that was left between life and death was one breath, and I had to respond the same way the native people said a man must live his vision or be a walking dead man; but She has never judged me. This Voice directs toward life, creation, beauty, meaning and truth. It finds what is real and expresses it through anyone that cares enough to listen to it, but that's what it requires of each person it speaks to, we have to, 'Care' with every atom of our heart, with this willingness to let go of everything if that's what it takes, that's all 'sin' is about. Love and Care are the same thing, one is the cause the other is the affect. It's not so much a brow furrowing effortful caring, it's like loyalty to your lover, it's the voice of your lover and your response. But here is why I'm writing to describe it, because there are other voices speaking in their own dissonant harmony, a whole choir of them listening to and believing what can be called, the voices of destruction. Sometimes they are heard and spoken by other people to you. Sometimes they are thoughts you believe are your own and sometimes they succeed to get people to act on them and then we have tragedy after tragedy that our modern world is afraid to call evil because then they would really have to make a free-choice. Here are some of their characteristics.

They usually have a twisted or rationalized element of truth. They are always insistent and accusatory, they never feel good although if you've been listening to them long enough you will lose the ability to know what good feels like and you can become addicted to them and to those that speak them. They berate and serve no purpose other than demoralization and destruction. They will use any and every means they can, even pity to get you to believe in them and to get others to believe what they tell you about you too. They want you to feel a never-ending guilt, a kind you could never feel sorry enough to satisfy because the voice is too proud to forgive. I'm talking about real presences with real voices that want to overwhelm you, but you think it's you or if they come through another person you think it's them. It's not a matter of reasoning with them because they are unreasonable you will only go in circles. No matter what you do, even something seemingly good, if it is in response to their condemnation it will bring no good, because it is for the wrong reason. To respond to them is to affirm them. There is no sifting through them or figuring them out, it's a matter of discerning their dissonant lack of beauty and meaning and recognizing their dark purpose and the affect they desire, and then refusing to react. As soon as you recognize they are not the Voice of Creation, the only way to get them to stop and avoid their destructive intent and affect, is to refuse them, and if you don't believe in God, God help you, because what they really are is a, 'Curse;' hatred is always a curse, love is always a blessing. When you refuse every voice accept the Voice of Creation the Voice creates through you. The more you do it the more it becomes the only voice you want to hear, it is always peaceful and still with a deep energy that pulses and invigorates, again much like the energy we feel when we're in love. Responding to the Voice of Creation takes faith, passion, enormous energy, and a different kind of 'effort' because it's like falling in love. But here's the thing, the only way we can hear it is to resonate with it, like all the rest of creation does, that's all 'moralities' about.

The Voice of Creation tells the truth and confronts me with myself and it can be painful because it Illuminates my Conscience and I'll see where I'm not responding with love, but it never shows me my 'sins' or my 'lack of love' in a way that discourages and demoralizes me, even when it breaks my heart it awakens a sorrow out of nothing but love and its whole purpose is to show me the way and encourage me and help me have faith in love and in my true self. When your own thoughts speak this way they are speaking with the Voice of the Creation, when they aren't, they are cursing you with the voices of destruction, refuse them the same way you would refuse them to set foot on your land. If they won't go, you need help and it's there if you humble yourself enough to ask for it.

Pride doesn't like hierarchies, but nature both relative and divine does. I see Earth's hierarchy everywhere, the social structure of the buffalo is just one example of billions. Every atom of everywhere is part of a harmony of hierarchy, and in the unseen angelic world the hierarchy is infinite, it is the Communion of Saints. To me it's like the mystery of the Trinity, we are each an infinitely sacred eternal individual and we are each One. In the voice of God, His Son and the Holy Spirit who is one with Mary through Holy Matrimony and through His Mystical Body, and through God's flesh and blood with all of us, I hear and feel the Voice of Creation. They aren't disembodied voices, they belong to Persons, like you and me, I know them by their names and they know me by mine, the same way I love you and you love me. They speak a perfect Triune harmony, a Trinity of Love, with no beginning and no end, but each with their own Voice listening to the Voice of Creation and singing in harmony with Gods and ours. They don't sing in harmony with His because they have to, they sing with His because they are overcome with, by and in His beauty and Love. His beauty is irresistible to anyone that hears it, that's why I listen to it, but if somebody could sing me a better song we'd all be bound to listen to that, that's called being committed to the truth, there is no allusion to personal perfection in that commitment, it's the opposite, it's a state of sincerity and humility that allows a person to 'Listen.' The way to beauty is beautiful and those that walk it are beautiful, they see beauty where it is invisible, through faith, where it is covered in hatred, accusation and condemnation, of others and of themselves, through love. The measure of truth is love. I want to walk in Faith, not a faith in the world of man, but Faith in the Love of Man, Who's Voice of Creation keeps saying, "Love; love no matter what, no matter what you hear or see, no matter who the voices of others and of your own thoughts tell you, you are, don't believe in them, don't believe in what you don't believe in, believe in Love with me, really believe, enough to see what happens! See how they hated me and accused me and condemned me of everything you've ever done and how they still do and how I kept and keep loving and believing in you. Believe with Me and in Me and you believe in you, until my Voice is yours."

'Free Will'

WINTER 2014

In the darkness, I learned to feel angels. They weren't the kind I asked for, they were the kind I was giving my will to. They taught me the hard way, to tell the difference, between the feeling of Death and Life, of Darkness and Light. It is the feeling of the presence of Beings, different 'species' of Angels, very similar to how I felt creatures in the wilderness. They don't care how positive I am or how 'good' I am, they care how honest I am. If the only soldiers you know are angels, ask one of them to hear your confession. If you're feeling oppressed, harassed, hopeless, addicted, in anguish, 'stuck';

~ The problem is your Spirit, and the answer is Angelic

If you're not feeling the deepest peace exuding beauty like being in love with every holy thing around you, and free, where you're will is yours because it's Gods, where your thoughts are discoveries, gifts, like living words in the book of life, that amaze you, not only for what they mean, it is the realization that they are actually True, and that the truth is better than you could dream, where you feel the power of angels around you, peace like a whispered song that's yours to hear, and if the lion has not become a beautiful fear;

~The problem is your Spirit, and the answer is Angelic

Believe whatever you want, you have to

You can't escape it

But then instead of trying prove you're good, prove the Truth is, prove Love is, prove God is, to yourself.

In his last words he cried, "Father, why have you forsaken me?" He gave his Being, his Spirit, he gave everything, the way a mother would for her child. Angels bowed down and knelt in an unending prayer of the adoration of mans Beauty, and a man in the presence of those angels kneels in ecstatic Gratitude, for love that conquered everything and that nothing can stop, not even our hating him and what he asks of us, holiness. Through Christ, mans flesh is no longer limit, because it becomes Gods, and so does ours. That is the whole point. Limit like sin and like flesh, is transformed into Glory. In the first born of the Immaculate Conception and in all her offspring;

Glory becomes limits purpose.

But you can also believe they are just ideas
And make yourself an idea along with them...

The night before he was betrayed
In agony, he prayed
The same prayer three times
He didn't want to do
The greatest thing he ever did
And God sent him an Angel
To console him
That's what they do
You feel them
As the presence of His power
And as subtle as smoke
Rising in the redwoods

God has angels
God prays
I pray for God
His planets are heavenly bodies
He veils his Bride with the Sun
The stars are light breaking through
The lace of her wedding gown
We have no idea
How Holy God Is
But we will

There is nothing worse than to be in the presence of angels of darkness. They work their way in by lying to you, to take your will from you, but they are their own downfall, because they prove that God exists and is a Being, not an idea. This is why they hide until they are commanded to reveal themselves, name themselves, and answer the interrogation of those Christ gave authority to over them, don't believe me, believe them. When hell breaks loose, things fly across the room, beds levitate, atheists become incontinent. You don't have to believe in them for them to be as real as you. A lot of things that are hard are just the life of a soul in a body, but my humble advice is to pay very close attention to the nature of your dis-ease, and ask for help, so maybe you won't have to learn the hard way along with those around you. Ultimately it is a call to rise, and become another kind of man and woman, the kind who's will is truly free. That is what holiness is, pure, ecstatic Freedom.

Many of my friends are stronger than me. I watch them with admiration and I'm trying to learn from them. I try to focus on how holy God is, and how good the truth is, instead of how holy or good I am.

The Communion of creatures I follow is holy.

We share a Mystical body

The only requirement is honesty

When this is my first desire, I am an artist.

Gods will is Free

He asks us to be

He asks for the passion of a lover

He asks for everything, because he gives everything

His reason for being Man

Is his Bride

The martial art of Angels is the wielding of 'Free' will

'Why'

Is it your question or your reason?

Is anything real? Is it an atomic accident? Is it a nameless force, whatever I decide it is? Is it a living being like you and me whether I decide it is or not? Does it matter, do you care, do you guess and agree and disagree? What makes any of it matter to me, is why. What's real for me is why. I've always wanted why.

Are you spiritual or an atheist? Do you think you're a Christian or a Buddhist, or a mixture of ideas? We're free to choose, when you do, do you ask yourself...

Why?

How do I know whatever I think I know, in the end, isn't it because I believe it, isn't it faith? And whatever that faith is, whatever it is I decide to believe and believe I don't believe...

Why?

My why is alive

My why are beings I love

My why is the beauty of

Why they love me

My why is who

My why is you

In every child

With a Cross

And a mother

And a question

That's a reason

One man's accomplishment

Freedom

From doubt, death, darkness

From evil

Overcome by Love

The question worth asking

The answer worth giving

Living meaning
The only one
That makes everything real
Is why

'Ours to Hold'

An artist gives his being
For the beauty of it
Reaching to touch the One
That turns those that touch him
Into artists too

True to Our Nature

Ideas can be partially true, kind of like people. I've had good intent, but intent is like art and love, partial is never enough. Everything creates in its own image, You and I, male and female, Gods image. You know in this weird way, our divinity lives in the separation, love lives there like life, separation the oneness of God, sovereignty the price of freedom.

We are more like God than we think. God is free too. Nobody can force him to be true to his nature, he doesn't even have to be love. I think people feel like somebody's forcing them to be good, like God's saying 'Love me or burn.' But what if it's not one or the other, to love God or not. What if I love anything or anyone I want and what I want the most I love the most. What if that's my 'God?

What I ask myself is, what is worth wanting and loving the most? What and Who is beautiful enough to be my God? And then with my whole heart, mind and soul I've wanted to want it, enough to find if it's true. It hurts to find out it is, but it's too beautiful to resist. I want my life to be my prayer, in the wilderness I came to call it 'Wandering in the Spirit.'

What we love we become. What we love becomes our creator. But for a great mystery, I have yet to love my God enough to become much 'like' him. I ask to experience and express his beauty, to become his body and blood, I want to bleed it and be it, and then I fail tragically and you know what, even that makes me more like him, because humility is beautiful. I realized in the Monastery, the holiest person I ever meet will be the humblest person I ever meet.

I'm in love with him like a father or a woman, or a child and a Mother, or Earth when I'm alone with her, or an innocent creature I hate to hurt, but I've had to eat to live. Does a lion feel bad for his nature? I don't think so I think he feels true to it, and so humbled, he can't even judge himself.

'We Are Altars'

I wanted something different
I didn't want symbols
I wanted what they symbolized
I wasn't looking for friends and singing
Or for good ideas
Or for someone to inspire me
I found that in everyone everywhere
I was looking for the mystery
At the core of my being
I wanted the sacred
I wanted God
He found me in the wilderness
We tracked each other to ourself
Alone with the whole universe
He gave me his word
With his beauty
Quiet like distant wind
In the trees
From Condors wings
To Thunder and lightning
And a silence too still
To wonder
The highest thoughts distractions
Can we be quiet for a minute
And listen
Like Earth
With faith the world was losing
I sought the sacred and I found it
Everywhere when I found it somewhere

Love is never limited by loyalty
Whatever is holy is good
It is never either or
But always and only more
Like a child or a woman
We are altars
Kneel at mine
I kneel at yours
To do what Christ did
With Her
In Her
Become one flesh
Don't believe in either or
Believe in more or nothing
I pray to offer myself with him
To become who 'I am'
Not a symbol
God's blood in Man
Earth the altar
Sanctified by creatures

'We'd Love What We Wanted'

I stopped thinking about people
The good things we did
Or bad things we did
And the name's we said
We did it in
I walked onto Earth alone
I asked God to speak to me
Even stones spoke the truth

I wandered with creatures
I believed with them
They didn't lie
They didn't sin
They didn't hate
But our souls had flesh
We killed what we ate
The grass in every blade
The deer the lion the snake
True to our nature
It humbles a soul
To carry a body
I had nothing and everything
The whole Earth to myself
Alone with them it felt like heaven
I found the utter joy of peace

Then I thought of people
How if they came
They'd destroy it
Compared to the heaven of Earth
The world seemed hellish
With wounds we inflicted
Instead of praying we were thinking
Did we love each other
Or what we wanted
What was free to all on Earth
We sold our souls for in the world
And I'm one of them
Putting Gods love aside
I loved what I wanted

But if you were there
On Earth
With me
Alone
We'd see
The brilliant burden of the Light
How love is the height
Of every thought, word and action
How not being good enough
Has made us even better
At forgiving
And living for innocence
That sets souls free
Alive to be holy
To pray with Gods Body
And die
For each blade of grass,
We'd love what we wanted

'Fight'

As an artist
I've spent my whole life reaching to express beauty
To the extent I have loved
I've created something
But I look at a flower
Or a snowflake
Or you
And I feel an ecstasy

Everything is an expression of its Creator
Look around
Every living thing is an artist
Creating in its own image

The most important part
'The Heart,
Of all things'
Is, "Why?"
The Reason

I describe what I believe
To express the beauty
Of
"Why"

I don't want to
To convince you
I want to want to
To convince me

Like a flower
Gives her scent
Beneath the heel
That crushes her

You might think you understand
My faith
But I don't think you understand it
Anymore than I do
I can't begin to till I do
With my whole heart, mind and soul
Because it isn't a thing to be understood
Anymore than music is notes to be read
But a Being to be Known
We cannot Know ideas
We can only Know
Who thinks them
Each other
Beings
The only way I can know you
Is to love you
And to love you
The way God does
Is the only way
I'll begin to understand
Christ's Faith:
"The hope of loving that way"

We might not cherish a human
When its old
Or before its conceived
In the womb
Or in the world
Maybe when it dies
We'll see
But I look at each living thing
And see something holy
Sacred
Unexplainable
That we exist
Free

Like God
What he shows me
Is me
His treasure
His work of art
His child
His Mother
You and I
Becoming totally vulnerable
He proved his unconquerable power
To Himself
For me
To see
That in his body
I may do it too
And say with every breath
"It is done"

But this is the reason in time
I want to share
We are not a worthless treasure
We are the prize
Our soul His
The masterpiece
Alive
Forever
To rise
Or fall
Into the hands of God
Or whoever
And whatever
We love
More
We live
With no idea
Of how sacredly, critically, infinitely precious
Every second of breath is
Its value exists
Whether we know it or not
Even right now
The same way a lion does

To a deer
The unseen world
Of angels fallen and exalted
Souls condemned and set free
Is much less different
From Earth
Than the same

Do you think your soul is unwanted?
When all around us
Is a frenzy for a morsel
History is ours and our ancestors
Shared experience
Of time
When it happens it does
It has
It will
It unfolds
To Fulfill

This is the reason
"Why"
It's not to feel good
Or to get what you want
Go ahead you're free
Believe in anything you want the most
We have to
We can't escape it
Earth is in-between
A 'Worldwar'
Of Worlds
That are Real

Hitler was a paper hanger
His authority wasn't his
There is no armistice
With his Fuhrer
His serpent strikes her heel
And She, the New and Everlasting Eve
Queen
Of Heaven and Earth

Crushes his head
With her beauty
Her holiness
Her Love
Her Son
Her Creator
How can I waste my thoughts
When I have pierced her heart
To reveal them?

I fell on its sidewalks
I tripped in its cracks
Hell is paved with the dead
Heads of priests and religious
That turn away
From the Sacred & Holy Communion
Of their ancestors
To devour and vomit
Consecrated souls
Sucking them down like toilets
Drawn in sin by demons
Wolves in shepherds clothes
That serve up their own flesh
Not Gods
Learn to tell the real
By being one!!
It's not pretend
Nothing is
Not a single second
We can't fight a little bit
For both sides
And if everyone waits to be saved
Who will be left to help them!
We are not saved against our will
But saved by being given the will
Of Christ
No one has to take it
But that is what he gives
It is one will or the other
Not an illusion
Or a positive idea

Freedoms price
Is the objective reality
Of choosing
Heedless of opinion
Death or life
The way my father and his friends
Gave theirs for ours
War
Can't you see the smoke
Rising in the temple
Don't you hear the drumbeat
Echo in the halls
Valhalla is the middle ground
Between heaven and hell
Choose Loves side
And help each other!
Fight

'The Most Important Thing a Man Can Have'

My uncle Albert would brush invisible crumbs off himself kind of like Art Carney on the Honeymooners. He was big and nice and had a kind of low i.q. level. One day my Dad came home from school and went up in the attic where the model airplanes he built out of whittled apple crates hung from the ceiling. They were detailed, scale models of real planes of his day. Albert had gone up there earlier and smashed them all. Dad was heartbroken, he'd put so much work and love into those models. Dad told me, "Poor old Albert, I knew he didn't understand what he'd done. The other kids used to beat Albert up, he'd come home all beaten up, and he was bigger then them. One day I told him, Albert, you've got to hit those kids back!" He said, "Okay Richard, if you say so." The next day at the bus stop, the kids were making fun of him and pushing him and Dad said Albert socked the biggest bully right in the nose, and the bully started crying, and after that nobody tried to beat up Albert, and you know how that goes.

But Uncle Albert told me what the most important thing a man can have is, and that's what I want to tell you. Albert was a janitor his whole life at a high school in Portland. He retired and came to visit us in Santa Barbara. I was about fifteen. I remember he was standing in the hallway, brushing those crumbs off his sleeves and off his pants. He said, "Good morning nephew, ya know what the most important thing a man can have is?" and he looked at me kind of funny. I wasn't sure if he was joking or what, but I said, "Uhh, no Uncle Albert, I don't know, what is it?" In a low voice he said, "Leo, the most important thing a man can have"… (and then his voice got louder) "Is a good pair a shoes!!" I said, "A good pair of shoes?" He said, "A man can do whatever he has to if he's got a good pair a shoes."

Later that day, I told my Dad what Albert said. I can't remember what my Dad said. I told my mom and my brother and sisters and a couple of friends, imitating Uncle Albert and thinking it was pretty funny.

About two years later I limped out of the Sierra Madre's with pieces of my mule hide rattlesnake guards cut and tied to my feet. About a week in I'd gotten lost and had to come down off the side of a steep mountain range into a valley. My boots were falling apart. The whole sole of one ripped off so my foot was sticking out with the boot around my ankle. I sewed the soul back on the best I could with thread I made out of yucca plants. The spine at the end of each long leaf turns into a needle with the thread already attached. I had silver dollar sized bleeding, oozing holes in the backs of my heels, the boots would grind in the dirt and sand and then peel away, every step was so painful, I can still remember it. I had to walk backwards up out of the valley. I was supposed to meet my Dad 3 weeks after I'd left in the little town of New Cuayama. I was hobbling along the road when he drove up next to me. He looked at me kind of funny and said, "I guess Albert was right."

'Be Small'

No matter what you say
Some people will agree
That's why it's so important
That what you say is true
I can think whatever I want
What matters to me is
Does God think it?
With cobalt body and golden wings
She fought her prey beside me
And inches from my eyes
I watched her paralyze
For her larvae lives a tarantula
I laid there in the sand all day
From the burrow she dug
Like a dog for a gopher
Till she laid her eggs
Buried her prey
Kicked leaves in its place
And flew away
While I watched life like this
A rattlesnake snake slithered by
It took will over instinct to be still
And I was hungry
But I let him go his way
And I thought
What do I know?
Nothing
These being's are light that's alive
Like me

They fight to survive
I'd left the world where I'd tried to be big
For Earth where I thanked God just to exist
And I was amazed by it all
If you want to transform your world
Into the whole Holy Universe
Be small

'A Bridge'

After the war when my father retired as an aviator and Naval Commander, he became a scientific consultant. He designed, developed and communicated the implementation of technical systems, usually in the field of marine environmental safety and maritime battle systems. This entailed carefully assessing every aspect of the need, and understanding precisely, the abilities and limitations of technological systems he coordinated into answers.

Assessing need, answering it and then describing the implementation of that answer in writing, so that others could carry it out, required precise clarity. He insisted on that from himself, looked for it in others and tried to instill it in me. He wouldn't tolerate flawed logic, circular reasoning or conclusions drawn on relative assumptions. His words were punctuated with silence. He insisted we communicate so that we said what we wanted to say as accurately and as clearly as we possibly could. That means first discovering exactly what it is you want to say, and then saying it in a way that means it, and not something else.

Certainty is a conclusion he only came to after exhausting every reasonable possibility. To come to an accurate conclusion about anything and then express it accurately, requires reason above knowledge and 'precision' above everything. On multiple occasions in the war and in the air afterwords, he saved his crew and his own life by answering chaos with precise reason. To generalize anything with accuracy is to understand it precisely. Whatever it is, art, history, matter, science, atomic and sub-atomic physics, human nature, religion or spirituality, there are two pre-requisites to an accurate answer; love of truth, and precision. When I look through this prism, I find the world is the opposite of the Earth.

In past chapters I've told you something my father never mentioned and didn't give much credence, he was a genius. Intelligence is not knowledge, it's knowing the nature of answers. My father believed with my holy ancestors. He knew what he believed, his faith, and he was as faithful to it as he could be, his love, but I wouldn't describe him as especially 'spiritual.' Our religion is what we believe and what we believe we don't believe, our spirituality is our experience of it. He was more cerebral than emotional. My mother was very intelligent in the opposite way. She was sensitive, emotional, artistic and 'spiritual.' I think I became a bridge.

> To be a bridge lay down
> And love both sides
> Be where they meet
> And touch each other
> Across the divide

As an artist, an author and a man, I want to be a bridge between Earth and the world, Spirit and flesh. I want to track beings across the ancient bridge between life and death. A bridge serves a purpose with beauty. It draws from both sides across what is deep and dangerous. It's a place some people go to die, and others cross to live. It carries value. It joins opposites.

My book ends with deep, extensive links into knowledge, evidence, subjects, people, places and phenomena few people today are aware of or know anything about. Studying them opens us to a new world. I approach life and work as an artist, but I exhaust reason to come to conclusions. I don't rest certainty on the relative. Much of what I've been tempted to use in order to prove my point, I've left quietly till the end, for you to discover and decide for yourself. Cross the bridge, I can promise you, the other side is fascinating.

'Falling'

I remember thinking it's impossible, how can anybody be true to that kind of love? I thought of God and of Jesus as more masculine than any man could possibly be. Then I saw myself through a Virgins eyes, the way she saw her Son, and he saw her, and God changed, I changed too, but I still feel wimpy compared to anyone truly holy. It reminds me of the way Chester came to me in my dreams trying to give me his power, I was afraid to take it, until the day he died and I breathed his last breath.

When things happened out on Earth alone, I wanted her nature, everything that happened, and every wild animal, felt pure and innocent, it was a peace that was power. They took me into it. Nothing disturbed it, even the fear was beautiful. I wandered with all of it, I thought this is Gods living creation and he is creating it in front of me, for me, and I am, a breathing, sweating, loving part of it.

I'd come back out to the world, weak and as strong as I'd ever been, not macho, masculine. I wanted to see how long I could last, fast and be a prayer. If it wasn't for work with the band, it was hunger that drove me out, sometimes I was skin and bones, not like Christian Bale, but I'd burn up any fat in the first week and then burn muscle for a month. I'd eat snakes and fish and then see what they saw, in flashes, shooting through the waterlight over the stones or slithering on the ground behind my own heels.

In time I saw the only way to be lost was if I couldn't get to water, my thermometer went to 120f and sometimes it was pegged by 9 a.m. At the end of a long Californian drought, a lone condor watched me for a day and a half, I'd crawl out of the last wet beaver pond and fall asleep under a tree, he'd land, hop closer, and check to see if I was good and dead yet.

All the animals would be going to the same water hole for miles in every direction, even snakes, and I would too. I made mule hide gators. I've been struck at many times and hit a few, but they never sunk their fangs in. Rattlesnakes are usually as surprised as you, that's why they miss. Anyway, I feel this resistance when I talk about it because I think it might seem like I'm trying to sound tough. But I told you, I'm wimpy, animals and holy people are tough, that's not why I'm telling my story, it's because it was so amazingly beautiful to be alive, to exist as one of Gods creatures. I've lost him tragically at times, but then I see I was never really gone. In a way, he loves me the way my friends do.

I saw how everything is conscious, plants have feelings and emotions, life eats life, creatures have to kill each other, but out there, there was no hating, no lying, no betrayal, no compromising, no dumb ideas for the world to swallow. At first I was scared at night in the open, on the ground. I couldn't see things moving around me, but it wasn't like the world where my fears were buried so deeply under other fears I didn't know what I was afraid of or why. In the wilderness I listened, and I heard why. After a few years the wilderness was home. I had nothing and I was happier than I'd ever been in my life. I felt honor I've seen in the eyes of Native men before the white men destroyed their culture.

In every group, hypocrites and selfish people attract each other and move like moods do through a person. In every name, there are people that mean well but who's intellects aren't formed by a love for the truth, so they're kind of...dumb. A lack of love for the truth results in an inability for us to identify what's worth thinking. Genius is thinking what's worth thinking. The peace of God is an order so perfect that only one thing can disturb it, the pain of our rejection, and that's why I began to write this.

I said I used to think it's impossible, to respond to Christ with his own nature, I'm just a man, with insatiable appetites and disordered passions, a human. You gave your life and every breath to us when we hated you, to show us we couldn't make God stop loving us, what kind of man can do that... Sometimes, living for this peace and innocence feels like a battle against myself, and instead of peace, I feel conflicted for not being able to resist what I experience as temptation to do things that are beneath the truth and love, things that aren't the way the Earth and my Creator are for me, but because of something that happened in the wilderness, that I've lived for, whatever I've felt, even anguish and heart break, even the edge of despair, gets turned into a prayer, into art.

Holiness, love that is pure and perfectly powerful undisturbed peace, beauty that keeps building and bursting and overflowing; is art. Holiness is the art that makes life art and living things creations. Art might not seem important, but it takes my whole heart, mind and soul. Reaching for beauty is reaching for God. It's hard, awkward and unnatural feeling at first, like playing the guitar. It takes faith. You obey your master, you trust your teacher. You have to keep believing, I can do it, I can create something beautiful, if I give it everything, and it's worth everything, because it's real, it's true.

I have to maintain that faith and fill my heart with it, but, at the same time 'judge' every nuance of my creation and discern the gradients of beauty. I have to want to recognize the infinite ways I'm missing it, lacking it, not aware of it yet and not caring enough to reach for it and touch it, like a man and a woman that actually love each other. It takes your whole life. You sense with a sensitivity that grows, and eventually what I thought was beautiful in the past, isn't anymore, and I have to let go of it. It's the same with the illumination of our conscience. Like art, it's reaching for the highest beauty to be, to think, to believe, to feel. Reaching for the highest beauty is prayer.

When God is a living being like me and you and the creatures, I experience art. I don't want to fall, I love the power of peace, but when I reach I fall. Falling isn't about punishment, but it is about betrayal. I love God the way I've fallen in love with a woman, I can't resist her, I want to love her the way he does. But in different ways, I fall, and she forgives me, and the mystery is, it makes me better.

The aspect of art that's martial, like a prayer in war, is a weapon too heavy to hold, like believing in God a little bit, or succumbing out of beauty into something forbidden out of beauty. God's love is impossible to hold, it has to be constantly sighed for. It's singing a song, it's loving someone, it's reaching, and it's falling.

'Mud Spelt Backwards...'

Is a way my dad said dumb. He didn't mean to be mean and either do I, but the funny thing is that some of the dumbest guys my dad encountered, were other geniuses. I remember him with this pained look on his face, saying, "How can somebody so smart be so dumb!" The genius club sent him the quarterly magazine, we'd read this dumb stuff, and then we'd sit their muttering, exasperated together, I miss it. I see now, the ones we were muttering about were using only one part of themselves, their mind, their intellect. We are created to use all our heart and all our soul too.

I've only seen my dad cry twice, when he told me Mom died, and once about the war, when he told me what he had fought against, was what others fought for. What Hitlers followers did made him angry, but with tears in his eyes, me too. It's hidden, but it comes again, contagious, it spreads like germs in lies and dumb ideas, but what I'm talking about is worse than dumb, evil perfects itself in the holiest places, through wolves in sheep's clothing. I've learned to recognize its presence the hard way. One of the most repulsive things about it is how lame and dumb it is, but it's why who you believe in is important. Who you believe in is the only one that can help you, or take you to hell. Whether we know it or not, it's really beings we follow, not ideas.

I've noticed doing anything creative is three things at once. Everything, including a good idea, is three things at once; heart, mind and soul. All three are free and also one, in a life giving relationship, like mother, father, son, a Trinity of love. Love is what Christ left us, not just his perfect words to argue about, but all his heart and all his soul. The most real things Christ left us are his sacred living mysteries. The most mystical of them is him, in his body. Christ doesn't make Earth and the body an illusion, he makes it real by sanctifying it, he makes it unlimited by glorifying it, he makes man the symbol that is what it symbolizes, his image, the image of God. In my experience, if it isn't real, it just turns into another dumb idea.

The world doesn't seem to have a clue, because the world doesn't pray, it's too far away from Earth to want to know what prayer is. Our bodies are a billion times more than what we think they are. To use them in vain brings condemnation upon ourselves, I know from experience. They are living arks, Gods blood vessels. Our bodies are the mothers of our soul. Life is the souls gestation and death is the souls birth and it's real and it's important. Like Earth, our body is where the angels sword comes down and every human being, beyond ideas, beyond language, even all alone in the jungle, knows their Creator and makes a decision, of who they want to believe in, who they want to love, who they want to follow, who's creation they are, who they want to be. We don't track thoughts, we track who thinks them.

No one is born dumb. We are taught to be dumb, the way white people are taught to hate black people. Being dumb is something you have to insist on, like prejudice. It's desiring something else more than the truth, and it's refusing to be precise because you don't want to see, not because you can't. It's an unconscious desire for nothing but the basics, instead of the beauty and passion of detail, it generalizes everything, it says what is similar is the same, it's beautiful enough now lets not get in trouble, but the worst thing about insisting on being dumb is that we believe ideas that aren't true and then teach them to everyone else.

Coming to conclusions that are true sets me free, that's how I know if they're true, but the world teaches me that to enslave myself is freedom. Divine Reason like love, is not relative, no one and nothing can take it away from you but you, its reason is the reason for all other reasons. It is a desire, an art, a path and a way of wisdom that can only be carried and passed on in living holy beings. We can excel in relative and even in holy knowledge and be dumb. Being dumb is a lack of love so I know, I'm dumb, with all this stuff, I've been the dumbest person I know, but the souls I track are artists, and they ask me to grow. Being dumb is a lack of formation of everything beautiful about a human being. It's the difference between the world and Earth.

For me this is intelligence; before thinking, doing, saying or believing anything, ask why, have a reason, only the most beautiful reason you can find, forever.

Why is a question I can't answer, but a reason I can have. I track souls that turn why from a question to a reason. Sincere, loving, faithful people can be 'dumb', by wanting something else more than the truth and not caring enough what it is we are faithful to or why. We become bad art. Before I believe anything, I ask myself why, is this the most beautiful thing I can find to believe, and if it isn't, I don't believe it. Presented with two things to believe, I ask my Creator, which is more beautiful, this is discernment, the Holy Spirit is the artist. What is more beautiful is always what is more true, that's what the souls I track do.

I'm not a leader, I'm a follower. I really am a Soultracker. My holy brothers and sisters, the angels, and the creatures of Earth, teach me, they live to teach us all, the most beautiful reason, why. The hierarchy of souls Christ left and leads is an infinite gift, the opposite of the limitation the world believes. The worlds why is a question no one can answer, Christ's why is a reason, no one can take away.

'It's You'

Am Wi was seventy years old and four foot nine inches tall. My dad came home one day and she was way up high in our lichee tree, he said they were both laughing as she tossed the fruit down to him. We all thought she was wonderful. Singapore in the 70's was an exotic mixture of old and new, east and west, the open Orchard Road market was full of the freshest food, brought in from surrounding Kampongs and from the sea that morning. Orchids breathed into the monsoon washed air and mixed with the squeals of pigs and clucks of chickens men bled in concrete pools there. They arrived in rattan baskets on the backs of Honda P-50's. It was virile and real and I had to get used to it.

It wasn't until my brother came to visit that we found out Am Wi could speak english. We'd been there for almost a year by then but we thought she was speaking Chinese. I have a great brother, as a kid in Monterey he taught me to read and in Singapore he taught us to speak Am Wi's language. He translated her words for us and pretty soon we were all speaking it too.

There was this big hairy, red spider that would come out of a hole in the ceiling when she took a shower. She turned on the hot water to show my brother, and it crawled out. She said, "Am Wi no! whoo-lie seepiedah, tooooo many feet!" Richard said, "Am Wi no like spiders, too many feet" Once he showed us the way she said things, it was easy, but we didn't understand a word she said until he helped us.

At dinner one night my dad said he'd had a meeting that day with the president, Lee Kwan Yu and the minister of defense who's name I can't remember. They said if he left the American company he worked for and came to work for them directly they would pay him four times his present salary. I remember overhearing him talking with my mom about some of his colleague's disrespectfulness to the Singaporean's, with a tone in his voice verging on disgust. The president's offer was for more than his genius, it was because he recognized my Dad respected people.

The memories inspire a prayer in me of respect too. If I could see the best in every person, enough so they could see it too, I'd be loving them the way I want to. It's funny because for me to be able to see the best in others I've had to keep facing the worst in myself. That's been agonizing at times, there's a lot to look at, and it hurts. Lately, it seems like we're supposed to keep telling ourselves how great we are, but it doesn't work for me. It doesn't work to tell myself I'm rotten either, I'm not fit to judge me or anybody else, so I focus on the good in others and how holy God is, and I track the souls that love the way I want to. All the negative or positive self judgement and judgement of others becomes kind of meaningless and 'my' thoughts seem like noise.

Most people are trying to love others and help others. My friends help me everyday. But there is a lack of precision, in what we decide to believe, like trains of thought that never reach their destination. The world's going faster and faster, with the people, waiting to jump off when the breaks are gone. Common sense, miracles, visions, apparitions, messages and the prophecy of almost every tribe and path, foresee a time like no other, a time where true survival skills are of the soul. I know what it's like to be hungry. If you were afraid you might starve, wouldn't you rather starve loving each other, instead of hating each other, and isn't it love we're starving for anyway.

Every soul on Earth enters a wilderness, a desert of the heart. To be born and become a man is what God does, and a woman gives him birth. They are inseparable. To live and die here for love is glorious no matter what anybody thinks of us. To simply take a step here washed in the water of Earth's blood calls on a kind of courage demons don't have. One person at a time, facing ourselves, to pray, from the heart, really pray, our souls already know what it is, it's how they breathe and see and rise up out of us to overcome everything that's not true, to become light to darkness.

We're already Soultrackers, prayer is our way. I look back and prayer is the most beautiful thing I've ever done. Nothing in me lives up to anything, and I don't care, it can't stop me, we are a million times more than what we think we are, we are a prayer, and prayer is more than thoughts and wants, prayer is love. To pray is to love God and be so small my universe becomes infinite. It's beyond asking, to give, everything I am, even just for a moment, a second, to be honest. To pray is to say, it's not my weakness, and it's not my thoughts,... it's alive, it's you.

'One Again'

I know we're One
My separateness from God
Is my likeness to him
If it weren't for love
God wouldn't be
A he or a she
He'd be alone
God gave his own flesh
To become a man
And man gave his own flesh
To become a woman
We begin and end as one body
It's not an illusion
Life is real
We are real
It's out of love
We're separate
It's out of love
We're free as God
Out of love
He took form
To touch
Her beauty
And be one again

'Impossible'

I want to reach for something that appears impossible, but I've learned over and over, every sacred mystery is the opposite of how it appears.

When I was eight years old in Monterey, Miss Dahlberg, our young, pretty fourth grade teacher, asked us to make a list of all the things we thought were impossible and turn it in the next day. Every time I thought of something, I couldn't do it, because I thought, to say something is impossible, is to be 'certain' of something. A little exasperated, she said, "Leo, can pigs fly?" and I said, "Well, I know it's really improbable Miss Dahlberg, but I don't know for sure it's impossible" She shrugged, but I remember a little smile on her face I thought I saw again years later on Mona Lisa in the Louvre.

Later, when I began wandering in the wilderness alone, I finally thought of something impossible... not having sex!! arrrggghhh! I was lying on my back in a high Portero of oak savannah and huge sand stone rocks the Chumash call the first people. It was their Garden of Eden, 'Sipoxi', the House of the Sun, where they believe the Great Spirit first put them on Earth, and where condors soar to carry their souls back to him.

That day, I glimpsed between the world and Earth and I heard and said to myself, "I am here to be a holy...man" That was kind of weird, but I thought, yes, I want to be a holy...man. What that meant to me was a man that 'really loved', but for an exquisitely beautiful reason I'll describe later, the next thing I thought was, "Wait a minute, would that mean I'd have to stop having sex and girlfriends" "That's impossible!" It was so impossible that I didn't even take it seriously. It was a quick series of thoughts that ended with me wanting to be a good guy, but not a holy...man, because I thought it was impossible.

Femininity, breathes fragrance into the mist's of Earth, and gives birth, to beauty in men, they are the male source and destination, the force of nature is a female, sublime, daughters, virgins, lovers and mothers, tears that hear, sigh and whisper, they surrender to overcome, I'd be dumb to resist. Their beauty is impossible.

Holiness is impossible beauty, impossible to touch and impossible to resist, the moment before a kiss, that waits weightless, cusped in the palm of a hand and held, like a wave posing to crash forever, like legs on a ballerina, arching and floating, in arms, that embrace her to release her, but never forget who gave her to you, who she belongs to, the same One you do.

I've tried to live like a rock star, like an Indian, like a monk and a monk on vacation, like a man, a husband, a father, I've tried to live like a body, and I've tried to live like a soul, like Earth and like the world, but it's taken me fifty years to live like a bridge between everything.

I've always desired the impossible, that is what art is, to me, that is creativity, to live in a mystery and let it stay one, unknown. Playing guitar, music, songwriting, asking to be judged, feeling naked in front of people and singing; besides petrifying me at first, it was like electricity. I'd listen to musicians I loved and think, I can't see it, but I can feel it, how do they do that? I wanted to with my whole heart, mind and soul, I still don't 'understand' it, I hardly know a relative thing about it after a lifetime of learning what it is about music that isn't relative, the part that is alive. I've just touched it, like a woman God gives me, to fall in love with. I want to live for beauty, for love, to see love in everything real, in people.

Veiled old woman, kneel with a smile at me, your prayer is for the young ones, with hope and brightness like gazelles. I picked one flower forever, I married her in a harvest and lost her in a storm. Now how will I walk through the field, they float like spirits around me, flowers of a feminine fragrance, budding open, to beautiful to pick. The only way I can resist is to find something more beautiful, and give it to them.

The kind of power Chester showed me, offered me, and finally breathed into me, is the kind I get from God. It's having faith in him, so he has faith in me, so he can trust me with the power of the beauty he reveals. It's like walking around with lightning in my heart, it can be scary, because a man can hurt people, and a woman can let a man hurt people. When you reveal beauty to someone, even their own, you become like kites in a storm. The path of the soul is single track and ancient, one soul following another like the path of the buffalo, together, we follow it alone, to join everyone and everything. What makes us one, also makes us alone, what makes us one makes us free, what makes us one makes us like God. That is the responsibility of holiness. It's impossible to touch and impossible to resist.

God and People

My purpose is to express meaning, not to judge people. If I did want to judge people I'd have to judge myself first and the show would be over; what I want to do is love people. There's a vast gradient of what people believe, experience, express and do and I know people of different faiths and people that don't even think about God much that are giving, loving, sincere, kind, generous wonderful people. I also know people that think they believe in God and act lame and I have to include in that category at times myself. That's part of why I'm writing this. It's like helping someone to be a better artist by being a better artist, it has nothing to do with telling them they're bad, but everything to do with expressing the beauty of meaning. For me, the meaning of truth is beauty the same way that God is Love.

Usually when people think about God and religion, they don't; they think about people. I hear it all the time and it perplexes me. "Believers' and 'nonbelievers' both do it, they judge God by people. God is who God is if God is, and religion is a description of who God is. The perfection of description is art. Symbols including but not limited to words are our medium and 'Meaning' is what they exist to symbolize. Meaning is the purpose of symbols, and everything here in time, space and form is symbolic. We are the symbol, the image, of God. If we don't find 'Meaning' in what we see, we aren't seeing what it's there for.

If God exists I want to know God. The only way I can know anyone or anything is to love them, because what I love I become and I can only really know what anything 'is' by becoming one with it, that includes God. I remember at the end of a long prayer quest alone in the wilderness, this 'event' happened to me, I described earlier as the 'Angelus.' In it, I became my music. My music wasn't something I did, I was it. Religion is a description of reality. What matters about religion is the perfection of meaning it describes and how perfectly it describes it. It is art when it creates the thing it expresses, in you; it becomes what it symbolizes.

People do all kinds of lame things in relation to religion, but to say, I like spirituality but I don't like religion, is a misunderstanding of the meaning of the words. Religion, no matter who's, whether it has a billion believers or one, whether good or bad, is the intention, it is a description of 'what you believe.' Spirituality is the experience of it. It's the difference between knowing about music and playing it. It's the difference between faith and faithfulness. Your religion is your faith, what you believe and don't believe. Faithfulness is your devotion to it, your love, your spirituality, your experience.

But overwhelmingly what I find is that most people judge the meaning of God and religion by people, and what people do and don't do. On the subject of God and religion one person will talk about the good people do and the other will talk about the bad people do. On the subject of religion it's as if they were talking about music and they said, 'What about all those bad musicians, music is bad.' Then somebody else says, 'No, what about those good musicians, music is good.' But music exists no matter what people do good or bad. A sunset exists, one person doesn't care, one person sees God speaking to her like a lover. Judging a religion by people that do the opposite of what it teaches is like judging music by bad musicians. It's dumb. Their will always be hypocrites and people that act lame everywhere in every group, so what.

What matters to me about God is does he exist and who is he. What others do, and what I have to do if he exists is a secondary subject. What ultimately matters is does God exist or not and if so what is God. If he doesn't what I and other people do is all that matters, and if he does, he does no matter what anybody does or doesn't do.

As far as people and what they do goes, if they say something is true they should be able to prove it. That's what a saint does with his life, he proves what he believes is true. But no matter how profound his or her proof is, there will be people that don't want to believe it because they think they want something else more. I've thought before in different ways, you can't argue someone into being a better artist. You can't badger, condescend and accuse someone into being a better lover; you can only inspire them by being one yourself.

Does God Know What He Means?

To understand anything meaningful, I have to believe it. But I don't have to believe in anything dumb, that's what my intellect is for, to consider only the highest most beautiful thing I can find worthy of belief. I can't have the slightest idea, the slightest feeling, the smallest insight into who Mary is, until I decide to believe what she believed. If you care, I can give you a hint, she believed in God, she became his Bride, He filled her with Himself, Grace, and she gave him a Son that created her, and she gave us her Son and loved us as we hated him, didn't believe in him and killed him, she allowed her heart to be pierced to reveal the thoughts of our own, because she loves us the way her daughters will when they realize who and what they really are…

Everything about God and all his mystery is like that. If you're still asking yourself is this really true? You're missing the point and wasting your time. You have to ask yourself, 'What does this mean if it's true?' Find out what it means to you if it's true and then the only thing that can ever be more true is something that is more meaningful, more beautiful, more of the same. That's why I ask everyone, if you disagree with me or find error in what I'm saying, help me! by offering me something more beautiful and meaningful.

Whatever it is you believe, the meaning-fullness of it or the meaning-lessness of it, is what ultimately determines whether or not it is 'True.' All we can begin to know is, 'What it means.' Meaning is the measure and purpose of truth. To have even the slightest understanding of our purpose, our meaning, of God, of his faith, his mind, of what God believes, of who God is, of God's nature, the nature of truth, of love, of our true self and the immense reality that we exist! is to willfully enter a sacred mystery, and the only way we can enter the Sacred is to Believe.

Do you watch a movie telling yourself 'This isn't real, I'm not going to enter into the story and believe any of it because it's a movie?' No, your entering into and believing in it is what allows you to discover its meaning. The question, "Is it true or not?" is one no one is equipped to know with certainty but only come to believe through 'faith.' This includes people who think they don't believe in anything and don't have any faith, that is their faith. Everybody's got their personal 'religion' it's just what they believe and what they believe they don't believe.

Man creates God in his own image and then doesn't believe a word He says. We want to know what God means without believing him; we can't. I can't know a word God means till I believe it. I believe Jesus knew what he meant when he said what he said and he cared. Believing what he said about life, reality, truth, love, God, himself, his body, and you and me, determines whether I can know what he means and this is the reason it's important; because 'He' knew what He meant! and he cared enough to let us kill him to prove it to us.

There are two ways to 'get along', one is to be committed to the truth with your whole heart, mind and soul until what you discover unites you, the other is to not care about the truth and replace it with opinions, guessing, compromising and voting. Anything holy in any faith is good and many faiths have similarities, but that doesn't mean they're the same. Because people have similarities are they all the same? Because music has similarities is it all the same? Only if you are satisfied with a pathetic mediocrity and don't care the way an artist has to.

The passion of Christ is that he cares. To be an artist, to be creative, to be 'holy' is to not just do what God says, but to do what God does, and the only way to do that is to believe, it takes faith to create. To believe is like being in love, it is to care, that's what makes it worth doing, but to believe in something that isn't true is meaningless. I think all we really have to be is sincere… down to the last drop of our blood, because if you care enough, you find that the truth is true, and miracles happen.

A true artist discerns beauty through meaning. The beauty he expresses is like a prayer who's meaning can be as silent as it is deep. It speaks beyond words and thoughts like these, but approaches the center through our intellects. Beauty and meaning are really the same thing, Truth. If something isn't true it's meaningless. People don't Not believe in what God says because they think he's not telling the truth, I think deep down everybody actually knows he is, they don't believe because they think what God wants is an obstacle to what they want. To believe in a God that wants something for you you don't want for yourself is to believe in a God that is meaningless and to believe that you want something more than the truth is to lie to yourself. When we all stop lying to ourselves, the truth will set us free.

There are a million ways to express what you believe, by silently loving someone, by being God's Bride like Mary was and is, by receiving God's flesh and blood in your veins really not symbolically and finding out if he was telling the truth when he said what he said and if he cared and what it means to you.

It's not a mystery I enter because I want to sing songs and feel good any more than Christ coming to Earth and Mary giving him birth was something they did so they could feel good. What makes something feel good is its meaning, even pain. That is the passion of Christ. I want to believe what he believed because it's beautiful.

'The Only Sacrifice'

I was 33 when I entered the Monastery wanting and expecting to live the rest of my life there. I had these strange tears day after day for months, not tears for sadness, tears for beauty. The sacred mystery of my Communion is usually one told by a world that has never entered it. They think about people and the good or bad they do, instead of God and their mystery with him. The world has ideas of what it is, I did too. Their ideas about it are usually negative and painted with enmity, my ideas are positive and painted with love, but in opposite ways, we're both wrong, because it's not an idea. The wilderness and the Monastery were the same in a central way. They were both sacred, in them I offered myself as a sacrifice....and I was rewarded.

Months before, I remember sitting in the dirt, sweating in the heat, but cold, weak, sleepy in the sun, and so hungry. I'd left promising I'd come back with an answer, whether I was going to stay in the 'world' and keep playing or follow this call I heard into a mystery and the wilderness. Water holes I'd never seen dry were dust. I climbed into the mossy crevice of a spring and channeled cold drips of water into my mouth one at a time. I had to come back with an answer and I had none.

I started to wonder, does any of this, faith, matter, does God care that I'm fasting, giving things up that are good for what's better, suffering, that I want to know what it's like, to be one with his Son? I know God loves me, I want God to know I love him! I want to know I love him. I opened up the same little bible I'd found under a big pile of boulders in the middle of nowhere when I was a teenager on my first vision quest, and I put my finger down on this, 'Without faith it is impossible to please God, for he that cometh to God, must believe that he is, and is a rewarder of those that seek him' For some reason it's not politically correct to believe God 'rewards' us, but he does. He rewards me for my sacrifice the same way my woman would reward me if I sacrificed for her, with her love. He leads me into the desert of my heart and answers me beyond anything I can imagine, because his being real is better than anything I can imagine. I pray to trust God so God can trust me.

I know, nobody's supposed to offer a sacrifice anymore, we're supposed to manifest our ideas of what we think we want, and we can; but we don't know what we are so we don't know what we want. Modern Christians think to offer a sacrifice is some kind of superstitious empty idea. But it's not an idea, or a positive or negative thought, it's something else. Not the something else we spend our lives doing so we can do something else; it IS something else, like a song or the wilderness, or a buffalo, or blood or life. The only way I've ever known, is to do it; to cross the bridge, enter the mystery, and find out all by myself, why I believe and don't believe, what is real. It changes everything.

God turns anything I give him to good, even my worst sins, things I weep over. He can turn disease, divorce, addiction and even the drooling of demons, into a sacred gift, a sacrifice. The dark night of my soul ended when I woke to this beautiful nightingale singing, and realized, it was me. I want to share things with you that are private. Some involve others so I can't, but confession takes the secrets out of a man. When I write, it's my Monastery and my Wilderness. I enter the mystery hoping you'll enter with me, to track the Spirits words, privately, in confidence, the same way we'd walk into the woods, because Christ says, you are my responsibility and I'm yours.

It's not ideas, or techniques, or even the stories, it's beings. It's more than the Spirit's words, it's the souls who speak them. They're alive, they're real, really, and it blows me away. There is no substitute for the Earth and the wilderness. I disappear and my soul walks with the souls that are already there, but I'm learning to do it in the world where most of us are kind of stuck, like prisoners, without meaning. I've never found a path as beautiful as the path souls leave, to track theirs is to find mine.

There is no substitute for this Communion of beings, human and angelic, it's like saying I can substitute someone else for you. There is no substitute for you because there is no substitute for God. Christ could have skipped his final sacrifice and still left us his wonders, his holy and perfect word, symbols of the truth, but he's left us more, he left us his sacrifice, his flesh and blood, he sealed his life with his love. I'd love him even if he never rose, loving him is its own reward, he shows me passion, he offers me himself. I forget the world, hypocrites, myself, and I ask to feel how he felt, how Mary felt, when you love someone, you identify with them, it's why the more aware we are of how others feel, the more self aware we become. Think about only what's worth thinking about, that's genius. When I accept what he offers, I offer what he offers, Life, the only sacrifice beautiful enough to mean anything.

'Precision'

In a dream I saw the immense cost of imprecision, and it's all because we don't care. A God that is willing to be killed and feel forsaken, is one that asks me to use my mind for what it's for. All it takes, is to want to, enough to chose one thing over everything else, truth. Somewhere, even in the darkest heart, we all know truth is not an opinion.

He chooses what he gives his mind to, if I told this mountain lion, "I live as if nothing's actually true, I can't know so I guess" I think he'd say, "You're pathetic, you're passionless, you waste what I see every second."

Christ said, "Ask, and it shall be given to you: seek, and you shall find: knock: and it shall be opened to you." "You shall know the truth and the truth shall set you free." To know the truth is to know my nature the way the lion knows his. My nature is the embrace, the kiss, the mouth, the mind, the heart, soul and body, of God. It's not an idea.

Today, we think it's nice to say the spirit world is everybody's own opinion, but the world of spirits is as legalistic as music and as precise as a mountain lion. It's as far from an opinion as you are. It's another mother nature. One millimeter is the difference between strings resonating with each other in the precise unity of harmony, or the ugliness of deadening dissonance. Precision doesn't limit anything true, it describes it the way I want to describe you.

God believes he is capable of dying at our hands and by our betrayal. Either God is an idea or real, he's either dead or alive like you. Sometimes I don't know whether to smack or console, be gentle or severe, but I know one thing, I care. He doesn't show me hardness, he shows me passion, like a lion, he doesn't have opinions he has love, if you don't believe he is who he says he is, don't give me your opinion, give me someone more beautiful, more passionate. If you do, help me, be a lion, to use my mind for what it's for, precision.

'Into The World'

Last week I left the stillness of the Earth and rode into the world. I'd forgotten how much I love what's good in it. My eyes kept welling up and I thanked my friend for taking me with her. Her eyes welled up too.

The week before, I'd watched a film on Liberia's cannibal warlords, Charles Taylor, General Butt Naked, armies of slave boys and girls. The insanity was unimaginable. Some people doubt hell exists, I don't, cause I've been there, but if I did, there it is right here on Earth.

My actress friend told me I'm kind of intense, I said that's the pot calling the kettle black, but I am. I look at Earth from far away and think, I'm there, I hear the birds sing, I breathe, if I had guts, if I had passion, if I could be as gentle as a child and as brave as a man, I could help that place, if I don't I'm a coward. It can be daunting and I've been one. I tried to drink anguish to oblivion, I couldn't bear the thought of failing.

Everything good I've ever done came from a Spirit, I've seen exquisite angels floating behind my friends saying, don't be afraid. The world doesn't understand what I believe or why I believe it, most of them are just sure they don't. They use people as excuses instead of reasons why. When I think about God I don't care if the whole rest of the world are perverted hypocrites, they can't take away his beauty. His words are true. I believe in the real ones I've met here, people like you.

Somebody went down there and did something that changed everything. He put an edge on me to sharpen, not to harm anyone, to cut through a lie they're told and believe, and to track with my soul. It means being a child, a helpless human being, it means believing, only what proves itself true. I don't know if you need love or something to break you, I've needed both. The next time you judge, please be precise, don't think you're certain unless you're willing to die for it. Don't use weak and selfish people like me as an excuse. Don't settle for some stupid partial truth and non answer. Help me and everyone else. Please give me something beautiful, give me yourself, like he did.

'A Confucian Slip'

Thoughts are the tracks
Souls leave
Like mine and the animals
Faith is the beauty souls reveal
And faithfulness our love
Thoughts to souls
Are like tracks to animals
When they know I'm tracking them
They'll stop and look back
They check me out with everything they are
I've seen it with mountain lions and wolves
I don't keep my nose on the ground
I hear the ravens and blue jays
And wander with the Spirit
If I love them
Eventually they'll wait for me
They share the path
With Soultracker's

My thoughts are gradients of light that is life and existence. Light is what Love gives, what everything is made of, it is 'Being' out of nothing, out of a 'humble moment'. Love is better than anything I can think to want or imagine... In this way yes, the material is illusion, symbolic, in this way, yes, Love takes all that accept it, in our own ways, with our own beliefs and ideas, to the same place. But does this mean matter doesn't matter? That belief is just a tool? Does this mean I'm the judge of illusion and reality? Can I be? Do I want to be? I can only judge by beauty, what I will believe, I'd rather be loving and loved, like a child.

Precision, definition, knowing, believing, and following can appear as limits on freedom. Many think ambiguity is freedom, that because God is infinite light, their is no identity and the details of matter don't matter. But I think the opposite, because every sacred mystery I've ever found is the opposite of how it appears. That's why it takes my faith at first to see through, beyond and behind it, to the living thing that is expressing it. That's tracking a soul. God is love, everything real is made of love, but this doesn't mean that what we believe and who we believe in, who we follow, 'doesn't matter' It doesn't mean we aren't real. It doesn't mean be satisfied with the basics and just get along with each other, tolerating each other is not loving each other. There is so much more, and it's alive.

To me, it's about beauty. Love is art, Love is as complex as anything in the universe because it is life itself. Because we are all vibrating infinitely through every cell and thought and pulse out and beyond the galaxies, doesn't mean that we're just vibrations and that reality is just perception, that nothing material is 'real', that no belief is closer to the light than another. What fills me with hope, joy, inspiration, creativity, love and trust is the exact opposite. Everything matters as much as everything else, and everything, every single thought and belief and way and idea and person and stone matters precisely and infinitely. The details, especially about something I decide is beautiful enough to believe, matter to me, and when I let them, everything becomes more and more beautiful.

Reason is beautiful. It's not tiring, it's inspiring. The thing that is tiring and uninspiring for me is to oversimplify everything so it's easier, to make general partially true statements without assessing everything first, in detail, the facts, or to think I want to 'be God' and assume Gods authority. You know how a woman becomes one with you, with a man, that's how I love to become one with God. I think he finds it as irresistible in us as a man does in a woman. I don't want to be the judge of reality. I want to be an artist.

Love makes you an artist, and there's nothing more beautiful. I think after this hard time, the whole world will live for the beauty of love, the world and the Earth will be the same place, where all creatures are the friend of who is expressing us. I believe we will know our Mother and Father and they will be like us because we will be like them. Complaining about our weaker ancestors and using them as excuses to divide and leave and not believe, while ignoring the holy ones, is like complaining about our family.

God doesn't have to be Love. God is free to be whatever God wants. Light isn't forced to exist. The only appropriate response is to humble myself and if I'm not grateful, beg to be. God is free like us and God chooses to be love, the same way we do, to rise like a Cathedral of light and become his bride, it's infinite but it's also a baby and it's also you and me sitting here wanting to help each other.

It takes everybody facing ourselves, it gets exponentially easier the more of us decide to do it and I think almost everyone that's reading this already wants to, and already knows this stuff somewhere in their soul, but I also think a lot of us don't know what thinking is for, what we are, why we can be here, we don't think thoughts out to the source of their destination; who is thinking them. We don't care enough to follow the tracks to the animal, and see where they're leading, into the light or into the dark. Love rises and unfolds into life now, forever in front of us, a billion times better than we can ever dream or imagine, when slowly, we realize, it's true.

Earth makes the body strong, but the soul is made strong by loving God, that is what prayer is, the souls food is Gods blood, the souls passion is God's love, it consumes and gives birth to beauty, living beauty, alive, in us, it transubstantiates and transfigures, glorifies and incorrupts. He knew what he meant when he said what he said and he cared, that we do. To guess, vote and argue about what his word means is dumb, and he's not dumb. He left us souls to prove what it means.

When the world starts believing that truth is good, that God is love, it will begin to be able to recognize beauty because it will begin to see with its soul, I think it's speeding up and happening already. We will start making it much easier for everyone that's stuck and suffering and lost and confused. Whatever path we follow, is laid by living 'souls'. My responsibility to you and everyone else is to choose only the most beautiful souls as those I follow, and to determine that in precise detail, they leave the most beautiful thoughts, perfect reason, they walk into the light and love it in sincerity more than power, in trust more than will, in humility more than wanting.

I don't know anything, but I believe in the most beautiful One I have found, and the ones that believe with me. I listen to the souls that are already there. I'm more of a fool than anybody I could call a fool, I feel bad sometimes about calling ideas stupid, because I'm stupid! and because I don't want to offend anybody, but that thing where we insist on being dumb, it's so unnecessary and lame. It's insincere. There is no intellectual integrity in it. Face the truth the way an artist faces beauty. It's like my classical guitar teacher yelling at me and saying, 'Play it with Feeling!!" and me thinking, 'huh..oh...Yeah! you're right!!! Thank you!!!!!! Wohoooooooo! I get it! Yell at me all ya' want!!!' I was ten, he was Chinese, and he actually yelled, "Prrray it with Feerrring!!" A Confucian slip.

'Kintsukuroi'

(n.) (v. phr.) "to repair with gold"; the art of repairing pottery with gold or silver lacquer and understanding that the piece is more beautiful for having been broken.

'KINTSUKUROI'

He said, "My mission is to alleviate the suffering of every guitar player in the world" I said "Where are you?" He said, "It's easy, there's a halo above my house, guitars players from all over find me" That's really what he said, and then he added, "There's a map on my website."

My friend heard about Gary Norris from a singer songwriter who doesn't let anybody mess with her guitars, so we brought him three of mine. They were critical, in close to terminal trouble. All I was hoping was that he wouldn't kill them. The only person I trust them with is my friend John Mooy who lives in Santa Barbara and I hadn't been able to get to California to bring them to him. They call guitars axes, but I treat mine kind of like chainsaws. They go through the Canadian winter in my wood stove heated cabin. I've made my living pounding on them and always treated them like tools, but I love them like animals that have carried me through a war.

He opened the coffin and raised one out, my old American acoustic Fender. I've had to put down animals I love and my herd gives me and others food that I consider medicine. Learning to grab hold of myself has been a hard process. Death is the climax of life, I don't like to be overly sentimental about humans or animals or guitars and I don't polish mine all the time and stuff like that, but they feel like spirosexual instruments in my hands, and I don't desire to sleep with others. We've been loyal to each other with all our faults, the bond becomes kind of like a spirit or a third life. My hope, desire, love, pain, beauty, blood and sweat has dripped into their wooden bones.

My friend since our first days as professional musicians, *Pat "Good Times" Milliken*, used to laugh and insult my Fender, calling it 'Kindling!' Mine was buzzing and hard to tune and he had this amazing Martin. I couldn't explain why

I loved it so much. I've bought and played six thousand dollar guitars, but I always come back to this one. There was this deep tone in it I couldn't quite hear but I felt in there, buried under a ton of imperfections, like me.

Gary was looking and measuring and making the kind of sounds a doctor makes when he's discovering what's wrong with you. Then he started to describe to Lori and I how a guitar works and how the strings are meant to resonate with each other like bells sustained in the wood. He said, "You'll be amazed when I'm done with it, the whole thing will sustain and resonate and the strings will be in perfect harmony with each other" He plained the neck, replaced the frets, made new bone nuts and a bridge he inlaid like a hip in the saddle. He worked for three days and nights and then called us to come and get them.

Kintsukuroi; 'to repair with gold and understand that the piece is more beautiful having been broken'. Some people recognize this in each other. I've been broken to pieces. I thought I'd failed and I'd always be damaged. I've wanted to be strong since I was a kid, and I felt so sorry for being weak, that it almost killed me. There was all this advice of how to think, how to forgive myself, how to fix myself. I tried some of it, but their reason didn't hold water, none of it resonated through me like a bell, I just felt like a crumby broken bowl, that dropped itself.

I was a little afraid to touch her. I held my old Fender and stroked my fingers down her tensed strings. They rang like the Angelus, like the big iron bells I fixed one day for a real priest on Our Lady of Mount Carmel. All the strings ring each other now and sustain each other through the body and the wood. They feel like vocal chords. You know how they always paint angels with harps. They're always playing and singing this heavenly music. I've heard it before, in the wilderness once, I became it, half light, half matter. I was broken, but I'm better than I was before. You can be too. Sorrow melts the gold and purifies it, the Creator re-creates his vessels. He loves them with all their faults, he grabs a hold of himself and lets them break, so they can become perfect in his eyes and broken in their own. Faith was how he allowed me to be like him, because God is broken too.

The world is going to wake up, souls will resonate in perfect harmony and Earth will sustain us. Pray for the strength to break and start new, cross the bridge, trust the one who made you, his daughter says pray till prayer becomes your joy, follow the halos, God is a passionate artist, he doesn't care how hard it is, he asks us to be like him, but then, I've seen it, his angels bring his friends to lay living lilies at his feet, and kneel before me with grace I can hardly begin to describe, if you break with him, he'll fill you. Trust him and you'll help everyone around you resonate. Even if we break, everything is going to be okay, and so exquisitely beautiful, for having broken.

'Beautiful Reason'

There's practical things; like skinning a buffalo or making fire, handling a gun and other tools safely, finding water and food. There's knowledge; like detailed historical facts and the personal accounts of those who were there. And then there's perfect reason; not what to think, but why. I love perfect reason, I find it beautiful, I don't know how many others do, because I've rarely seen it change minds. I think people are so stressed out by the world, they just want to 'feel better'. I felt so horrible I tried to drink myself to oblivion, I was stuck and attacked, I found incredible answers, not the ones the world gives.

Part of what I had to do to feel better was to feel how I felt, what I was afraid of, what I was using my whole life force to resist so that I wouldn't even see what it was, and face it. I was afraid I had failed to accomplish what my life was for and I didn't see how I could. I felt like I broke the most beautiful thing I ever had, my family. To live, men need something to die for. Hitting bottom is where you have no choice but to confront it. I decided to express it creatively, meaning in a way that was beautiful enough to help somebody else, but I wanted to write today about a certain aspect of it. I think what I see stronger than ever in so many of us is a thing we all say we don't believe in, but don't realize we are, Prejudice; judging before we know what we believe is true.

Like white people hating black people, we're pressured into prejudice in hidden ways and we do it without thinking, we don't quite realize how afraid we are, we don't seem to use our mind for what it's for; choosing what's worth thinking. We love feeling 'right' more than the truth. We present the worst people in whatever group we're against while ignoring the good ones and ignoring the separate issue of whatever it is the group confesses to believe, or if they even know what they believe. Facts and reason seem to threaten and upset us, but almost never change our mind.

We mix things up, guilt with culpability, sin with sinners, we mix up everything! People think they're thinking about God, but they're thinking about people and the good or bad they do. People have been doing good and bad stuff for a long time, so what, I stop thinking about how holy I am and I think about how holy God is.

I wish you could go into the wilderness alone, and forget the world like I did, and be the first man, the first woman. Everyone should be able to, but even if we can't, we can still enter 'The Heart of All Things' not by following good or bad ideas, by tracking souls that are already there. That puts you on a path of a tribe. It's a tribe that will take anybody that wants the courage to love as much as they do. It's walking into a whole other kingdom with friends that are the most amazing inspirations, and leaving tracks in this one, and they aren't ideas! They're as real as you and me. Really! They don't need any help being real, they just need us to shut up for a couple minutes and listen.

We think we're thinking and talking about one thing, but we are mixing that thing up with a bunch of other things. I see it all the time, and frankly it's kind of exasperating, but we don't have to do that. Once a person sees the limitless beauty of Precision, that is; paying attention to detail and caring, the way you'd pay attention to the most beautiful eyes, you look into to find a soul, and give yours, it's not 'work', you want to pay attention because what you see and find is beautiful!

My dad loved truth like a woman, more than himself, he wanted to put her first. It's a deep joy to communicate with someone who loves the truth more than being 'right'. Like a woman, first you have to commit yourself, believe in her and love her and then your love sets you free; if it's True. In a way, I think most people today don't actually believe anything is true. They assume that to know something is to limit it. For me, knowing truth is being in love with God instead of my ideas.

I'm just an old dog, but I'm a loyal one, I track my best friend and wag my tail, a Soul, he tells me the truth, and says it's alive like me and him. The world thinks truth is an idea, a bad one. Most of us seem to operate under the approval of the collective conscious, and overly sentimental emotions, cut off and removed from Earth, our intellect and our Spirit. Instead, we think thoughts of what we think we want without knowing, caring or thinking about what we are. We question everything, but never precisely. Our lack of conscious thought results in personal attacks on people instead of an insightful evaluation of who and what they are following.

Do you think about what you are and why you're here and if anything exists that is actually true all by itself free of anybody's or everybody's opinion about it, if their is love, meaning and a purpose so sovereign and beautiful you can have it and be it and give it, no matter what happens around you? That question and how the answer came, was a miracle, the tap root of my tree, and in a way, I had to be willing to die to get it. Telling it and the others out of context is like tearing up the roots, so I planted them in the ground of a book.

In a dream a few nights ago, a friend asked me to join a protest against something that at first seemed like a good cause. On the way to support it, I met the people that were the target of it. The protesters were attacking them personally, in a way cursing them, as bad people. As I spoke with them, I realized they weren't that way at all. In this dream I saw a force of destruction moving through our lives and our world like a bulldozer. It is the unconscious yet willful 'Imprecision' of prejudice. It doesn't pay attention on purpose. It doesn't think to create, it reacts with lame emotions, and it causes 'Misunderstanding' that grows till it spreads between almost everyone. Most people have no idea what I believe, they think, if you can call it that, arrrrghhhh!, I believe something very different if not the opposite of what I believe, but it's like they don't really want to know, instead they want to tell me what they don't believe. I think a change is coming.

There is something important the souls I track have learned about love, faith and the mystical life of the Spirit. It is that Love is Art, the creative act, all our Mind, that is, our intellect, not a little bit of it generalizing everything, satisfied with 'the basics', and circular non-answers, so we can strum some chords, get along and be hokey. All our Heart, that is, our Love, because it sees its lover and wants her with every beat and pulse in its veins. And all our Soul, our entire being surrendering like a bride that would give her life for her groom, all of us, seeking the beauty of truth and seeing and giving it glory because it is breathing, loving, creating and alive like us. God is alive, everything real is alive and I'm pretty sure everybody knows it, but their afraid of it, because they're prejudiced.

In the dream I was painfully disappointed in myself for forming an opinion without knowing if it was true. I woke up praying to use all my faculties, my whole heart, mind and soul, harmonized, together, in beauty, with the Communion of Souls I track who prove what they believe is true with unequaled miracles, to seek the truth, by listening and loving as a prayer, precisely, carefully, choosing only the highest, most beautiful reason to believe anyone or anything.

'The Bear'

He was a big, beautiful shiny black bear with a brown nose sniffin' muck he was pickin' up with his claw outa' the river. I heard him comin' cause he crunched a stick. He looked carefree and happy like he was singin' a bear song, doh doh doh dee doh, all alone like me. I wouldn't a let him come so close, but I was lonely and kinda sad, I wasn't afraid, I already felt like I gave all I had, so I had nothing to lose. I felt that way with mountain lions and monks and fake monks and Tunnel Rats that chased people outa' the woods with an axe, and did much worse things than that. I was as free as the bear, but I wasn't carefree. Bears need to be bears and men need to be men.

Men need to bleed for something alive, their song is different, like the lonely one I heard an old Indian sing and beat on his drum at night in a storm through a winter alone, wandering, breaking the tips of branches the sun dried enough to burn in a stone, stove I made by a grass thatched hut I slept in. The world will know when it prays, for beauty instead of ugliness. I looked and listened across the river and she roared, me and the Indian, all alone, crying for everybody else.

Perfect reason is the one who's meaning exists in itself, it's the one every other reason is relative too, the one we miss the same way we do the mystery we exist. Perfect reason is reason for the rest. It's not a thing to think, it's a heart to love, it's beauty I consume to become a living food. Perfect reason is the one no one can take away because they can't stop it from giving. It's a Spirit like the Sun and it has One, that it loves and that loves it, and nothing and no one can stop it. Men are made for glory they don't know they become from the inside, like a child in a womb of a bride, Pride would not bow down to; a Woman. Earth doesn't know what one is, but it will, and then all its relative reasons will become relative to the meaningful for the meaningless, as they wonder at the beauty they missed. They'll say, the woman, the bear and the Indian knew... and I was there.

'Funny'

I'm not serous all the time, I'm serious! I write about the deepest, most beautiful thing I can find, but nothing feels quite like making a friend laugh where it goes to the next level, kinda a like a donkey.

I was at my friend, 'Not That Joe Walsh 's' dinner party, and I was making his friend Roger laugh at the dinner table with my John Wayne and Cookie imitation where they're out on the trail and Dukey is getting lonely and thinking Cookie's lookin' kinda cute. It's pretty hilarious if I don't say so myself and I was doing it just right.

I can't remember so good but apparently I was very funny when I drank. After diner, Joe and Roger were out on the porch finishing up some kinda concoction I'd invented. I knew they were gonna miss me cause I was so funny and wonder where I was in a minute, so I climbed up on a thing where a lamp was, in a dark corner waiting with a kind of humpy Lurchish look. They walked back in the room and didn't see me, I was looking right at them and then Roger looked up and said, "Gulp, what are you doing!?" "I'm a condor waitin' for somehtin' good n' dead to eat." You had to be there and drink my concoction, you would have laughed that way like a donkey and I would've felt good. I had a lot of fun when I drank, and it wasn't all bad, people need to loosen up! But really alcohol's like playing with a loaded gun, and I'm so happy I'm so happy without it.

I woke myself up laughing in a dream a few days ago. I was playing with Kenny Loggins at the Santa Barbara Bowl, he was singing and I was playing my Silvertone. We we're rockin' out. I wish Bonnie was in the dream too, she used to say I was a 'Stud.' Anyways, when somebody in your band is rockin' out, it's nice to walk over there and look at him, and dig it. I was doing some thang' on my guitar that was fun and Kenny came over and was diggin' it, which was cool, but then he started doing this 'Bump' kinda thing on my leg! I was goin', "What's he doin?!" but I thought it was so funny at the same time, and I was all embarrassed so I was kinda ignoring him, and I knew he wanted me to look at him and kinda dance around like I dug it but I didn't!

I hope you're laughing, I am!

'How I Pray'

I didn't know how to survive in the North when I moved to Canada. People that grew up here taught me. There was ice, snow, and the cold, on skin and machinery. There was farming and buffalo, how to work up and seed a field, how to hunt, skin, gut, cut, eat and use all of an animal, and many other things we do to live here. At first I thought of it like a science with one best answer. Life here has turned out to be much more of an art than a science, which is a big part of why I love it so much. I experience God as art more than science. Science looks at what happens, God looks at who is looking.

I've had a few people ask me how I pray. It humbles me to be asked. I've prayed a lot, but I've been a weird example. My life has been more beautiful than I could ever dream, and as hard as I can bear. I've needed a lot of help from my friends, and I've been lost. I've lost my family once and my faith twice. Each time, I didn't know I'd lost my faith till I got it back. I think I lost my faith because of my passion for it. I don't believe because somebody told me to, it has to be real, I believe for the honor. I went into the wilderness to find God, I did. I believe for the beauty. That beauty gives everything and asks for everything, it's not easy, it's art. God became his creation and lost his faith the moment before he laid his life down for it. It is the most beautiful thing he had to give and the most agonizing thing he had to lose.

Few people have had the experience of actually being lost. It's a very scary feeling to be lost in the woods, without food, and especially without water, but there are things you learn from it you can't learn any other way. When I look back on my lost faith, it was kind of like being disloyal to a lover. Both times, without being fully aware of it, I turned to something or someone else. Loving God is not something you can turn on and off, anymore than loving your woman or your child.

We think of lots of reasons we don't want to pray, because we don't know what it is. Praying is loving God, I can't know anyone I don't love. When the world loves God the world will know him. I didn't know what music was when I started, I still don't really, but I loved it for the beauty, and I believed, and I did it. Prayer is like that.

Praying for me is loving someone, so much that you become one with them, like I have the few times I've been in love. Praying is also like Wandering in the Spirit, wild animals, learning to survive, playing the guitar, singing and writing songs, and over the past few years it's become like writing a book and like living and breathing until prayer becomes my joy.

You can't know a person or an animal or an angel deeply without loving them, praying really is loving God and his creatures. It's a neat thing, like art, because as long as I commit myself to the truth and I'm sincere, even if I'm not that good compared to somebody else, I'm an artist. I loved that about being alone in the woods too, there's no comparing. Alone on Earth I felt like Gods only son. The souls I track, from all different tribes, all wandered alone on Earth in the fast of a sacred and 'sacrificial' prayer, it has been central to the most powerful things in my life, to miracles, it's tragic that the world has lost this prayer.

To a certain extent, I remain cryptic on purpose. I empathize with human animals because I am one. I'm a little scared to scare anybody, but the state of our soul is of immense consequence every second forever. The herd has a collective conscious. We are being affected by creatures we can feel, but we don't see, because they are beyond form, pure intellect, angels, of the light and the darkness. They are as real and as practical as mosquitoes and wolves. I feel like I have to whisper, one human at a time, or people spook at the partial truths, imprecise proposals and illogical assessments they've been taught to swallow without thinking them through to their end. Our spirits are being broken by this system, but somehow, I feel the whole herd waking up, I feel Gods grace pouring into us. Maybe people are praying….

Soultracking is praying by getting as close as I can to the souls that are praying with me and for me. Souls that love passionately, love God as inspiration, as beauty, art, as a man loves a woman. I pray by tracking souls, with my intellect, my heart, my being, my body. They are real, animal, angel, human, I smell the fragrance of their bodies, I look for their tracks everywhere, I breathe their breath, I wake up in the woods with them looking down at me, I hold on to them, I pray for them and beg them to pray for me. I love them, like I love you, and they love me.

Brad Pitt said Angelina Jolie was getting 'sick', she wouldn't eat, had bags under her eyes and no energy, felt sad and uninspired and didn't want to work. Their relationship was on the verge of separation. He decided he was going to do all he could for her to feel how much he loved her and how beautiful in every way he thought she was, he poured all his love out on her and she healed, and so did their relationship. I guess a lot of girls would be happy if Brad Pitt gave them the lovey dovey's! But a similar thing happened to me when I was sick. I didn't need more advice, therapy or books on 'ways to think'. I needed love, and my friends and my sister and niece gave it to me. It works in our relationships in both directions, and for me it works with God. I have to love him, believe in him, find his beauty and express it, in order to prove he is in me and I am in him. I have never found anyone more mystical than Christ and the Communion of souls I track. I wanted to find God, so I found the most beautiful mystery I could every second. Prayer is to become part of it.

In the wilderness alone, there weren't any people, good or bad, so there weren't any excuses. There wasn't any culture, no social statements, no one to judge or be judged by, no one to argue about God with, no political issues, no one to offend, no language police, no one to blame, no one to take care of me and provide me with lifeless food, and no one to trade my power and dignity to for it. I was the first man, and the last man, all the good or bad people could do whatever the hell they wanted in every name they do it in. I had no excuses and I didn't want any, and I still don't. To pray beautifully and feel what it is, ignore what the world says and think for yourself, care enough to prove it to yourself. I live for the beauty of loving the truth and I endure the liars, perverts and hypocrites in every group as predators, victims and meaningless noise, but not as an excuse. I walk with the souls I find that are willing to at least try, to pray, to love. I admire them. I feel exasperated sometimes, but always very sorry for the rest.

There was a 'mute spirit' that would throw a boy into fire and water and make him foam at the mouth. It's in the bible somewhere and you can find it for yourself. The boy's father and the people were both in awe of Jesus and in doubt, they asked him if he could help. He seemed terribly exasperated and worn out by them, and said something like, 'What's wrong with you people, how long do I have to endure your doubting and unbelieving?' Jesus said to the boy's father, 'All things are possible to the man that believes.' The father said something interesting, "I believe, help me with my unbelief" Sometimes I've thought I'm not good enough to pray, or that my prayer's aren't good enough, that I have to fix myself before I can pray, but I've found prayer to be about being honest more than being good. Whatever doubt or lack of love I have, I give that in my prayer too. He cured the kid, they asked him how he did it, he said, 'This kind of spirit can only be driven out through prayer and fasting.' It's not just us that pray, God prays. God prays... We're supposed to help him, to me that's having 'God within' that's being one with God, helping him, believing him, loving him, the way we're supposed to do for each other.

The journey of the vision quest, alone, Wandering in the Spirit, in the wilderness, living close to the Earth, wanting to live 'like an Indian' since I was a kid, the Monastery, all of that is a, 'Fast.' Fasting is a central part of anything I have to say about prayer, about the Earth, about God and creatures, faith, life, death and my story. It's also hard for me to do very well in the world. Once I'd take that first step into the journey, the wilderness itself would enforce my fast, and that made it easier on me in a certain way. The subject is deep and big and needs to be treated separately. Food, how all your other problems dim in the presence of hunger, what it is, what it means, how to get it, what it takes, has been a central part of my life, but it's also the mystery of sacrifice, what every animal does so another can live, what only life can do for life, what Christ did for us the night before he was betrayed. We are meant to consume beauty and become it much like all the creatures that are true to their nature do.

I pray to God, but I also pray with God, I give my whole being to him, like the father of the possessed boy who said, 'I believe, but help me believe.' I give him my doubt and sin, not presumptuously I hope, sincerely, humbly, I confess to those he breathed on and sent as the Father sent him, and that he left me, souls I track, they are the caretakers of infinitely powerful sacraments, soldiers with weapons even demons submit to. The whole thing is so incredibly different from what the world says it is, it's the opposite.

I use my intellect to choose what is most beautiful. There are different oracles the world offers us to choose from, but I realized in the woods, I could throw deer poo on the ground and read the synchronicity of truth and the future in it. Everything is sacred when I commit myself to the truth in it. The problem is, I separate myself when I rely on myself to figure it out. Some think this is 'spirituality' but I find it complicates unnecessarily and creates avenues for error. Instead of seeking power and knowledge and then trying to figure out what to do with it and what I think I 'want' and how to get it, I put myself totally in his hands, I put All my faith in Christ who is perfect, in his Love and in his holy Communion, the way I give all my love and commit myself to a woman and my family. It's beautiful and it's hard, like art. How do you do music? It takes the life and blood of an artist to answer.

I don't picture Jesus as the hippy I've seen on t-shirts. He still seems so infinitely tough to me, so impossible to live up to. I know he doesn't want me to feel that way, but I believe he deserves a respect so sacred that it stills me, it puts me in awe. I think I'm beginning to see the dust of his sandals, I'm learning to rely more and more on his perfection.

I must make 'Everything' a prayer, even if I only have one tiny atomic sliver of will to accept and want the truth, I say in that sliver and with that sliver, 'God, I don't love the way I want to, but I know you can do it, nothing is impossible with you, not even me and my weakness, please give me your love, your will.' I want Christ's faith and I want Christ's will. I want to believe what he believed.

When I hear the people say God is within, I agree, but usually I feel like what they really mean is, God can't be himself. They say God is everywhere, but it seems like what they really mean is, God can't be anywhere. I believe God is the true artist, he makes himself his art. There's all these crummy examples of Christian's, like me, and there's all this peer pressure to be embarrassed. I understand, I'm embarrassed for Christ, at the hypocrites and hokeyness myself, but I try to ignore the meaningless tracks and follow the beautiful ones. The souls I track bring tears to my eyes with the beauty of their love. When one drip of Christ's blood, is ours, it will drop the entire universe to its knees, and then, we will really see, God is within.

There are as many ways to pray as there are ways to love someone. I express my love through my words, my thoughts, my actions, my hopes and dreams, my interest, my body, my work, my intent, my 'art' and most of all through my sincerity. Prayer for me is a journey into sincerity, the same way love is. It seems like a lot of us are cynical, angry, judgmental, proud, way too easily offended, overly sentimental, purposely imprecise, and prejudiced toward a two thousand year old Communion we know nothing about. All that stuff feels terrible to be. Sincerity can hurt, but it feels beautiful. To me, that's a good enough reason to be sincere.

The prayer of the Mass, is the prayer Christ said he turned himself into the night before he was betrayed and crucified, to transubstantiate the unfathomable into form and man into God, to show us what reality is, to show us who and what we are, and to show us that nothing we can do can make God stop loving us, or make God stop existing. I know, I must appear like some kind of weird creature or barnacle to believe in this two thousand year old prayer he said, and then sealed with his blood. I believe he knew precisely and exactly what he meant, when he said what he said, and that he cared. I believe it because it is the most beautiful thing a man has ever shown me and because every denial I have ever heard of its reality has been from a creature trying to limit his Creator. Your and my Creator is unlimited, and alive, and real and I know in my depths, I can see it in all the tracks, the world is about to get a glimpse of God. I believe it like the air in my lungs and the light. I pray nothing will make me turn away from the beauty, the way nothing made him turn away.

His last prayer and what it does, is the most mystical, the most romantic, the most heroic act on Earth and in Heaven, for a million reasons I try to tell you one word at a time. Every word I say, leaves out so many, but maybe the most important one... is you. It's like loving you, believing in you. His last words are a prayer I believe in to become, to love, to lay down. I believe him, that not only Gods spirit, but Gods blood is in my veins transforming not only me and a whole Communion of souls that love, but time into eternity, symbol into what is symbolized, memory into now, prayer into God, Earth into Heaven. I have the most beautiful reason to live and breathe and die I can find every second. Every member of my tribe, every soul I track and that tracks with me is as important to me as you. He said, "To be full of my joy, love each other as I have loved you" That was and is first, no matter what, that's why and how I pray.

'Find Yourself'

Soultracking is seeing through the eyes of who is leaving the tracks, the animal, the soul. You see the imprints an animal leaves as if you're looking from inside the animal. The tracks of the animal are like the tracks of the soul, because they are a reflection, reversed. The animals mirror is Earth.

This is the quality of a souls tracks too, of the Sacred, the Mystical, the Holy. It's always a surprise so I think it's helpful to repeat, it will always be the exact opposite of how it appears, the opposite of what you think, of how it looks, feels and seems, every time. This means to find the joy of freedom, I must look through the pain of fear, through the mirrored, reversed reflection. And to be honest, I haven't met many people who have prayed for the passion, and the grace, to really look in the mirror.

When I love God a little bit, it's not God I'm loving, it's my idea. No matter how positive my thoughts are, they are not even the dust he leaves his tracks on. If you don't feel him, if you don't believe in him, if you've never heard him calling you, to be like him, then you should be crying in the dust for him to, I did. And he did. God is real, Heaven knows, Earth knows, the creatures, the weather, the stars know, and the world is going to find out whether it wants to or not.

You have grown up in a world, brainwashed with subtle torture like I was, to accept prejudice planted in your mind without you ever being conscious of it. In the wilderness I forgot the world, I forgot my culture, like Adam, like the creatures, like the first man, all alone, innocent, with the indescribable beauty of a living, breathing, Earth and the creatures God was giving birth, for you, and I felt for me...to show me who I was, who We are. I was able to forget everything I thought I knew and start over, and I found a tribe of souls, that love. They live and follow a path, like the condors and the buffalo, and you and me, to God.

When I was born, men that loved the world more than Earth, were infesting, possessing, raping, indoctrinating, and taking over the throne of my tribe and its Medicine Men. The smoke of the mystery of iniquity was like a foul incense I smelled in the Monastery. I've seen it rotting from inside the animal. It's roots are strangling and choking anything and anyone holy, left. None of it is how it appears. They told us the tribe was about the world now, not God, and either we could go along or get out. They say love, love, love, but it's not what you think, it's the opposite, and it's mixed up like a haunted funny house, with no humor in it at all. It's the perfection of lameness, it's so incredibly dumb, it must make wisdom weep. They are deceived by a realm of souls possessed by a type of angel some are not aware of, and some have darkest business with.

The Mystery is limitless beauty my words are only molecules of, secrets Soultrackers read. We can't leave. How can we abandon ourselves? Our body and blood, the Living Ark of the Covenant Christ said he left us, to guard with our souls, our faith, our humility and our honor; his Bride, his Glorious love, the blood the souls I track prove is what he said it is. We couldn't leave without it, without Him. It isn't an idea, it's alive, and without it we'd be no different from the world that was taking us over. Our life and our blood is what he gave and what we give each other and the Earth, like the animals.

The Sacred is the difference between truth and opinion, God and ideas, Earth and the world. Our blood is the difference between life and death, and somebody has to be willing to die for it, not kill, because like I said, every sacred mystery is the opposite of how it appears, from the Cross, down to the slightest detail of the subtlest thought. Don't tell me why you don't believe it, you're on your own, you are a faithful follower, your god is whatever you want the most and you worship it religiously. Ask yourself what the hell you are, or ask for help, if you're sincere enough to have the slightest doubt, do whatever it takes to find out. Be an artist, Earth needs you.

I am a gentle man, I've never wanted to hurt anyone on purpose in my life, and only will to defend those that can't defend themselves. My purpose is to love, but if you decide to look in the mirror, you'll need help like I did and do every day, every second, to pray till we're a prayer, to be the Communion of Souls I track and I'm not being figurative, they are not myths we think we control, they are alive, like the animals, like you and I, except that they love more. Their tears are joy, their voices song, they point at truth, not themselves. They use their intellect for what it's for, choosing, only the most beautiful thing they can find to believe, like love, beauty that has no limit. They know where their honor, glory, and passion dwell. Nothing stops them, not hell, not death. They love truth like they love each other. Look in the mirror for their tracks, and you will find yourself.

'Chip Monk'

I sat at the edge of a fork in a river I loved. It was early in my experiences alone in the wilderness. I'd never felt this way before, and after this, I never did again. I'm ashamed to use the word bored, in a kingdom I explored, but yeah, kinda bored, thinking, what should I do next? Then I thought, wait, I can do anything I want to, I can go roll around under that bush, or follow a bug.

I decided to take a step onto the rocks that were islands in the water, like archipelagos that could take me to different parts of the river. I didn't decide where to go, I'd just wait, and see where I went. Sometimes I'd stand on one island for ten minutes soaking in everything, sometimes a minute, and then see which island I landed on next.

Up stream along the rivers edge I saw a cute little Chip Monk. He was pulling the grass seed heads down with his hands carefully one at a time and eating the seeds and then letting them bounce back up and choosing the next one. His hands were like a humans, and when he did what he was doing he looked like he was praying. I'd wait till he was behind a rock and then jump a few rocks closer so I wouldn't scare him.

I was about forty feet away when he looked at me, and then jumped across seven or eight rocks that were surrounded by water coming straight up to me and stopping perched on a rock about five feet away. He stared in my eyes without blinking, both of us on our islands. He kept staring at me and after a while everything got quiet around me, and I was struck, by the beauty, the pure peace and innocence of everything, including me and the Chip Monk. I thought, this is what life is supposed to be for us on Earth. My next thought was the world, and all its dis-ease, greed and un-forgiveness. I thought it was like heaven and hell, and a tear began to well, and the moment it fell from the lid of my eye, the Chip Monk blinked, and ran back to pray in the grass.

That's why I called my first CD Heaven and Hell and it's the first time I experienced what happens when we wander in the Spirit. Earth's beauty is like the sweetest, most beautiful girl I'd ever seen, why would I want anyone else. What is the reason to believe anything, if not for beauty? That's the reason I believe in Christ, he's as beautiful as Earth in a man, the way we can be and the Chip Monk is. The way the souls I track are. The way I want to want to be enough to do whatever it takes to be. The way we all are meant to be. The way Earth is; Beautiful.

People make all kinds of excuses for not believing, the dumbest one of all is other people, who cares, there's hypocrites in every group, I care about God, but it's like they think they'll have to give up something they want more, than beauty. For me it's all art and the discernment of beauty. With God we are creators, artist's. Why would I believe in something less beautiful than something else? Love makes up for a multitude of sins, but it can't make up for excuses or insincerity, because they aren't beautiful.

You're probably to busy, surviving in the world to survive on the Earth. You're probably to busy taking care of your family to wander in the wilderness and live in a vision quest, but I'm learning to wander in the Spirit here, I want to share what the souls I track say. Most of us have never experienced Earth alone and wandered in a prayer, like the other creatures, where existing itself is the infinite gift. To be honest there is no substitute for it and if you can get away to do it, you should. Every second is infinitely precious when I live for beauty, it becomes living for Gods nature in man, in you and I. The chip monk, the mountain lion, the condor, are a species of creature, as are the myriad angels and man, the only difference is, he's true to his.

'The Most Beautiful Thing You Can See'

When a woman sees God in her man and loves him, her man begins to see him and loves him too. For her to see him that way takes faith. Only her soul can give a man the respect he doesn't deserve, but longs to. They come together as one and the child that proceeds from them is the life of the Trinity. It's always in 3's that the Trinity expresses itself in the act of creation. A family is its symbol on Earth.

An artist learns to encompass three things at once; God or "Everything", The Son, or "His body" and the Spirit, or "InSpiration." His body is the instrument he plays, with his whole heart, mind and soul.

This thought is not relative, not in pieces, pieces can only make, not create. This form of thought is buried in, 'The Heart of All Things,' an artist enters it from the Center, like a spider in the Orb of her web. The spider perceives all relative knowledge in the center. The artist beholds divine knowledge in God's Center, not in pieces, he becomes it.

This is what happens when I consume beauty that takes on limit out of love, God's flesh and God's Blood, and know what it is, by believing it. The Creative Act is describing what you see truthfully, and the most beautiful thing you can see, is God.

'A Different Way to Live'

I want to give the most beautiful thing I find, describe the most beautiful thing I see, say the most beautiful thing I hear, precisely, in the most beautiful ways I can. Focusing on beauty is a different way to live.

Soultracker's make love life, and life art. You don't have to cut off your ear, but you have to be willing to, to be passionate. My story became art, when I knew who it was for; my friends. In you I heard my voice, because I know, even with our different ideas about life, truth, and God, we want people to love, and give each other something beautiful enough, to stop being afraid.

The world is far from Earth, thinking thoughts of what it thinks it wants without knowing what it is and getting them. It's too proud to pray. It shows up in everything, in our hearts, in our relationships, in demonically inspired acts, in the weather and the planet, because they're alive. What is alive has a heart and Earth's is getting hard enough to crack. It's about time I guess.

The souls I track know the forces of nature are governed by angels. Every atom of reality is moved by an angels will in love with Gods. The guardianship of our body and soul is theirs, the way our souls have custody of our own, but nobody believes in them, not really, they think they're an idea, and they stay an idea, to argue about or ignore, until we love them. Padre Pio said they have as much faith in is as we have in them, and he proved it was true over and over. His whole life was proof, and thousands more walk the exact same path, tracking the whole Communion like the path of the buffalo. You don't know what happens in their lives, it's like this big unguarded secret, it's all there, don't you even want to look? Even when I think I believe in them, I discover I only know what and who they are to the extent I love them, and everyone else. I trust enough to be broken. It's the same with God. It's loving the Soul of God like a lover and in your lover. For me, there is no knowing without loving, Cutting off your ear is letting go of everything, and finding out what's left, is real, because it really is, alive, like you and me.

I have a chance to say what I hear, but it's so misunderstood, so delicate and majestic, so sacred and holy, so solemn, so beautiful and alive, like kneeling in the wilderness, that for someone like me to say it, it may be only God will believe it.

'One at a Time'

I wanted to be the real thing from the first time I heard 'Light My Fire' in the back of Dad's Ford Galaxy. You know how that dead Indian's spirit went into Jim Morrison when he was a kid, I felt like Jim Morrison's spirit went into me. Then I heard Jose Feliciano's version, and I loved the Spanish guitar. I was eight.

My creativity has always been tied and driven, by the the Earth, places are like people and angels to me. I believe places are intimately bound with angels the way we are. Monterey, Carmel, the Big Sur Coast, with my sisters and brother older than me and in the middle of it, the art of it, and the culture, there is so much good in those things, but there's a demonized angel the world has that twists it, for the same reason men become dark and twisted. Man is the only creature on Earth that isn't true to his nature, and this angel wasn't true to his.

People of the last few hundred years think the spiritual world is much more different from ours than it is. The revelation of the dis-enlightenment was Materialism and Relativism, they became mans new religion, the shared experience of what he believes. In Materialism, reality becomes things instead of beings. In Relativism, beings become ideas instead of living creatures. The wilderness taught me that everything is alive. I forgot the world there, I wanted to live like an 'Indian' since I was a kid. Alone, I learned to Soultrack and Wander in the Spirit and miracles happened. They are there for anybody willing to do whatever it takes. Miracles change our reality forever, they are a huge responsibility and if we don't live them, we become 'walking dead men'. I know because I have.

Earth makes religion about God, the 'world' makes religion about people. Religion is simply whatever we believe and believe we don't believe. Everybody has one. People give what they believe a bad name because they don't care enough to know what they believe. We seem to believe in myriad ideas instead of a living being creating myriad creatures out of love. Our choice is really between beings that think the thoughts, not thoughts themselves. Thoughts are notes. True religion is like music, a bridge between worlds, felt but not seen, it speaks from beyond the surface symbolism of words and ideas. Music is angels touching our skin with their light. They don't just play music, they are music. We don't seem to realize that we are unable to stop believing. We nail ourselves to whatever we want the most and it becomes our god, our religion. What is important about religion to me is not the good or bad people do, but that we believe only the highest, most beautiful thing we can find to believe every second, no matter what people do. When I commit myself to that, I commit myself to what God has to be to be God.

There are a million beautiful things to say about it. Time and space limit us to one word, one symbol of a symbol, at a time. I wanted the sacred. I wanted to find out if God was real. I thought it was dumb to use hypocrites as an excuse, some people weren't hypocrites, and the animals all around me weren't hypocrites. I offered every breath, my life, my self, as a prayer, as a creature. I said I'm not leaving till I prove I love you. People tell me what they believe they don't believe. It seems meaningless to me, they don't give any real reason for it. It doesn't make any sense. I want to commit myself to the highest most beautiful thing I can find every second, and find out for myself what real is.

There are a million things to say to someone who can listen as if they're the first man, the first woman, the way I listened alone, forgetting the world, wandering with and becoming, another creature. From the first miracle, I found I was following a tribe of beings that had gone before, following their beauty, their God, Love. But I was a kid with no Medicine Man, no one with authority, just a bunch of people guessing. I found the Oracle of our story under a pile of boulders. It is a perfect living word, that means everything, but also one thing. By itself it has immense power to be understood and misunderstood, to unify or divide. It is not meant to be separate from the tribe who's story it is and is becoming. The only way to know and not guess, is to follow the souls of those that prove its word is true. They are the Communion, they are the tribe I track, by the drops of blood they leave all the way back to the first track, for me to find them by. I don't care about my ideas. All the lying hypocrites in the world can do what they want. They make themselves meaningless.

But here, in a body, pulsed my sexuality, the people of tribes on Earth. My art welled up out of the Earth, but it was almost always for a woman, I loved them and their inspiration. There were a few I fell in love with, and they knew. They took me inside themselves, but also here on Earth, we were creatures together, becoming aware, learning.

Even though I loved them the same way I lived, wanting to give everything, looking back I objectified the female. Men can really enjoy being men with women, in our whole being not just our bodies. A woman can bring out the masculinity in you, like a flower opening to the sun. She can love you in a way that makes you come to her, stay, and stop at nothing and no one. Not even doors.

I worried about them, I loved them with my wounded nature, I didn't want to hurt them, but I thought an artist, a man, a musician, had to go to extremes all the time. We shape each other by our shared experience and belief. I was a product of my culture, both the good and the bad. Life has been a path of asking my soul to take over my body and when I speak romantically, I don't mean it to be carnal. Being masculine was leaning over till you wore holes in your exhaust pipes, drinking whiskey out of a bottle, it was being able to fight, even though I never wanted to start one it felt good to end them. I wanted to be strong since I was young, but it wasn't a competition. Going into the wilderness alone was between me and God, nobody distracted me, I was an only son, proving myself to myself and discovering what it means to know. We think we're giving something up, but we're being given more, and it includes our bodies.

After fifty years, any machine would be a clump of dust, but not a man. A coyote taught me what my body was for, it's what animates animals, to carry my soul around. Now I'm seeing what my soul was saying all along, from the very beginning, but to hear that through the world, the culture today, is almost impossible. It only magnifies why I can't judge anyone. I judge beauty instead.

The souls I track are alive. I put my face in the dust God breathed them out of. I taste the drops and I want to bleed them too, for you, for me, for beauty. Out there I said, I can be afraid, or have faith, I can be afraid or be a prayer. All around me I see my friends being prayers without knowing it, missing it somehow. You can't track souls without getting lost, and losing them is losing everything. It takes risking your life, offering up everything, both the good and the bad and the unknowing. Beauty is the proposal of the intellect to the will. The marriage of the Bride and God. He never asks her to repress, but only, to never settle for less.

An artist gets people to look. A Soultracker, walks in two worlds at once and anybody that wants to enough can be one. If I can get your attention through my art and my life, it's to point down their path like I would to a sunset. It's all art and it's so much more than I thought it was when I was younger. It's almost to good to believe, but it's true. It's a woman that will crush Satan's head. The Immaculate Heart will triumph in the end. Her Son is her Creator and she loves Him the way her daughters would love her sons if they knew. I'm not worthy of her eyelash, but she loves me anyway. Everything will be okay, no matter how hard it gets. We walk down this beautiful path together, but we each have to start, one at a time.

'Strong'

The other night I felt how strong people are in a real way, the most fragile. To me they're strong because they want to love with all they are. I felt how vulnerable love is, in its beauty, it quivers like a feather and a flame. I want to hold it and make it safe, to reveal its passionate face, but it means risking everything.

When I say Soultracker, it's a real thing. It's a Way. It's different, like anything good I have to say, I didn't think of it, it came to me, the way animals in the wilderness do, the way everything comes that's true. Truth isn't thought, it's revealed. A Soultracker 'listens' with all his senses at the same time, even the senses of his soul, he gives his whole self to it as art, but it's really through the surrender of prayer, to know what to listen for comes. A Soultracker knows he's weak, so he prays all the time, by looking for the beauty of the meaning God is giving him.

To me holiness is reaching for the highest beauty in every aspect beauty exists. When I see that it's art, I reach for it like art, then my weaknesses aren't about good and bad, they're a gradient of how much I'm willing to love, the same way an artist progresses. His master tells him the truth, to help him recognize beauty and reach for it.

Beauty is a living guide, she is so much more than we think she is. Beauty is the way God reveals his heart, but also his mind. It informs the intellect, and inspires the will, like looking into a lovers eyes.

When I refer to the One in a Trinity as, 'He', I don't limit anything, I become real. God becomes a man to show me what I am, and I think ultimately, he does it all for a woman. He put the whole universe in her hands because she was humble and he wanted his love to be born out of her. Why would he want to accomplish it all himself, and why would she either, he knows he can do that, what good is his creation if it can't love like he does. I think he wanted to put his faith in a woman and love her, and that he chose the right one. It seems like everything I see is the opposite of what the world tells me, but to me, it's much more beautiful than what the world tells me, that's why I see it.

As an artist, I have to think for myself without excuses about what anybody else did or thinks or claims or said. I have to love truth enough to verify everything, with precision that is beautiful, facts that prove true, only unequaled miracles, authority that doesn't guess and that even the demons confess, beg, and submit to, the souls and lives that are or were there, bleeding and breathing, living ultimate answers. That's when I see I already have it all, and I live in it to give.

Truth can't be chained by anything or anyone. It's light darkness can't comprehend, the way evil is crushed by a woman in the end. Like light to darkness, truths objectivity makes the presence of one, the absence of the other. To question with precision is to let myself not know. That's what a Soultracker does, he seeks exquisite precision, with everything at once, finding meaning in the beauty of the tracks everywhere, in the stillness of a prayer that is love.

All our issues are the same issue with the same answer. But, a person is real too, and when they're heartbroken, loving them is light. When I was sick, it was love that helped me, much more than any advice. I become aware of how fragile God is when I love with everything I am. I know what it's like to feel your soul drop out of your chest. All around me I see people loving, suffering, but they don't know why. They've lost faith in God and look for it in the selves they think they are, and they feel empty. It's selfish, it's ugly, I've got a lot of it, it's meaningless except for the pain it causes others.

I want to use every gift I've been given; my body, my sexuality, my spirituality, my intellect, my heart, my soul, my land, and all that's happened to me, in hope someone will listen, and see the beauty of a path, where souls walk to heaven, like bridges for each other. I want others to see, they are bridges for me, for us, not to judge each other anymore, to forgive, and believe in the best instead, to love, and be friends, in the purist sense of the word... of God.

'Big Balls'

Playing music together back in the 80's was really fun. Everybody knew each other. It seems more serious and tense now. Guys in a band learn to communicate with looks and sounds. Pat and I could have conversations in a strange zzzrrrrpp reeezieepp language. We had codes for everything from amorous delight to crummy stuff. Santa Barbara was California meets Spain on the Riviera.

He'd had open heart surgery when he was sixteen. They put in a valve, with complications that caused a grand mall seizure and epilepsy, but none of that stopped Pat from laughing, in fact it made him laugh more. Pat had balls. His motto was, 'Full on Fearless.' In this picture he's making a sound like, "EEeeaawwwaaarrrgghGhhGhheeeeeeeEEEEE"

Basically what it means is, 'Been there done that' and 'Fududududud' followed by 'Goodtimes' 'Oh! ohhh, man dude,' 'Epic!'

A few years before he died, I got him going with my theory that girls didn't really care about the size of a mans wiener. What they really cared about was..... oh, how can I say this, when I've thought I'd die a monk in a Monastery, or alone in the woods, and I pray all the time...but it's an emergency situation today. People need to lighten up!! Take a chill pill! Everybody is so stressed out and afraid of what they think's coming. I've examined my conscience, it may be deficient, but I'm convinced God wouldn't mind, well, I'm pretty sure. I'm daring to think God might even laugh at what I think I'm going to tell you. Pat and I laughed so hard that day we cried.

He'd heard about my theory for a long time and knew it was a tongue in cheek sort of a thing, and he cracked up when I'd talk about it. I'd get a grasp of the subject from all different angles, but anyway, what it was, was, that I thought what girls really liked on a man wasn't a big wiener, but great big hairy balls! It had kind of a double meaning.

I was trying to talk him into going with me to the bumper sticker place on State Street and getting them to make us a bunch that said, 'I've got great big hairy balls' and then sneak around at night and stick them on a bunch a bumpers. I thought, it would be a positive social influence, with people driving around and looking at each other funny instead of having road rage and everything. We told some girls about it. I don't think they thought it was as funny as we did, but guys did. Guys thought it was really funny! Well, musicians did.

I can hear him making that, "EEEeeeeeeeeaaaawwwwwrrgghhhheeeeeeE" sound right now. It came from the John Wayne and Cookie imitation, the late great Jack Folks turned me onto. Jack is a whole other story for later. Anyways, I'd do this thing where Dukey is getting lonely and talking about Cookie being kinda cute. I'll do it for you on my audio book!

You know why I started to write about laughing all the time, because I was thinking about crying all the time, not sad tears, tears of joy. As a teenager, I cried tears of joy just driving down the road. Then I encountered evil and turned into a walking dead man for a while.

Those tears poured from me in the wilderness many times, and for two months straight in the Monastery, almost every time I'd enter into prayer. I found out later they call it 'the gift of tears'. It's like you're right on the edge with everybody, you see how precious and good and bad and scared and happy and sad they are, miracles happen and reality changes, you see how utterly amazing everything is, that we exist. I don't know what else to say, but it's hard to get me to shut up. In a Monastery you can go around crying all the time and nobody cares much.

I fell in love once a couple times. It's always accompanied by phenomena. I have to wait, like you do for an animal. A Soultracker, a gift, a heart with lips God sent me, apologized the other day, "I'm sorry, I'm crying" they were tears of joy. I said, "Forget about'it, I feel like cryin' all the time!! but I can't cause I'm a buffalo rancher! I'm supposed to be Crusty the Ranch Hand!

If I keep doing what I'm doing, I'm going to lay down and become a good bridge. I have something to give, whether anyone esle believes in it or not. It's not mine, I just see it, like the woman I fall in love with, I believe in a beauty I can't resist, so I don't worry, I pray.

When Pat died, I decided to live. Everything was broken and falling apart. I learned things about hell and what the creatures are like that live there. Now I know no matter how hard things get, we're going to be okay, because I believe in the most beautiful thing I can find every second, and I keep finding it.

'Mother's Day'

I sat with my mom and rubbed her arm. It was so simple and made her feel so much better. I wish I had done it more. She was nervous, but gentle like a deer. She was so vulnerable, it could manifest as fear. Some nights she'd wake up screaming, terrified of something. She loved me. You can't love your mother too much, and I think God feels the same.

When I watch a movie, I enter a mystery, but if I wanted to, I could keep saying, this is a movie, it's not real, it's all illusion, I don't believe this, and in a limited way I'd be right, but I'd miss anything beautiful it had to say.

I want to describe something with a real, but limitless foundation, using symbols of symbols one at a time, names of images, words, for a world that doesn't want to believe in what they can mean.

I entered a Mothers story, a Woman's story, Mary's story. I decided to believe who and what she believes and feel what she feels. She showed me what a woman is. A woman is the most beautiful of all creations, without her, no creature is given expression. God creates through a woman and saves through a man. She is the eyes and the heart, the soul, that most beautifully loves her Son. Her humility crushes the proud in its wake. Man either hates her, or becomes her child. I am her child, to die for her is to live, as her Son lives.

Earth's Spirit is a Mother, milk and a garden. But the world follows the spirit of a kind of man, relative to everything, ultimate to nothing. He turns living beings into dead things, and makes a god of his ideas. Our nature, as creatures and a tribe is not of his world, but of Earth and the stars and angels with heaven.

We are artists because our Creator is, and everything creates in its own image. We are his medium. The souls I track are a tribe of Spiritual Bohemian. Our passion is for Gods flesh and blood. Earth, water and sky are real because of the love a man sacrificed for them. I don't live to transcend them, I live to make them sacred. When I see how she looked at her Son, and he looked at her, I want to love that way too. I live for the highest and most beautiful thing I can find, and like God, I find, it is a Woman.

'Addiction'

My life is about love and the meaning of its beauty, between a man and a woman, Earth, God, and a tribe of souls I track. I've gone so far off their path there was no way back, so I had to keep going forward. Life is not what I thought it was, it's who, it's all living soul's.

I've written some about how I broke in my book, but in another one, I think I'm supposed to take you to the edges of hell with me, where hope no longer exists. Freedom is the ability to choose, it can be taken by ignorance or force. The aspect that is battle is fought with creatures more like Earths than different. They are as real as bears, with natures. The difference is they are like men, in that they chose not to be true to theirs. To a certain extent they are slaves to the sin of others. Life eats life and death eats death. I want to take you where I went, so you can taste it, and glimpse it from within, and then taste the Answer. I keep finding we all have the same problem in different forms, with the same cure, and it's not some half way, thought technique thing, it's an actual cure. I think I've found a way to take you into the mystery of it with me, and show you how, with help from friends that loved me, and the friends I track on the other side, I crossed it, to become a, 'Bridge.' It's profoundly different from almost everything I've heard on the subject.

In the limitless way of every sacred mystery, where everything becomes the opposite of how it appears, the breaking, became a gift, the gift of breaking open, of a painful sacrifice, everyone pays, but few experience the power of offering.

Oneness is the opposite of what the world says it is. When I 'Believe,' I step into the impossible, but keep living on Earth, for the sake of the world. I track the Light that is everything, and also one man, infinitely beautiful, like you, and me. The spirit of the world-man says oneness is every idea and everyone becoming the same, but the Spirit of the Earth-man, a Soultracker, says, oneness is becoming like God, infinitely individual.

Oneness is the likeness to God that is the separation of sovereignty. Oneness is freedom, the freedom of infinite responsibility, the 'ability-to-respond'. To me this is what the holiness of love is about. As simple and as complex as beauty.

Prayer takes everything, and breathes it into beauty, every moment into meaning that is so utterly beautiful, it is its own freedom. It is my lover. The point of prayer is to find who's there. The Trinity of Love, for me is a joining that reveals our nature to each other and ourself, as Gods nature. Love makes each of us a snowflake and a fingerprint, so delicate, the whole universe rests on us.

The world-man presents me with ideas reflected nowhere in nature only a kind of manufactured idiot can believe. We are deceived by ignorance, because we follow lost souls and a kind of angel, like men, to proud to serve. We track the world instead of Earth. These demonized angelic beings are pure intellect and seek flesh, offered to them through our will, and the will of others, with predatory strategies, of corruption, lying in circles, prejudice, a strategic lack of precision, and eventually the strategy of unlimited and merciless violence.

People talk about just making a choice, but I don't make a choice for a bear or a mountain lion. They're free, like me. If I leave my food for them or do something stupid, they'll eat it or me. Angels are 'creatures' like rabbits and snakes and bees, but born and bound by laws of a different wilderness. I live in a world where everything is alive, where ideas are only the dust of who thinks them. At the end of every track is the animal that leaves it, that's who I want, and who I want to be, because of the beauty.

I 'Pray' to the First Light, with all the creatures, on Earth and in Heaven, souls, I track, present with me on the path, the mystical tribe of my Holy Communion; "I've seen how weak I can get, I don't know what to do, I have all these desires that are less than the beauty you hold up for me and everyone, but I don't care if it's impossible, You're Holy, see my heart and make me yours!" and they do, and he does, for me, for you...he really does.

As an artist, especially a performing artist, I sometimes feel like I'm pointing at myself, I've said, an artist is his own pimp, but I don't feel like I belong to me, I think each one of us is meant to be a bridge for the others. I hope you'll confess to these beautiful souls, and ask them to help you too, like a child, because they are the cure, and Earth needs us.

'To See Her Beauty'

Addiction is the worship of a false god
A fake that creates in its own image
A spiritual Impersonator

Every 'sin' has a 'spirit'
And so does every addiction
It's not about a substance
And it's not about you
It's a raping of our will
And a voice that isn't yours
You're listening too

In a fight for your life
Over your soul
The Will is a weapon
Who possesses the will
Possesses the person
To own our will
Is to learn what it's for

Truth, our heart commits to
Truth, our intellect seeks
Truth, we love like God
More than the world, more than life
More than ourself
God went to hell for
Truth, that sets a freewill free
To use our will for its purpose
Is to know Who and What we are

They are one and the same
Gods will
Is to show us our own

Addiction remains a disease
On till demons plea to leave
By our stepping into a 'State of Grace'
The only true honor
The act of true passion
Of true love, of Honest sincerity
That turns God from our judge
To our 'InSpiration'
That turns our question from
How holy am I?
To how holy is God?
Holy enough to love
Those that hate him
And his offspring
And Just enough to let them
Make themselves in their own image
The only guarantee God comes with
Is the truth

It's not you that's addicted
It's the self of another spirit
One you think is just your idea
And you think your ideas are you
Like you think your ideas are God
They'll go away
You can stop doing what they say
When you stop asking yourself questions
You can't answer
And pray

Don't be ashamed of your anguish
It's there because you care!
God doesn't live to not suffer
God lives to love

Where we resist, he embraces
Where there are demons, there are Angels!

They are real, like you
And they feel the way you do
When you're true
When you're in love
With the one
You kiss

This is prayer that is joy
Finally, something real; Art
Prayer is belief in perfection
The revealing of our self to ourself
In Gods eyes, ours
and in ours, each others
Prayer

Sink in, under the covers
It's real, you're here, pray
Make your prayer a vision quest
Your soul a wilderness
Your heart a desert
Where you Wander in the Spirit
Till you find living water
Find out for yourself
If God is real
And then, don't bring me an idea
Bring me God

Don't be a fake
You can't absolve yourself
It's a meaningless idea
To hear your confession
Let your lover be your priest
On the bed of Gods Bride
Your body and soul
Your will and your mind
Kneel down beside her
To see her beauty
Be blind
To darkness
Be light

'Hitting Bottom'

I woke up in jail like I'd been dropped by a stork. They let this great big Indian in. He took off his shirt and paced the length of the cell. There were about ten of us in there, they were talking in this gangsta lingo that sounded incredibly obnoxious to me but now they were quiet. He was big and muscled and I noticed scars on his chest from the Sundance. He used a phone on the wall and was trying to comfort someone that was sick and dying. He reminded me of pictures I'd seen of warriors before the white man destroyed their culture. We were chained together a few days later, I told him and tears filled his eyes. He said it was so hard for his people, everybody was lost, I nodded in agreement and tears filled my eyes too.

I'd been raising buffalo in Canada for twelve years and come back to California to get my U.S. meat business going again and try and save my marriage and my life. To save my marriage I had to succeed and make money and to save my life I had to stop drinking. We had lived ten of the happiest years of my life. Everybody saw how in love we were. Ten years of snuggles and laughing with my son and then it was like I was caught in a perfect storm, the same storm my own dad got caught in, in his late forties when alcohol morphed into a monster. I felt like I broke the most beautiful thing I ever had. Losing the respect and love of the woman I loved like family was killing me. I didn't understand what was happening to me until a year later when I heard Father Malachi Martin, an exorcist for thirty years, describe my situation exactly.

It was a few nights before Christmas, I wanted to come home, she didn't want me. I can't blame her, I was so confused and so weak, addiction was a fight for my life, like a pet Vampire. I'd never spent a Christmas alone. I sat in a bar called the Wildcat and drank till they closed, and then I drove, and fell asleep and ran off the road. I remember looking down at these stupid flip flops and then up at a few hundred other men in jail with me and thinking, 'I'm one of them' and then words came to me, "Whenever you helped the least of your brothers you helped me" and I thought, I'm one of the least of my brothers, and in this weird way I felt honored to be one of them and I thought if you're in them you must be in me too, and then he began proving it.

'Sacred'

I don't know why I didn't care what people did, when I thought of God, I just wanted the sacred. It's like it was always art to me and no matter how many bad musicians there were, they couldn't make music bad, it only took one good one to make it beautiful. I wanted my life to be something beautiful, and it was, Earth had moods like angels. Then I encountered evil, and felt like it took away my beauty forever.

I thought I was ruined, I thought I could make God stop loving me. God, I pray with my whole heart mind and soul, you will give me the words to say how you feel, to express the infinite, love that is light. How can I express a billion beautiful things at once, one word at a time, one world at a time, how can I express the souls I've tracked loving you?

When you meet someone God sends you, to be yours, to believe with you, to be your prayer, so you can be hers, he gives you a way of speaking without words, love that is art, eyes that are ears, hands that are brushes, a tongue that paints. Art is sacred, it's alive, we are Gods art. When we want to be his, we're not good or bad, He just hasn't finished painting us.

I hold her next to me and pray, with all I am. I want to give myself away, the way he does, but we're spooked horses, I feel the world around us, nervous, scared, brainwashed and spirit-broken, they don't trust anything and I feel it, as prejudice to my breed. I'd buck my soul off my back and run home, but not a woman's, she's Earth, even God needed a woman, and Earth needs me like a woman needs a man.

Creatures, Angels, Condors, Buffalo, Priest's that bleed, Visions of a Woman Clothed with the Sun, call the world back to the love of her Son, they whisper; "Pray.....no matter what, pray anyway....make everything a prayer no matter who you think you are, no matter how bad or good, no matter how many bad artist's there are, prayer makes you a beautiful one. It's not the craft, it's the art we care about enough to bleed. It's all art. Our purpose is to be as beautiful as Heaven and Earth, by being humble, our love is limitless. The way our souls sing is to pray."

Wherever I am, help me enter the Heart of All Things, and be still, opening, my life, my worries and my doubts, my quests-ions, my innocence and guilt, show me what I've done and failed to do, and I ask the blessed Virgin, all the angels and saints, and you, my sister, my lover, my brother, to pray for me, a kid, a man, for the lost, for all of us, together, to the Light that is one of us, and change everything, one at a time, like flowers that open up to the sun. Our Creator, the beautiful living Spirit, the Soul and Divinity, the Sacred, Body and Blood of a New Man, that loved with everything, is yours and mine, the New Adam and the New Eve, Man and Woman, animate this breathing child, this creature like a bird, like a spider and a horse, I'm everything and nothing, all I want to do is point, away from myself, at the One symbol that is what it symbolizes, the real and eternal presence, of a prayer that hides in the middle of everywhere and nowhere, being, exactly what he said it is, Sacred, like him, dying to love, and not believed in.

I look at the ugliness I've done, by not caring enough, like bad art, the selfishness, fear, the burden I've been, the weak willed one, the prodigal son, vain, and I pray anyway, and He blesses me beyond my wildest dreams. I don't ask for anything but his love, and he gives it to me, by showing me the pain of it, and the beauty, till it overflows and becomes alive, like his own Immaculate Spouse, a breathing, beating, pulsing, pounding heart, looking back at me and loving, and all I've ever really done, was ask.

'Love'

Like two creatures
Like animals that nurse
Like waves hold lips
And clouds hold rain
As if an atom out of place
Would change everything
It's a miracle for a man and a woman
To fall in love
The way God does
With each of us
Our most intimate whispers
Are prayers
I say for you
And you say for me
It's meant to be this way
For man and woman
Like light from the ends of a tunnel
Meet in one place and one time
Our bodies are souls with eyes
In skin that holds life
From death
Rise like a flame
Breathe my breath
Out and in again
Spent
So every moment
Every smile, every word
Every thought, hope and dream
And even our pain
Is making love

'Communion'

True lovers believe in each other. They give themselves heart, mind and soul for each other. A man and a woman join by having faith in each other. It takes all my life and the effort of caring, the way it does to become an artist. The difference between craft and art, is love. For me, art takes love, art is love, the life giving Holy Spirit of God that creates and moves in all things that are true and good. I want that Spirit like a wife and a friend. For me this Holy Spirit is Gods presence. It is a living, breathing, feeling Spirit, as a Mother, as Gods spouse, joined in the faith of love as One God, the unfathomable, sovereign, free One, that all of us share in fully and wholly, the way a family shares in love.

I think God wants us to believe in him, needs us to believe in him, the way a child does, the way a lover does, so we can create beauty. It's taken tons of faith to create anything beautiful in my life, to write a song and sing it for people, or to write a word I think is worth saying and say it, to give up the world for Earth, to go alone into the wilderness and to pray and learn anything true. I was petrified to play for people in the beginning. I didn't actually overcome that fear completely until my last encounter with evil and the creatures that dwell in its dark wilderness. It was alone in that wilderness where I came to realize everything is alive, existing for the purpose we choose to 'believe' we are created for. I think what we believe is infinitely important, it's why I only believe the highest, most beautiful thing I can find every second.

Do you remember how Christ couldn't do much in his own town because people didn't believe in him. They said, oh, he's just that carpenters son and that meek woman's kid. I can hear them not having faith in him and trying to get others not to, like, 'yeah right, he's gonna save us by believing?'

It takes faith to create, it takes faith to love. Faith is respect and belief before I or somebody else manifests beauty. A person has to really believe, that they and the ones they love can do it, even when they have no idea how and it seems impossible. It's not something that's planned and thought out in pieces, it's something I have to give myself to totally, like I want to as a man to a wife. The way I do it is by praying for it.

A man and a woman can believe in their union by praying for it. It's so sad when a wife stops believing, and I can understand why, I know men do things that are terrible. I became an alcoholic, that was terrible, it was so weak and selfish, I didn't yell at anybody, I crumbled. But in spite of myself, my friends loved and believed in me, love was what healed me, not anybody judging me, telling me how dumb and bad I was or how to fix myself.

I don't care much about my own ideas, but I care passionately about the ideas of the souls I track, a perfect Communion, those that have gone before me in beauty, and proven they are there, where it is I want to be, Heaven, a 'place' where all of us love each other like breathing, where we all know our purpose for being, loving each other as God loves us, that is no matter what, even when we hate him, judge him, don't believe in him and kill him. It's here for anyone that lives it, but it's lived on Earth creatively like art. It's primary skill is the development of a will for only the highest beauty, in every way beauty exists, in all things. It becomes a passion for seconds and a distaste for the ugliness of wasting them with useless thoughts about meaning-less things. It becomes our reason and purpose for existing.

The souls I track make love art. To them, nothing of its nuance is too subtle to taste, to touch with an eyelash. They are as precise in their purpose for thinking and believing as a planet and a star are, for existing. They are as precise as lovers reaching, with every touch and breath, and half breath, held, to touch our soul with our body, in communion.

'What Makes It Perfect'

Anybody can point, even me. The problem is we point at ourselves and our ideas. The experience of Soultracking came with tracking animals into visions. A Soultracker points away from himself and his ideas to the animal leaving the most beautiful tracks; the souls. They are real. I love them more than their ideas and they love me more than mine.

What is it about believing in God that is different from believing in a man and his ideas? When I was eighteen, I got badgered out of a vision I had on Earth, into a 'brainwashing' seminar based on the ideas of a man, and of the world. I've tried to describe the profoundly negative effect it had on me. I know it's not positive to say anything's negative. I'm not saying I haven't learned profound things from evil, but I don't have to start a war to know it's hell.

The sliver of why I'm asking you this question is what I hope will pierce your heart out of love, so we might save others from the piercing of their hearts, out of malice. The reason's men want people to follow them might appear altruistic, but in the end, any man that says follow me and my ideas, is not worthy of the dignity. I'm happy to serve, ask questions and follow instructions, but never, ever, submit your person, your true self, your soul, to another man, unless you believe with all your heart, mind and soul, he either is God or has Gods undeniable authority. Make him prove it in every way anything is proven. Even demons knows that much. I learned it from them.

Believing God is everybody's idea, or isn't as real, free, alive and sovereign as you or a mountain lion, is prohibiting a meaning from existing. It's trying to define a Being like you and me, as an idea. It's trying to make the definition more important than the meaning. I ask myself what does God have to be to be God, and then I look for Gods tracks everywhere, every second, in everything. Soultracking is the prayer of an artist.

It seems obvious to me God has to be the highest beauty in every way beauty exists, to be God, otherwise he's just a dumb idea and a waste of time. Beauty isn't the object, it is the meaning. Beauty is what it does, beauty must be alive to be God, because we are. When somebody tells us how to think, their handing us a hammer, not a vision to build, or the awareness of why. An artist has to transform thinking into the revelation of creating, believing into being. Thoughts, good or bad, are only paint and notes. They are tracks, not the animal that's leaving them. I've always wanted to find the animal, because the animal is alive like me, the animal is sacred like me, the tracks are the mystery, the animal is the mystic, like me. Even though the nature of his thoughts are perfectly beautiful, I want to know and love the animal, the mystic, the soul I'm tracking, infinitely more than his ideas.

When I say I don't track ideas, I track the souls that leave them, it might sound trite, but I'm dead serious. It's what makes a world of zombies. The world proposes and argues about thoughts and ideas with no awareness of who and what is thinking them or why. It defines things it thinks it doesn't want to know by directing its intellect toward everything but the truth it is afraid of. I don't believe in or accept an idea that I don't experience as perfect. What makes it perfect?

The beauty of the soul that thinks it.

'Thinks'

Three times the hair stood up on the back of my neck when there was no way I could have known what was there. I found out in three different ways. The first was at night in the chaparral, with a coyote yelping out its last breath's. I remember the full moon and saying to myself, 'this is the sound of death' and then this blood curdling cry, it sounds like a woman screaming. I remember every time I've heard that cry, out there in the night, after they kill.

The second time my hair stood up was along a river sleeping in the sand. I felt more at home alone in the wilderness than in the world. I slept and dreamt with power, sometimes when my body was its weakest. Night is filled with sounds out there, life, moving in and out in circles like ripples on a pond. But this night I kept waking up reaching for the knife I kept under a rolled up shirt I used for my pillow. I felt a foreboding presence I never felt out there, except for when this psychotic Vietnam vet was around. He was tormented and a murderer. I wrote about my experiences with him in a previous chapter called 'Tunnel Rat'.

I slept beautifully on the ground alone at night in the pitch black, with a bear sniffing my toe. Another time, something small, maybe a fox or a coyote, smelled blood on my knife, and kept pulling it away from under my head. I'd reach out and grab my knife and put it back under my head and go back to sleep laughing and then it would do it again. The grass was too thick for me to define its tracks in the morning.

But this time I kept waking with the hair standing up on my neck, scared of something. I'd listen with my whole being, where any thought, good or bad, is only noise, that interferes with hearing. I'd listen for the circles going in and out, creatures communicating and reacting to each other. At dawn I woke to the sound of a smack and splash in the river that I knew was either a mountain lion or a bobcat, pouncing on a duck. When I got up, I found a large male mountain lions tracks in circles in the sand around me.

The last time my hair stood up was with the first mountain lion I'd ever seen and have seen three times since then. The first time I've described in an earlier excerpt, where I saw a buck deer save himself and three does by facing the lion with his antlers. I was in the House of the Sun, the Chumash Garden of Eden, when it happened with the hair on my neck again. I turned and saw him a hundred and fifty yards away walking under a big black oak in the California savannah. I stalked up on him that day in the deep grass and we looked each other in the eyes. My hair stood up again, it was a physio~spiritual kind of feeling, relatively unrelated to any conscious thought.

The reason I'm relating the way I've felt mountain lions is because through a kind of gauntlet I went through in my late forties, I learned what angels feel like, the dark and light ones. Soultracking is real, angels are creatures, as real as spiders and eagles, each species with its own animating soul, when you quiet yours, you can feel. When I stand up against the dark ones, they flee, but it takes directing my faith, will and love, the three combined. It takes the love of truth that is 'Awareness'. You have to know they aren't ideas. They and their human slaves don't just give up, they fight for their prey like any predator. I feel their presence, subtly, but as clearly as the sound of a buffalo's breath.

I used to think the deep deja vu's, the moods that drift like mist in redwoods, the fog rolling in off Monterey Bay, the inspiration and oneness I felt when I gave everything to a woman, all emanated from within my mind and my thoughts. I sought them by myself and in myself that way, as if they had nothing to do with the presence of creatures, but they do. You may be quiet and still enough to feel angels of light in the mist. Or when out of the blue, you feel a sudden invisible oppression, or a person harasses you, with pressure and threats, it's not your thoughts, or even theirs, it is the influence of another kind of angel, directly, or through their human pawns.

When I learned to feel their presence, and what kinds of souls they have, my whole world opened up. I stopped thinking meaningless thoughts and started hearing and feeling treasures I could hardly resist if I tried. I was freed from addiction, whether to a substance or pattern, something they are almost always involved in. But you probably don't believe me. You don't think anything is objectively real or true, or alive, really, especially a God, with feelings you would have to feel responsible for, like a woman you love, like loyalty. You can think anything you want, but your betrayal is reserved for the heart, of someone that loves you.

One of the most emancipating discoveries of my life is that everything is free and alive, like I am in the wilderness and more and more, in the world. Life is infinitely more than thought, than mind over matter, it's heart over soul and soul over mind. I track living beings that are as real as you and me. I don't really care about my thoughts or yours, what you look like or can do, I care about you, and your love of the beings in your presence, that's what they care about too.

We don't have to say a word or be or do anything, to turn our life into a prayer. Every person on Earth has enough sacrifice and passion, enough blood, breath and flesh, to walk here, bathed in the water of Earths tears. Just to be born of a woman, we die for what we live for, when we live for love, we are heroic beyond our deepest dreams. The rest are free in the darkness to not want to know the 'Truth' and to believe in what they don't believe.

If something happens without Gods permission, God isn't what God has to be to be God, he's just our dumb ideas. Wolves can't take down buffalo without the animating soul that is life in them. You don't have a fricking clue how you exist, you're either believing or guessing. I've worked my whole life to create something beautiful and it's dust to a bug, because the bug is alive.

Evil has been crushed, by a woman, created out of her Sons love, and Heaven waits for time to tell. Listen, beyond good and bad thoughts, they're here, already, now, the saints and angels are praying all around us, 'Waiting,' for a few to turn their lives into a prayer, to take their ugliness and disease, their despair and unforgiveness, their hurt and hopelessness, their anxiety at a future torn apart by the perversion of eternal souls that believe they are bodies here to get what they want at any price; for us to join their Holy Communion.

We each have the universe to offer, our life, our heartbreak, our worry, even our sin, our lack of love; we can turn it all into the most beautiful prayer, by wanting to, by praying with a God we actually love. When you are a prayer, you become the most beautiful being on Earth no matter what you or anyone else 'thinks.'

'Freedom'

All wills but Gods will
Offer me something
For my freedom
Gods will offers me freedom

I struggled with this, like I thought I had to give up something I wanted, I felt like I was 'trying' to choose what was best, but a beautiful transformation took place through a trial. It was as if I had to lose my will to find it. I lost my will to the spirit of an addiction. The same thing happened to both my parents at the same age, and they went through something very similar, having it almost destroy them, yet emerging 'free'. If you are addicted, and almost everyone is, you can be free, more free than you can imagine. No one is as free as someone who has earned it.

We love our god more than anyone or anything else. We are faithful, loyal and obedient to our god. Everything real including our god/s are alive, and whisper to us as 'wants'. We follow them, their way, their voice, their wishes, their thoughts, we become inhabited by them, we become what we love, made in our God's image. This is what happens in addiction, to anything, a substance or behavior, it's originating from a living being exercising its will in us by us giving ours over to it bit by bit. To give my will to anyone but God, is called 'sin', because it enslaves me. I speak from cold, brutal experience. It's not about 'thoughts' it's about who is thinking them. If they aren't of the highest love, they aren't the thoughts of God. All people that live close to the Earth know, everything real is alive. The freedom I have is the choice of who I follow, who I Soultrack, who I give my will to. God is free the way God is love. Freedom is something we only experience by the act of 'being' free, like art and creativity and love. To discover Gods will is our will is freedom, we're still on Earth, but the inner struggle disappears. That is the Cross, the 'burden' of light every living thing is under, that is the inescapable free choice we don't have to vote for. Existing obligates us to it.

For me, Freedom is the state of being Sovereign, what God has to be to be God. Freedom is the difference between Loves will and all wills in the error of wanting something else more than freedom. Grace is the gift of 'Response-ability,' to respond to our ability, Gods love, to want to become united with the Free Will of God, the gift of the desire to become one being, even one flesh. If we believe what Christ said is true and want it, our body becomes his to live and love and even save with. That is what a 'religion' and a priesthood is about, about making the spiritual material and the material spiritual. It is about making reality sacred, life giving, alive. My 'religion' is about breathing life for, from and into the dust of Earth. To save the Earth, we must sanctify ourselves, there is no other way.

Our free will is Gods, that is what Christ came to show us, but we don't believe him, we'll believe anybody but him. It's like we worship the shadows instead of the light and we become them. The only way I know to see and become free is to become a prayer. I was able to do that alone in the wilderness with the creatures Wandering in the Spirit. I've begun to bring that vision~prayer~quest into my life here in the world. Approaching Gods beauty as an artist, helps me. It humbles me without discouraging me, it's a work of love.

Wherever we are, it's hard to face ourself, each person needs help, I needed tons of love and help. When I went through my trial, my friends of different beliefs, didn't judge me harshly, they loved me, and they helped me, it gives and takes a lot of faith to be a prayer, they were prayers. My prayer is to make them grateful they did, and I'm doing it, the best I can and the only way I know how, to be a prayer. When you are a prayer you are free, you are honest, but prayer is like music, I have to want only the highest beauty to reach it, I have to reject what is less to experience the best. I enter the sacred mystery, and take responsibility, in place of resistance and excuses, I give one second of my self fully, I am sincere for one second, I take my will away from all other wills for one second and give it to God and he turns that one second into eternity right here, until all our seconds and every breath rests in this peace that is the deepest joy. We become a different kind of human-being, wanting what's worth wanting; to give, with the will of God. Every holy soul and angel comes to our aide and rejoices.

I was broken, all I had left was sincerity, that's enough. The more we trust them the more they trust us, with miracles. They are real living beings, it's them we have to be true to, not ideas. It's like being an artist, it takes everything and gives everything, that is the essence of what art and prayer is. All wills but Gods offer us something they tell us is worth our freedom. God offers us Freedom.

'Yet'

What is most beautiful about you, to me, is not your thoughts, no matter how high they are, it's you, your soul. Since my first step onto Earth alone, I've been learning, thoughts are important, but it's not about thoughts, it's about beings.

I ask, and I listen, but in the world, almost everything I read and I'm told to believe, is about ways to think or to not think. It says, 'this is the way things are or aren't, if you think or don't think this way, you'll get what you think you want.' We don't know what we want because we don't what we are...yet.

What I want is the being that is the life in me and you. I touch that life and feel that life touching me through my love with it, and then with my soul, I track it. It is both creature and Creator. What I want, is who thinks the thoughts; the Life, the Being. The life I can love the most is the most beautiful life, the life that lays itself down for me and that I pray for the love to lay myself down for, this life is in all of us, if we 'want it'. It is the life that proves it's true, that I trust with my entire being and that only raises my dignity to give myself to and want to obey, because it is, Holy. When I refuse to reach for less, I reach out and embrace a Communion of real, living, beings,

Human and animal

Angelic and Divine

Soul and flesh

Angels don't think to get what they want, they are pure spirit and pure intellect, they are what they want. They are the adoration of their Creator. Everything becomes what it worships. Angels are as real as Earths creatures, they are the gaze of the Holy Spirit on his living creation, the gaze in the eyes of Jesus and Mary, because she Believes in him and he believes in her! The world can believe and not believe whatever it wants, but it can't take away their holiness. Their gaze is a sea of love, mercy and compassion, and a joy angels, children and the sincere can know. We aren't separate from what we want, we are what we want, the way birds fly.

The only thing that separates all of Gods holy creation from each other is our desire to love each other, we are the medium of Gods art. This is the sacred mystery of the Trinity and of our incarnation. Christ hasn't come to escape suffering or transcend an illusion, he has come to love. This is the purpose he offers us. The world says everything is relative, but He has come to make everything real. How? By sanctifying it. Our purpose is his, to sanctify Earth with our breath, life and blood on her altar, that is the way to save her, her creatures and each other. This is the glorious burden of light, it is the power of Gods angelic sword, and sometimes it hurts, because it means caring as if eternity and everyone else depends on it. I've learned the hard way, that reaching for anything less, is not weakness, but betrayal.

What's most important about our intellect is that what it thinks is worth thinking. That discernment is its purpose. Thoughts worthy of thinking are not really 'thought', but revealed, by asking with our intellect, actions and wants, as a prayer. What's most important about our thoughts is that we don't believe error with them. This is what faith is, to believe only what is worth believing, only the most beautiful highest thing we can find, to believe. I trust the intellect of those that prove they know, with unequaled miracles, the Communion of Saints, human and angelic, they are standing right beside us, praying for us, waiting for us to love the truth. Why would I trust the intellect of someone who's just guessing or voting and reinventing the wheel with new hubcaps, that's what the world does.

To love the truth is endless revelation. To actually love the truth, we don't have to know it, we have to believe it exists, and want it with our whole heart, mind and soul, our whole being, like an artist believes in beauty, and seeks it, looks for it, discerns it, feels it, and then with life, begins to become an expression of it, but I have to commit myself to it, then it finds me. It doesn't mean now we're fixed, it means now we've decided to love someone that is sincere. Christ promises that if we seek the truth we will find it, and it will set us free. That means loving the truth, like a lover, like the most beautiful, humble, passionate, woman, first, before and above everything else. There is nothing better than being free and no one more grateful for it than someone who became enslaved like me.

It's so sad, such a tragic waste, the cause of purposeful cruelty, meanness, vicious pride and faith in evil beings that lie; that our world doesn't love the truth. Earth does, her creatures do, the planets and galaxies do, light does, beauty does, music does, love does, joy does, innocence does, life does, God does. It's not that the world doesn't believe truth exists, it's that it thinks it won't like it as much as what it thinks it wants more. This is why the world doesn't want God to be a being like us, with feelings and a heart we'd have to care about. It's why we think we want truth and God to be everybody's opinions and ideas. For me, a God that's an idea is a dumb idea. The truth is who thinks it and loves with it. The truth is a living being I track and find, that loves me more than I can comprehend, it's too good to be true, because it actually is true, that's what the miracle does, it proves what is true. But we've got to take a step! We've got to decide, I want to track the beings that leave these tracks, and that means learning to recognize the tracks of the beings that don't and deciding not to follow them. A Soultracker learns to identify tracks by seeing who's tracks they follow, where they come from and where they lead. The reason there is only one path, isn't because it's not fair, it's because it leads to one place, a living Being that loves with a living heart and soul, not with an idea.

Truth is the gaze of God on his Son, of a Child on Creation, his Mother gazing on him, her children, the Garden of living creatures, a family, human, plant, animal and angelic. Through the laying down of his life for all he loves, even his Body and Blood become the truth, where symbols end and reality begins, sacred, a new creation, because God exists in you, with a heart, and because He says it is. History, ourstory, no matter what unseen beings or events unfold, the realm is Gods, all being transformed into something so endlessly beautiful in every way love can exist, that we haven't dreamt a molecule of it...

Yet.

'Real Thing's Are Alive'

I think back
In coming through
To unexplainable peace
Thick deep gratitude
At how hard it was
To lose myself
In an addiction
Hell
Where we believe
But don't have faith
Where the ghost's of damned souls
And the angels of things that fly
Through space and time race
Toward their own extinction
To see even God has an enemy
Love has hate
Light has darkness
Life eats life
It has to
I keep learning
Real things are alive

I could tell you the details
Of my disintegration
Give you good reasons
I could judge wolves
But they'd only be symptoms
Of selling my soul for a bribe
To let your enemy kiss me

Is he whispering to you
With some begging temptation
'Do it, whatever you want, you need it,
God is just your mind and I am too'

Now when I hear details
I see how they're the same
As what I went through
It doesn't matter what it is
What she says
What he does
It's all the betrayal
Of God
For a bribe
And this is where my gratitude
Comes breaking in like sun on snow
To be alive
Cold clear sky and buffalo
Like blood drops on the lily white
I know
My Enemy is Not Me!
He's not my soul
He's not my thoughts or weakness
He's not my body
He used mine
For his mourning bleakness
He hides behind another face
With hidden reasons to embrace
Which God do you believe in
Who is the fruit of your faith
Every sin has a demon
Every word you say
And desire
Is all inspired
By One or the other
The Devil believes in God
Judas healed the sick
But he's jealous
Because he's repulsive
He's bitter and angry about it
He fills his heart with lust

And then resents his ugliness
He accuses everyone but himself
He's not like you
He's meaner
You're free but you don't want it
Like me
When I was a believer
In a Liar
I'm not anymore
I've seen the light
I don't have to
I want to
Fight for it
I hope I die for it
If you could see what I've seen
Your temptations would be tempered
By living breathing beings
You wouldn't touch with a ten foot pole

Are you having a hard time
Do you rest in the sea of your doubt
Do you dwell in your drama
You need to see your worst enemy
I provoked him with grace
I felt his slap on my face
And woke up
Now I know he's there
He helps me
Have faith
To see
He's his own worst enemy
Not me

'Beauty'

I want to give the most beautiful thing I find, describe the most beautiful thing I see, say the most beautiful thing I hear, precisely, in the most beautiful ways I can. Focusing on beauty is a different way to live.

Soultracker's make love life, and life art. You don't have to cut off your ear, but you have to be willing to, to be passionate. My story became art, when I knew who it was for; my friends. In you I heard my voice, because I know, even with our different ideas about life, truth, and God, we want people to love, and give each other something beautiful enough, to stop being afraid.

The world is far from Earth, thinking thoughts of what it thinks it wants without knowing what it is and getting them. It's too proud to pray. It shows up in everything, in our hearts, in our relationships, in demonically inspired acts, in the weather and the planet, because they're alive. What is alive has a heart and Earth's is getting hard enough to crack. It's about time I guess.

The souls I track know the forces of nature are governed by angels. Every atom of reality is moved by an angels will in love with Gods. The guardianship of our body and soul is theirs, the way our souls have custody of our own, but nobody believes in them, not really, they think they're an idea, and they stay an idea, to argue about or ignore, until we love them. Padre Pio said they have as much faith in us as we have them, and he proved it was true over and over. His whole life was proof, and thousands more walk the exact same path, tracking the whole Communion like the path of the buffalo. You don't know what happens in their lives, it's like this big unguarded secret, it's all there, don't you even want to look? Even when I think I believe in them, I discover I only know what and who they are to the extent I love them, and everyone else. I trust enough to be broken. It's the same with God. It's loving the Soul of God like a lover and in your lover. For me, there is no knowing without loving, Cutting off your ear is letting go of everything, and finding out what's left, is real, because it really is, alive, like you and me.

I have a chance to say what I hear, but it's so misunderstood, so delicate and majestic, so sacred and holy, so solemn, so beautiful and alive, like kneeling in the wilderness, that for someone like me to say it, it may be only God will believe it.

"My Whole Life, It Has"

If you could betray your lover because you knew she loved you so much she would forgive you, would you do it!? That's what sin is, betraying your lover and yourself and come on, don't give me a crock, you know if you're doing it, I do.

The way the world is trying to overcome its guilt is by saying God is an idea, God has no feelings, he's not our lover, and if he's love he'll forgive so it doesn't matter. You've grown up in the same world I have. If you're younger than me you've got less to answer for because you inherited what we've given you, but what God who is Love is asking for is our heart, our 'Conversion.' To ask for this is to ask for the truth to be revealed to you about yourself. It's hard, in fact it kind of breaks you, it breaks your heart, but it's worth it. It doesn't matter how lost you are, I've been lost, I know. But you know what, there's an incredible strength that comes when you survive

The light of God 'Illuminates our Conscience' it makes us 'Conscious.' Becoming conscious of beauty brings with it a consciousness of what is ugly and the hardest place to experience ugliness is in ourself. But this is fantastic, in a way it is the most beautiful thing I will ever be able to tell you, because it has been foretold and it is not yet known and it is happening, A Woman, Clothed with the Sun, is appearing in Heaven and on Earth, her offspring are the lovers of her Son, who created her out of his love for her, and she helped me, she helps me still, she is everything I could ever dream a woman is at once, she is the New Eve, and I can testify in all my weakness and lack of love, and in all my desire to be a man, she will help you see what a man is, her Son. She knows who her Son is, God.

All she points to, lives for and sees is her Son, in everyone. She gives us her vision, her faith, with her heart. Really, not symbolically, not a memory, not an idea, not an educated guess or a vote, not only words, not something that doesn't matter; she is a Woman and she is, 'Full of Grace.' To be Full of Grace is to be without sin, she is the mother of the first born of the dead, the new Eve, she is real, a person, and when God becomes Man he is a person, this is the sword, this is the point, and the only reason that if you meet him, if he calls you, you must make a choice, like she did, because they are as real and as sovereign as you.

What I believe I can do is, with my whole heart, mind and soul, respond to the most beautiful thing I can find. That beauty never ends, but at some point each of us has to confront what we believe, and instead of preaching it to others, ask ourself, do I really believe it? Does it prove itself true? Am I living proof of it? I want to live to offer the most beautiful thing I can find to believe. The full beauty of that truth reveals itself the more I believe it.

I asked myself something one day and it changed my whole life, 'What if this is actually true? What if the arch-angel really did appear to Mary, and what if the Holy Spirit really did 'Fill' her with himself, Grace, and knowing her virginity, she conceived the Son of God, who grew in her womb and was born and what if every miracle that happened really happened? Just what if? What would it mean to her? To me? What would her experience of life be? What would it be like to have her heart? To love her Son as much as she did and does? To have her faith, her sorrow, her joy? What would it mean if it were all true and I let it be all it is, instead of limiting it by deciding to believe I don't believe it? And instead of being afraid to feel her heart because mine is still so full of lack, my lack of love. I say to myself, this seems impossible, I'm not holy like the souls I track, and then I go for it anyway, like music and buffalo and the wilderness. It's art, I want to be an artist.

Simeon, the old holy man told her, 'And a sword will pierce your heart to reveal the thoughts of many.' His prophecy has come true, her pierced heart reveals the thoughts of mine. No matter what you say or think, you've got a religion just as much as I do, they are just different, because we believe different things. It matters what we believe, it's as precise and critical as music. Do you want to know why it matters to me? I'll tell you most of all; because of the beauty.

I am in love, with a man and a woman. The beauty, the passion, the depth of meaning, the dignity, honor, glory and Grace, the limitless Faith, they have in each other, they also have in you and me, and in the Love they believe created them; they inspire me. No one has offered me an idea or another heart that is more beautiful, but if you believe you can, try, offer me something more beautiful instead of just not believing. No one has offered the miracles that have happened and are happening all over the world with increasing urgency and awe either. Only a very small percentage of people know about them yet, but it's growing and I will share the most profound at the end of this book.

The beauty of their love illuminates every other human being I see. It illuminates you to me. The beauty of their love illuminates my seconds, and makes each second grow more precious to me. Their love has turned the same seconds I could hardly endure when I was lost, when I betrayed their love, when I was addicted, into an eternal prayer. He said, "The Truth will set you free." My whole life, it has.

The following links will take you into a world very few people are aware of. If you close this book without carefully looking into these links you will miss treasures, and what the book was for, but if you look at them, and ask yourself, 'Is this true'? 'If it is, what does it mean'? 'How does it change my life, the world, reality, me'? You will be following your soul into beauty that is alive and has already triumphed over evil. That's what Soultracking is.

The Most Astonishing Miracles

http://listverse.com/2008/07/14/top-10-astonishing-miracles/
Signs From God
*http://www.youtube.com/watch?v=g_X3zHKRB6w&list=PLC20FECD89D96
    3364*
Interviews by Art Bell with Exorcist Father Malachi Martin Phd.
watch all the interviews, every one, you will learn things critical to every aspect
    of your life, very few people know anything about.
https://www.youtube.com/watch?v=ubLQzBZi5G8
Overview's of Medjugorje and Akita
http://www.dreamscape.com/morgana/encelad.htm
Marino Restrepo, mystic kidnapped by Columbian Guerillas
http://www.youtube.com/watch?v=cvwus4bTf0Y
BBC Interview with Conchita Gonzales, Garabandal
http://www.youtube.com/watch?v=JTOpIXXyL-I
2 Documentaries on Garabandal
http://www.youtube.com/watch?v=-SjPLiOCGpg
Garabandal~ the eye witnesses
http://www.youtube.com/watch?v=jlp2xFvuA3Y
Miraculous healing prayer with Father Suarez
*https://www.youtube.com/watch?v=8UP3LHBgtIc&list=PL7pUP5LyumxoDW9
    GENLuzsCD41cDTLtRV*
8 priests survive Hiroshima & the same thing occurs for Franciscan Priests in
    Nagasaki
http://infallible-catholic.blogspot.ca/2013/03/fatima-miracle-in-hiroshima-japan.
    html
Tears From Heaven
https://www.youtube.com/watch?v=ciTD4-Onjjk
The Message of Fatima
https://www.youtube.com/watch?v=cyC73Zn9fPw
The Song of Bernadette (of Lourdes)
https://www.youtube.com/watch?v=XbLs3iAgr5s

Believe ~ The Story of Fr. Zlatco Sudac
https://www.youtube.com/watch?v=7fi6NouPe3o
Interview ~ Fr. Zlatco Sudac, Bilocation, Stigmata...
http://www.stjeromecroatian.org/eng/frsudac.html